SCHOOL IMPROVEMENT IN AN ERA OF CHANGE

SCHOOL IMPROVEMENT IN AN ERA OF CHANGE

David Hopkins,
Mel Ainscow
and
Mel West

with a foreword by
Michael Fullan

TEACHERS
COLLEGE
PRESS

Published in the United States of America by
Teachers College Press
Columbia University
New York, NY 10027
USA

First published 1994 by Cassell, London.

Library of Congress Cataloging-in-Publication Data

Hopkins, David, 1949-
    School improvement in an era of change / David Hopkins, Mel
Ainscow, and Mel West; with a foreword by Michael Fullan.
        p.   cm.
    Includes bibliographical references and indexes.
    ISBN 0-8077-3390-3 (pbk.)
    1. School improvement programs – United States.   I. Ainscow, Mel.
II. West, Mel.   III. Title.
LB2822.82.H66   1994
371.2'00973–dc20

ISBN: 0-8077-3390-3

Typeset by Colset Private Limited, Singapore

Printed and bound in Great Britain

Contents

Contents

Foreword

There is a great deal written on educational reform and school improvement — much of it bewildering. Innovation, reform, improvement, effective schools, school effectiveness, restructuring, systemic reform all have their place in current literature. Taken in total, the writings are diffuse, providing little clarity as to the key elements and their interrelationships.

School Improvement in an Era of Change is an exception because it is clear and comprehensive in its treatment of school improvement. Hopkins, Ainscow and West have done a remarkable job in making the phenomenon of educational change coherent. They render the study and practice of change — both theoretically and practically — accessible.

Given the territory covered, the book is amazingly compact, representing a single place where one can view the whole field of school improvement. All the relevant research literature is addressed, making the bibliography invaluable in its own right. But the literature is incorporated in a way that makes it flow with the argument of the book from theory to practice.

Perhaps it is because the authors are so heavily immersed in their own improvement work that they have been able to make the broader literature 'come alive'. Some books are narrow, reporting on a few case studies in detail, others are encyclopedic, lacking the fine-grained insights arising from first-hand accounts. This book is both encyclopedic and fine-grained, containing scores of insights as a result.

The first major section (Part 2 of the book) is on 'theory'. Its five chapters provide a comprehensive and valuable primer on what the literature says about school improvement. The authors link classroom, school and school-environment perspectives on change. By the end of this section we understand how the different approaches to change interrelate, but more importantly we begin to see the powerful leverage points through which more fundamental reform can be achieved. We see that developing collaborative work cultures is the key agenda in bringing about sustained school improvement.

The second major section (Part 3) is focused on practice. It is here that the full richness of the book becomes apparent. Using a combination of the theoretical constructs developed in the first section, targeted excerpts from the literature, and front-line vignettes from teachers and administrators in the 'Improving the Quality of Education for All' project, Hopkins, Ainscow and West present a powerful investigation of the praxis of school improvement. Staff development, involvement, inquiry and reflection, leadership, coordination and collaborative planning are all critically portrayed, grounded in theory, but also in the descriptions, activities and reflections of practitioners. The limitations of conventional treatments of school improvement concepts are thoroughly explicated, along with new, more comprehensive formulations of what it would mean to embed these potentially powerful elements into the core culture of schools. Stated differently, a fundamentally new definition of school improvement is required (see my book *Change Forces: Probing the Depths of Education Reform* (Falmer Press, 1993)).

As the authors stress, understanding and doing something substantial about school improvement are a never-ending journey. *School Improvement in an Era of Change* takes us a considerable distance down the paths of change as a result of its powerful interplay of good practice and good theory.

Michael Fullan

Preface and Acknowledgements

Schools in the UK and elsewhere are facing demands for an unprecedented series of educational reforms. In responding to these external demands and in continuing to provide quality education for all their students, successful schools are seeking more effective ways of working both within and outside the classroom. This approach to planned change is called school improvement. We consider ourselves very fortunate to have been involved over the past ten years or so, at a variety of different levels and with many schools, in developing strategies and ways of working that can improve the quality of education for all during such an era of change.

Although we have been working on this book for some time, it is a testimony to the continuing rate of innovation that this volume is only an interim statement. The rate of change and an expanding knowledge base would make any other claim overly pretentious. In the book we have attempted to reinterpret what is known about planned educational change and relate it to our on-going collaboration with the schools involved in the 'Improving the Quality of Education for All' (IQEA) project. At times both 'academic' and 'practical', the book traces the evolution of our thinking and practice as we struggle to help schools make sense of the complexities of development during these challenging times.

In the same way as the book is only an interim statement, so we cannot claim to present a united front on every issue. The discerning reader will see our own arguments being worked out on the pages that follow; and that is how it should be. We rely heavily in the book on the metaphor of school improvement as a journey, and, true to this image, we at times have gone off in different directions. The values underpinning our work, however, as we hope comes through on the pages that follow, enable us to argue creatively within a common frame. That the three of us can cooperate on such an intense task as this and still emerge with greater respect for each other at the end says much for the power of collaboration within a set of mutually agreed values.

We have received a great deal of help during our journey, particularly during the early stages. Our colleagues have been characteristically generous with their time and wisdom. In this respect, we are extremely grateful to Tim Brighouse, Michael Fullan, David Hargreaves, Michael Huberman, Bruce Joyce, Matthew Miles, Peter Mortimore, Desmond Nuttall, David Reynolds, Geoff Southworth, Louise Stoll and Sam Stringfield for subjecting our ideas to such rigorous and challenging critique. Thanks too to Ann Kilcher and Michael Miller for their comments and advice, and to Caroline Bean and Ann Sargeant for their help in preparing the manuscript.

We are also indebted to our colleagues in the IQEA schools for challenging our ideas in a more practical way and being so gracious to us as we fumbled to make sense of their realities. We are particularly grateful to the following colleagues who contributed the vignettes to Part 3 of the book: Monica Adlem, John Brandon, Michael Cassidy, Gill Daly, Robin Dixon, Les Fearns, Jan Featherstone, Jean Graham, Mary Healy, Frances Howarth, Pamela Hughes, Karen Jones, Lyn Newman, Julie Payne, Suzanne Phillips, Carol Robinson, Malcolm Ward and Malcom Wright.

Although it may not always appear this way to our colleagues, we consider ourselves extremely fortunate to be working at the Institute of Education at the University of Cambridge. We have particularly appreciated the opportunity and space to experiment with new ideas and ways of working, and the continuing support and generosity of spirit that our colleagues have shown towards us during the preparation of this book.

Show-business award evenings and introductions to books such as this have a common failing: that in making so many acknowledgements the thanks appear gratuitous. At the risk of falling into that trap, we need to apologize to our children for the dereliction of parental duties, and in the hope that as we greet them again they still remember who we are.

David Hopkins, Mel Ainscow, Mel West
Cambridge, June 1993

PART 1

INTRODUCTION

Chapter 1

School Improvement in an Era of Change

We were recently in a meeting with heads, teacher union representatives, governors and senior local education authority (LEA) officers discussing an evaluation we had just completed of a large pilot project within the LEA. Although the project had been very successful, and the evaluation positive, the conversation turned eventually to the lack of integration between this initiative and others currently under way in the authority. There were no critical overtones to the discussion, we were just talking around the problem of innovation overload. It was then that we began to realize that, despite our pessimism, much progress has been made over the past few years in developing our schools and nurturing the teaching-learning process. We also began to realize that the conversation we were then having would have been inconceivable even three years earlier — the strategies and language have become more sophisticated and precise. Most probably three years hence our current concerns over the lack of integration will appear naive, as we see with hindsight that it has all been part of the process of development.

Schools in England and Wales are in the middle of a sea change. The current reform agenda is having a more profound impact than even the transformation that occurred in our secondary schools following comprehensivization in the mid-1960s. It is important to realize too that the nature of educational change itself is also changing. The weaknesses of the traditional 'top-down' approach to educational change are almost daily being exposed in our newspapers, and there is a growing recognition that neither centralization nor decentralization works. None the less, we believe that schools can still enhance educational quality in spite of a heavily deterministic national agenda.

As we work with schools within the framework of the national reform agenda we are committed to an approach to educational change that focuses on student achievement *and* the schools' ability to cope with change. We refer to this particular approach to educational change as *school improvement*. School improvement in the way that we define it, however, is not about how to implement centralized reforms in a more effective way. It is more to do with how schools, in an era of change, can use the impetus of external reform to improve or develop themselves. Sometimes what a school chooses to do in terms of school improvement will be consistent with the national reform agenda, at other times it will not. Whatever the case, the decision to engage in school improvement, at least in the schools that we work with, is based on clear evidence of what is the best for the young people in that school.

SCHOOL IMPROVEMENT

There are two senses in which the phrase 'school improvement' is generally used. The first is the common-sense meaning which relates to general efforts to make schools better places for pupils and students to learn in. This is a sensible interpretation of the phrase and its most common usage. In this book, however, we are principally concerned with the second, more technical or specific way in which the phrase is used. We regard school improvement as a distinct approach to educational change that enhances student outcomes as well as strengthening the school's capacity for managing change. In this sense school improvement is about raising student achievement through focusing on the teaching-learning process and the conditions which support it. It is about strategies for improving the school's capacity for providing quality education in times of change, rather than blindly accepting the edicts of centralized policies, and striving to implement these directives uncritically. But even this more specific definition is open to differing interpretations.

In his book *Improving Schools from Within*, Roland Barth (1990) distinguishes between two different approaches to school improvement that rest on sets of very different assumptions. He describes the dominant approach like this (Barth, 1990, p. 38):

- Schools do not have the capacity or the will to improve themselves; improvements must therefore come from sources outside the school.

- What needs to be improved about schools is the level of pupil performance and achievement, best measured by standardized tests.

- Schools can be found in which pupils are achieving beyond what might be predicted. By observing these schools, we can identify their characteristics as 'desirable'.

- Teachers and heads in other schools can be trained to display the desirable traits of their counterparts in high-achieving schools. Then their pupils too will excel.

- School improvement, then, is an attempt to identify what school people should know and be able to do and to devise ways to get them to know and do it.

Barth argues that such a set of assumptions has led to an approach to school reform that is based on a proliferation of 'lists'. There are lists of the characteristics of the 'effective' school, teacher and pupil, lists of minimum competencies, lists of regulations, of performance indicators and so on. We have a great deal of sympathy with Barth's concern about the dangers inherent in such an approach. What is dangerous and self-defeating about this view of the world is the mind set that informs it. Inherent in the approach is a set of assumptions about people, how they feel, how they should behave, and about how organizations work. It is an approach that encourages someone to do something to someone else: it is about control rather than growth. The argument is less against lists than against the values that inform them. Lists in our opinion can be helpful when they are used to inform action; but

3

even then, they need to be negotiated and subject to the teacher's (or school's) judgement.

Barth then argues for basing school reform on the skills, aspirations and energy of those closest to the school: teachers, senior management, governors and parents. He argues that such a 'community of learners' approaches school improvement from a radically different set of assumptions as compared with those of the list makers. These assumptions are (Barth, 1990, p. 45, our italics):

- Schools have the capacity to improve themselves, if the *conditions* are right. A major responsibility of those outside the school is to help provide these conditions for those inside.

- When the need and purpose is there, when the *conditions* are right, adults and students alike learn and each energizes and contributes to the learning of the other.

- What needs to be improved about schools is their *culture*, the quality of interpersonal relationships, and the nature and quality of learning experiences.

- School improvement is an effort to determine and provide, from without and within, *conditions* under which the adults and youngsters who inhabit schools will promote and sustain learning among themselves.

These assumptions neatly capture the essence of our approach to school improvement. As outsiders to a school, when we engage in school improvement activities we are concerned to *work with* rather than *work on* schools. Barth's assumptions lead us to some liberating ways of thinking about change. Schools, and those who live out their daily lives within them, are no longer the victims of change, but can take more control of the process. By using the opportunity of external change as a stimulus, they can subject the specificities of change to their own professional scrutiny and judgement. These are the values that we hold dear and that inform our approach to school improvement, as we hope will become clear in the pages that follow.

AN ERA OF CHANGE

Some twenty years or so ago 'change' was about working with new curriculum materials prepared by national or local agencies. Or it may have meant trying out a new teaching strategy. Most of these changes were *ad hoc*, self-determined, single innovations which by and large individual teachers decided to work on, or not, as the case might be. More recently we have not had the luxury of choice. In the UK as elsewhere, the change agenda has increasingly been set by national politicians, rather than being advocated by educationalists or support agencies. With the centralization of educational reform, teachers have lost control over change.

In the UK during the past fifteen years there has been an increasing emphasis on accountability and school improvement (in the common-sense usage of the phrase). The public debate on educational standards, which began in the mid 1970s, has become increasingly polarized, and resulted in a plethora of nationally inspired changes. A variety of legislative efforts to improve schools occurred during the 1980s, culminating in a series of Acts of which the Education Reform Act 1988 was the most important. These were consolidated by further legislation in the early 1990s.

While the detail of this radical reform agenda is beyond the scope of this book, it is worth briefly summarizing the four fronts on which this attack on the traditional organization of the school system was carried forward. The first was *prescription*, of which the prime examples are the National Curriculum and the schemes for national testing at 7, 11 and 14. Second is *decentralization*, and here local management of schools, the increase in the power of school governors and the demise of the LEA were the main policy initiatives. Third is *competition*, which was encouraged by the expansion of grant-maintained status for schools, open enrolment supported by the publication of 'league tables', and a general emphasis on the use of performance indicators. Finally, there was the *privatization* of those who provide services to schools. This includes cleaners, advisers, the creation of curriculum agencies, and, most recently, school inspectors.

As we move through the 1990s the educational agenda is increasingly being dominated by a concern to implement and institutionalize this radical reform agenda. This quest for stability, however, is being made against a background of continuing change, as expectations for student achievement rise beyond the capacity of the system to deliver. As a result, there are seemingly contradictory pressures for centralization and decentralization, yet it is clearly evident that neither approach works by itself.

Those of us in the UK, and particularly England and Wales, have been struggling for longer than most with the challenge of this centralized-decentralized dichotomy. At the same time as the national government has drawn to itself more power than ever before, the usual infrastructure of support has been eroded, and schools are finding themselves increasingly alone in the struggle to take charge of the process of change. This situation complicates and places great strains on school improvement efforts.

Despite these constraints, it is also an exciting and instructive time to be engaged in school improvement. We find it fascinating, if not unsurprising, that other countries are so interested in the British experience of educational change. At international conferences the British presentations are always fully and enthusiastically attended; and there is a steady stream of visitors from overseas to institutes like ours, who come to find out 'what is going on'. Whatever one thinks of our national reforms, there is no doubt that we are in the middle of a radical and ambitious attempt to revolutionize the character of an educational system and to redefine the locus of decision making at various levels. It is the radical and intensive nature of our reforms that interest others. By the same token, if our attempts at school improvement are successful in raising quality during such turbulent times, then it is likely that similar strategies will work anywhere!

The jury is still out as to the success of this massive, extensive and radical national approach to school improvement. The evaluation evidence to date

5

would suggest an uneven impact. It would not be unfair, we believe, to suggest that simply increasing the number of reforms does not necessarily increase their chances of having a positive impact on daily classroom life. Obviously this is a somewhat crude over-generalization, but the point needs to be made that doing more does not necessarily mean doing better. The intensification of reform efforts often results in 'surface' as opposed to 'deep structure' change. We are often left with the appearance but not the reality of change. The changes may have reached the LEA or school; but do they progress beyond the classroom door? To say this is not necessarily to imply criticism of the British government. The point is to emphasize the difficulty and complexity of implementing any centralized change. Whatever one's position on the content and character of our national reform agenda, there are lessons to be learned internationally from our experiences during this era of change. It is this radical background that provides a context for the book.

WHAT ARE THE AIMS OF THIS BOOK?

Our concern about the effectiveness and efficiency of a nationally imposed reform agenda; the capacity of schools to respond to these demands; our own school improvement work; and the vital importance of improving the quality of education for all — these are some of the themes that dominate this book. The book has four main purposes:

- to review the existing knowledge base on school and classroom effectiveness, educational change and school improvement;
- to define the approach to educational change that is generally referred to as school improvement;
- to illustrate our approach to school improvement by giving an account of the thinking behind the 'Improving the Quality of Education for All' project;
- to provide some practical advice to those within, and associated with, schools on how to manage the change process and engage in lasting school improvement.

There has been a great deal of knowledge developed and experience gained over the past ten years or so about how to manage the change process in schools. There is now, for example, a considerable consensus over the characteristics of the 'effective' school, and on strategies for school improvement that are based on sound empirical evidence and experience. Where this knowledge has found its way into national policy it is still only gradually being assimilated into our schools. One of the purposes of this book is to help further disseminate these key ideas and strategies. Reviews of research rarely resonate with one's own experience, as they are inevitably written one level removed from daily life. In this book we have tried to overcome this difficulty by complementing the review of what we know with descriptions of improvement work in schools with which we are currently collaborating.

IMPROVING THE QUALITY OF EDUCATION FOR ALL

During the past three years or so we have been working closely with schools in East Anglia, North London and Yorkshire on a school improvement or development project known as 'Improving the Quality of Education for All' (IQEA). IQEA is a school improvement project that involves schools in working collaboratively with a group from the Institute of Education at Cambridge, and with representatives from their LEA or with a local support agency such as Bramley Grange College in Leeds. The overall aim of the project is to produce and evaluate a model of school development and a programme of support that strengthen a school's ability to provide high-quality education for all its pupils by building upon existing good practice. The goal is enhanced learning outcomes for both students and teachers. The team from Cambridge provides training and support for representatives of each participating school, who, in turn, coordinate the project in their own schools.

IQEA works from an assumption that schools are most likely to strengthen their ability to provide enhanced outcomes for all pupils when they adopt ways of working that are consistent with their own aspirations as well as the current reform agenda. This involves building confidence and capacity within the school, rather than reliance on externally produced packages — although good ideas from the outside are never rejected out of hand. At a time of great change in the educational system, the schools we are working with are using the impetus of external reform for internal purposes.

The project in each school is based upon a contract between the staff of the school, the LEA or support agency and ourselves. This contract is intended to clarify expectations and ensure the conditions necessary for success. In particular it emphasizes that all staff be consulted, that coordinators be appointed, that a critical mass of teachers be actively involved in development work, and that sufficient time be made available for classroom observation and staff development. For our part, we coordinate the project, provide training for the school coordinators and representatives, make regular school visits, contribute to staff training, provide staff development materials, and monitor the implementation of the project.

The style adopted in the project is to develop a strategy for improvement that allows each school considerable autonomy to determine its own priorities for development and, indeed, its own methods for achieving these priorities. In this sense we (that is, all the partners in the project) are involved in one project within which individual schools devise their own projects.

WHAT IS THIS BOOK ABOUT?

Following this introductory chapter, the book is divided into three further parts. Part 2 — Theory is mainly concerned with what is known about educational change, school and classroom effectiveness, and school improvement. Too often we 'pretend to not know what is known' (Joyce Carol Oates, quoted in Glickman, 1991, p. 4), and this is especially true when it comes to educational change. In this part we review, inevitably briefly, the main lessons that have been learned about change over the last fifteen to twenty years. Chapter 2 describes the background to recent efforts at educational change and in so doing raises a series of challenges for school improvement. In Chapter 3 we overview the change literature in an attempt to disclose the main perspectives informing recent efforts at reform, and to emphasize the critical importance of individual meaning in the change process. In Chapter 4 we review the two main bodies of research knowledge that have a bearing on our work, school and classroom effectiveness. In our opinion these are the two crucial ingredients for enhancing student achievement. In Chapter 5 we describe in more detail the background to recent efforts at school improvement, how it is best supported, and which approaches appear most successful. The chapters in this part of the book present our attempt to review as economically as we can the knowledge base relevant to school improvement. In this we have tried to be critical but non-partisan: we have also provided a summary of key messages at the end of each chapter. In Chapter 6 we engage with the complex but crucial issue of school culture, show how this relates this to our ideal of a 'moving school', and on the basis of the previous chapters present a framework upon which our own school improvement work is founded.

Part 3 — Practice is, as its title implies, more action oriented. On the basis of our knowledge and experience we have identified six key conditions that support the process of development in schools. If these conditions are not present, then school improvement will not be sustained and change efforts will quickly become marginalized. Work on these conditions constitutes a major element of the training we provide for schools involved in the IQEA project. We begin in Chapter 7 by describing in more detail the school improvement framework that we used in our initial work with schools. Subsequent chapters in this section contain examples or vignettes from schools that we work with and summaries of key ideas. The six conditions dealt with in this section are:

- staff development (Chapter 8);
- involvement (Chapter 9);
- inquiry and reflection (Chapter 10);
- leadership (Chapter 11);
- coordination (Chapter 12);
- collaborative planning (Chapter 13).

In Part 4 — Reflection we present an interim and reflective account of how the school improvement process works in practice. In Chapter 14 we describe how some of 'our' schools have coped with the development process, discuss the predictable patterns that we are seeing in the ways that schools engage in cultural change, and by reflecting on our strategy outline how we go about supporting schools in an era of change.

In writing this book we have attempted to use the language of support rather than control. At times this has proven difficult because much of the language surrounding innovation and change, in the UK at least, is mechanistic, authoritarian and linear. Words such as renewal, growth, development and reflection capture our meaning far better than delivery, implementation and change. But as children of our time, and, on occasions, for reasons of expediency or habit, we no doubt have regressed into more conventional jargon; and for these lapses can only crave indulgence.

WHO IS THIS BOOK FOR?

We are great believers in Kurt Lewin's dictum that there is nothing as practical as good theory. Michael Fullan recently told us the story of the ivory-towered professor who wrote numerous books on education without ever once visiting a school. Eventually the professor was prevailed upon to spend a morning in a school and, much to his surprise, was most impressed by what he saw. On his departure, he thanked the headteacher generously for her hospitality and said that the visit had given him a great deal to think about. As he turned to go he was heard to muse to himself, 'I must see whether all this will work in theory'! We hope that it is already obvious that this story is not about one of us.

This book is not a detailed review or account of research, nor is it a 'how-to-do it' guide, neither does it contain easy recipes for success. In it we aim to steer a course between the specifications of research, the prescriptions of handbooks, and the dogma of experience. We aim to translate 'theory' into practice by using accessible language, by citing relevant research and experience, by providing examples, and by engaging in clear analysis.

We have written the book with three main audiences in mind:

- *those interested in school improvement and development.* They will be our principal readership, and we hope that there is sufficient practical advice in the pages that follow to help them face with a little more certainty the eternal question 'What do I do tomorrow?'. We also hope that the book is sufficiently 'theoretical' to provide strategies for sustained and coherent improvement.

- *practitioners in other countries interested in the UK experience, and support people more generally,* interested in school improvement. The book contains a sustained argument for, and an extensive example of, the school improvement approach to educational change set within a particularly radical and turbulent context.

- *students of educational change,* who may find the book useful as an introductory text. It provides a fairly complete and critical review of the current issues and literature, as well as providing detailed examples of school improvement in action.

It may be that the occasional 'policy maker' may come across this book. If they do, we hope that they will find within its covers some suggestions that may assist them in understanding the crucial distinction between the object of change and the process of changing.

We have not mentioned researchers, because this book is not based on research in the conventional sense. It is an account of our experiences with school improvement and the ideas and principles that inform it. As we continue to gather data during our work with schools, we intend in a subsequent volume to present the research evidence to support the strategies advocated on the following pages.

We hope that this book will also be read more generally. It should be read because as a society and educational community, we continue to 'pretend to not know what we know' about raising standards in education. National policy initiatives by themselves will not raise student achievement. Whatever their aspirations, many of our government's policies for school improvement will serve to reduce standards, not enhance them, for the majority of our students. If we are seriously concerned with equity in our educational system, in improving the quality of education for all, then the message of this book must be taken seriously — not because we say so, but because our children's future, and our society's, depends upon it.

PART 2

THEORY

Chapter 2

Perspectives on Educational Reform

One of the themes of this book is that change and improvement are not necessarily synonymous. Although it is true that external pressure is often the cause, or at least the impetus, for most educational change, this is not to imply that such changes are always desirable. Indeed in our opinion, some externally imposed change should be resisted, or at least adapted to the school's own purpose. We are also uncertain as to the outcome of the changes that are currently being attempted; some are working, others patently are not. Our fear is that the end result will only serve to increase the gap between 'good' and 'bad' schools. We have no evidence to suggest that accountability and increased competition, as strategies for improving the quality of education for all, actually work.

The increasing pace of change has led, as many as those who read this book will know, to a situation of innovation overload. There seems to be a common belief, at least among policy makers, that if one change is not having any apparent impact, then add a second, and then a third and so on. There are at least two problems with innovation overload. The first, as we have already noted, is that simply doing more does not imply doing better. If change is added to change, nothing gets done properly; people quickly get exhausted and then even what was going well deteriorates. Although this is common sense, it is surprising how often we fall into the overload trap.

The second problem is less obvious and perhaps more insidious. As Michael Fullan (1992a, p. 1) has noted, 'overload fosters dependency': which means that one's actions are predominantly shaped, however unintentionally, by events and by the actions or directions of others. Innovation overload is one of the most serious and endemic problems faced by an educational system. Unless we can begin to rationalize and sequence our change efforts, we will drain the system of vitality and the goal of school improvement will continue to elude us.

Even when change is received enthusiastically, there is no guarantee that it will be satisfactorily implemented, or that it will result in enhanced outcomes, however broadly defined, for pupils or teachers. Student achievement must be the *raison d'être* for any educational change. Unfortunately, because the process of translating policy into practice is so difficult to achieve, the reality, as opposed to the rhetoric, of change is often only loosely connected to the progress of pupils.

On a more optimistic note, we know of many schools that are taking the opportunity of this era of change as a chance to achieve positive developments in their curriculum, organization or methods of teaching. In many ways these schools are subverting change and confirming Peter Drucker's (1985) nostrum that 'entrepreneurs exploit innovation'.

This, then, is the less than auspicious background against which efforts at educational change are currently occurring in the UK. What is interesting, however, is that this general context is not restricted to the UK, but is a phenomenon common to most developed countries. In this chapter we explore in more detail the contemporary nature of reform and the problems with traditional policy approaches, in order to provide a backcloth to the discussions in subsequent chapters on educational change, the research on school and classroom effectiveness, and school improvement. In particular in this chapter we:

- discuss the nature of systemic change;
- review contemporary approaches to centralization-decentralization;
- explore the pathology of 'top-down' change.

SYSTEMIC CHANGE

As we began to hint earlier, even the contemporary situation of change is itself beginning to change. We are moving beyond innovation overload, which by definition is something we recognize as new and different, to a situation where change is endemic. Change is becoming all-pervasive; it is here to stay. We do not see much alleviation in the pressure for change nationally; but more than that, we see society itself becoming increasingly accustomed to, and expectant of, change as a way of life. Traditional responses to change are no longer coping with the situation. Developing strategies that help us handle single changes in curriculum or teaching methods, such as INSET, or even more sophisticated approaches that are supposed to help us deal with multiple innovations, such as 'development planning', are rapidly reaching their sell-by date.

What we require is radically different ways of looking at, responding to, and managing change. Michael Fullan (1992a, p. 2) has recently phrased the problem in a particularly helpful way. We quote him at length:

> Many of us who have pursued the theory and practice of planned change over the past 25 years have now decided to take a different tack. This change in strategy is based on the conclusion that educational reform not only does not work as the theories say it should, but more fundamentally that it can never work that way. Educational reform is complex, non-linear, frequently arbitrary, and always highly political. It is rife with unpredictable shifts and fragmented initiatives. I am afraid that this is the nature of the beast in complex socio-political societies.
>
> Moreover, we do not have the choice of avoiding change just because it is messy. One way or the other, new policy requirements, new technologies, changes in personnel, demographic shifts, political interest groups inevitably encroach upon the status quo. We are badly in need of a new mind set and lines of action that will enable us to survive and have a chance of progressing under these complex, less

13

than helpful conditions. There is no easy solution, and in fact I do not assume that we can move forward in every situation, or that we can stay moving forward when things seem to be going in the right direction.

We use the phrase *systemic change* to describe the situation in which we currently find ourselves, where change proliferates, is unpredictable, and is all-pervasive. It is a situation that requires a radically different response. The basic problem is that our maps of change are faulty (Fullan and Miles, 1992, p. 745). It is difficult to get to a destination if the directions being followed are incorrect. It is these faulty assumptions that leave one helpless, de-skilled and frustrated at one's inability to come to terms with a changing world. What we require is, to use Thomas Kuhn's phrase, a 'paradigm shift' in our approach to change. Such shifts in understanding and beliefs are difficult to achieve, but without them we will continue to wallow helplessly in the face of the inevitable.

One way of coping with systemic change is to make change everyone's business. As Fullan and Miles (1992, p. 745) comment, 'no change would be more fundamental than a dramatic expansion of the capacity of individuals and organizations to understand and deal with change'. We need to become skilful and knowledgeable about the business of change. Everyone within a school or college needs to become in some sense a change agent. Instead of change happening to us or being committed on us, we need to understand the process, and through understanding take control. We need to study the process and become more skilled in its use.

Part of this mind shift is the way in which we view change. As we will argue in Chapter 3, most of us try to resist change because it is threatening and uncomfortable. Instead of resisting change, viewing it as a burden or something to be suffered, we need to welcome it as an opportunity. As we move into the future, problems of all sorts will enter our lives. In order to survive, we have to adapt and modify our behaviour. We cannot ignore the problems, for they will not simply disappear. We must grapple with them and embrace them. In a sense, we must make them our friends and learn to live with them. Problems are our friends because only through immersing ourselves in problems can we come up with creative solutions (Fullan and Miles, 1992, p. 750).

We believe that school improvement, like the human condition, is largely about problem solving. It is about weighing and taking decisions and living with the consequences, before moving on to the next set of problems. By understanding this, and by becoming skilled in the process of problem solving, we can develop as individuals and also cope more effectively with the future. Although this is an appropriate response at the individual level, these insights rarely inform national policies at the macro level. This observation, as we see in the following section, is not restricted to the UK alone.

THE CENTRALIZATION–DECENTRALIZATION PARADOX

Over the past ten years there has in many countries been a tremendous increase in the amount of change expected of schools. This increase in expectations has been accompanied by fundamental changes in the way schools are managed and governed. In most Western countries there appear to be seemingly contradictory pressures for centralization (that is, increasing government control over policy and direction) on the one hand, and decentralization (that is, more responsibility for implementation, resource management and evaluation at the local level) on the other. This tension is making it very difficult for schools and local authorities to implement successfully innovations that make a real difference to the quality of schooling and pupil achievement. The key challenge, as a recent OECD report makes clear, is to find a balance between the increasing demands for centrally determined policy initiatives and quality control, and the encouragement of locally developed school improvement efforts. Three principal conclusions emerge from this report on decentralization and school improvement (OECD, 1989, p.2):

- The decentralization of decision making as part of school improvement establishes new roles and responsibilities for senior education officials at the centre and for school leaders, teachers and parents at the school level. As new roles are assumed, tensions inevitably develop. Approaches need to be put in place to respond to these tensions.

- Shifts of responsibility to the school level raise the possibility that some functions, formerly carried out at the centre, will not be effectively performed. Central authorities need to ensure, through guidance and support for pre-service, in-service, and community-based programmes, that those assuming new roles have developed the capacity to meet their new responsibilities. External support for schools, re-oriented to meet specific school-defined needs, also must be sustained (even if the services are no longer provided by central authorities).

- The management of change, whether at the centre or at the school level, requires a strategy which considers change as a dynamic and evolutionary process. Following from a clear vision of the expected results of the change, the strategy should anticipate tensions and difficulties but also allow for adaptations and adjustments as the change proceeds.

This type of analysis raises a number of questions about how central policy can be implemented and monitored, while leaving latitude for professional judgement at the school level: in particular, about the role of external support, the allocation of resources and the involvement of governors and parents. A general response to the dilemma of decentralization has been to give more responsibility to schools for their own management. Although this change goes by different names in different countries — 'local management of schools'

15

in the UK; 'self-managing schools' in Australia; 'site-based management' or 'restructuring' in the USA — the concept remains similar. Unfortunately, similarity does not imply clarity or specificity. Many of the policies seem to be either politically or ideologically inspired, or an *ad hoc* response to an immediate 'crisis' situation. Simply changing bureaucratic procedures or holding people more accountable does not by itself improve the quality of education for our young people.

The policies for the *local management of schools* (*LMS*) in England and Wales in the late 1980s were designed to increase the autonomy of schools in terms of their financial arrangements and governance. In general they led to a weakening of the traditional ties between the LEA and the schools. This initiative, which was as much politically as educationally inspired, was further buttressed by more recent legislation that has encouraged schools to 'opt out' of LEA control completely. Financial delegation, the increased role of governors in the running of the school, and 'opting out' have proven very popular with some, but their benefits in the medium to long term are still to be demonstrated.

The phrase 'the *self-managing school*' emerged in Tasmania and Victoria, Australia, in the mid-1980s, and has been adapted and emulated in many other school systems, most notably in Edmonton, Alberta, and in many areas of England. This approach was developed initially as a response to the devolution of financial resources to the school level, which by itself is no guarantee of school improvement. The aspirations of this approach can only be achieved if financial plans reflect educational plans, and if resources are allocated to support the priorities that a school has set itself. The approach, described by its originators Caldwell and Spinks (1988) as 'collaborative school management', aspires to integrate goal setting, policy making, budgeting, implementation and evaluation within a context of decision making that involves the school's staff, students, community and governing body.

In a similar way current approaches to *restructuring* in the USA (e.g. Elmore, 1990; Murphy, 1991) are attempting a more fundamental approach to educational reform by transforming the organization of the school in the quest for enhanced student achievement. The restructuring phenomenon is generally traced to the release in 1986 of two influential reform reports, *Tomorrow's Teachers* by the Holmes Group and *Teachers for the Twenty-first Century* by the Carnegie Forum. It is also being seen by some as a means of implementing the findings of, or legacy from, the school effectiveness research.

The restructuring movement in the USA provides perhaps the best and most researched example of the potential and pitfalls of this ubiquitous approach to educational reform. The studies so far conducted on restructuring suggest that simply devolving budgets or broadening the governance of schools is no guarantee of school improvement (Levine and Eubanks, 1989; David, 1989). Like many other initiatives, restructuring, and by implication LMS, appear superficially attractive and provide a useful banner under which to rally the troops or attack opponents. It will remain a superficial initiative, however, unless its 'deep structure' is implemented.

Elmore (1990) suggests that there are three commonly agreed components to restructuring:

- changing the way teaching and learning occur in schools;
- changing the organization and internal features of schools — the so-called 'workplace conditions';
- changing the distribution of power between the school and its clients.

Unless these three occur simultaneously, so the logic of Elmore's argument goes, there is little likelihood of marked improvement in student outcomes or achievement of the core goals of the school. These components of restructuring seem to us to have some general validity; yet they are rarely given much credence in national policies, which as we see in the following section are dominated by 'top-down' approaches to change.

THE PATHOLOGY OF 'TOP-DOWN' CHANGE

It is almost always the case that centrally imposed (or top-down) change implicitly assumes that implementation is an event rather than a process; that a change proceeds on autopilot once the policy has been enunciated or passed. This perspective ignores the critical distinction between the *object of change* — for example, the contents of the Education Reform Acts — and the *process of changing* — that is, how schools and local agencies put the reforms into practice.

The pathology of policy implementation has recently been described by Milbrey McLaughlin (1990) in her reanalysis of the large-scale Rand Change Agent study undertaken in the USA in the mid- to late 1970s. She found that many of the conclusions from the study still hold true today, and commented that (McLaughlin, 1990, p. 12):

> A general finding of the Change Agent study that has become almost a truism is that it is exceedingly difficult for policy to change practice, especially across levels of government. Contrary to the one-to-one relationship assumed to exist between policy and practice, the Change Agent study demonstrated that the nature, amount, and pace of change at the local level was a product of local factors that were largely beyond the control of higher-level policymakers.

According to McLaughlin (1990, p. 12) this general observation has three specific implications:

- Policy cannot mandate what matters.
- Implementation dominates outcomes.
- Local variability is the rule; uniformity is the exception.

The Rand study also looked at the strategies that promoted educational improvement, and here too McLaughlin (1990, p. 12) has a list of what does and does not work. Strategies that were generally seen to be ineffective were:

17

- reliance on outside consultants;
- packaged management approaches;
- one-shot, pre-implementation training;
- pay for training;
- formal, summative evaluation;
- comprehensive, system-wide projects.

Those that were generally effective, especially when used together, were:

- concrete, teacher-specific and extended training;
- classroom assistance from local staff;
- teacher observation of similar projects in other classrooms, schools or districts;
- regular project meetings that focused on practical issues;
- teacher participation in project decisions;
- local development of project materials;
- principals' (headteachers') participation in training.

As is apparent from these contrasting strategies, the relationship between macro-level policies and micro-level behaviour is paramount. Although policies set directions and provide a framework, they do not and cannot determine outcomes. It is implementation, rather than the decision to adopt a new policy, that determines student achievement. What is needed is 'implementation friendly' policy that is concerned with the process as well as the substance of change.

The central irony of many superficially attractive reforms is that they have no hope of enhancing the outcomes of students, which was their *raison d'être*. We appear to be living in an Alice-in-Wonderland world of educational reform where the sole rationale for many policies is the public support for them by a small group of ideologically committed politicians. Consequently there is no room for informed debate as to the coherence or likely success of one policy over another.

Innovation is like a carousel ride with 'new' ideas coming around on a regular basis. Educational reform consequently proceeds in fits and starts as various fads become popular, are adopted and then replaced. The problem of 'faddism', as Robert Slavin (1989) has called it, seems to be that innovations are rarely proven before they are implemented, or evaluated prior to wider dissemination. New initiatives are often adopted because they seem to be a 'good idea' and are not formally evaluated until interest in them dwindles. By then it is time to move on to something new or at least to an idea whose turn has come around again. A good example of this phenomenon is the recent controversy surrounding the teaching of reading, with polarized positions taken on the basis of belief rather than evidence. Slavin (1989, p. 757) maintains that:

Two major shifts will have to take place if we are to wean ourselves from faddism and increase the chances for responsible and lasting change in education. First, school districts [that is, LEAs] will have to demand high-quality evaluations of programs before they adopt them. Federal, state and local governments can assist with this process. Second, school districts will have to focus their staff development efforts not on one-shot workshops, but on extended training and follow-up for a smaller number of programs and practices of proven effectiveness. The emphasis in staff development must shift from scattershot presentations on what's new to systematic implementation of what works.

We do not want to argue at this point for a specific set of policies. We wish simply to emphasize the point that much policy decision making in education, by any rational criteria, appears to be capricious and based more on ideology than on educational substance. The main purpose of this broad sweep across the current field of educational change, however, has been to provide a context for the argument that there is a preferred way of meeting the challenge of educational reform — through school improvement. It is to a further consideration of what this implies that we turn in the following chapters.

MESSAGES

The context of educational reform in England and Wales and elsewhere is becoming increasingly complex. The dependency created by innovation overload clouds a number of important issues. The centralization-decentralization paradox, for example, encourages one to believe that the objectives of reform have been identified. It is dangerous to accept this, because if reform initiatives are to succeed, they need to be reinvented in local settings. Another irony is that the sea change schools have been involved in places more, rather than less, reliance on school-based development. There is also the danger in times of radical reform of attempting to demonstrate that a new system will work, at the expense of focusing on enhancing the quality of education. All of these issues, we believe, detract us from the central purpose of schools, which is increasing the level of student achievement, however broadly defined.

The other messages that we take from this discussion are:

- Do not assume a deficit model of change. Just because there is a great deal of change around does not mean that everything that exists is wrong. You do not have to be ill to get better! Successful change builds on the excellence we have already achieved and judiciously blends it with what we can achieve.

- Assume that policies are only a starting point. At best they provide a framework, at worst they set the school off in the wrong direction. Even with sensible, helpful policies, what goes on in the school determines what happens to students.

- The distinction between the 'object' of change and the 'process' of changing needs to be recognized. There is an implicit assumption that change is an event rather than a process. It is mainly because of this that the success of most centralized educational policies is unpredictable. There are two specific reasons for this: a lack of understanding of the dynamics of change, and a neglect of the internal conditions of schools. It is only through being self-conscious about the change process that one learns how to manage innovation, as well as how to implement specific curricula or teaching initiatives.

- Implementation strategies need to support teacher learning. Successful, sustained change at the classroom level is the result of teachers who are confident and committed to an on-going concept of professional development. Schools need to create the opportunities for teachers to meet together regularly to discuss aspects of their work, share ideas, plan, observe one another's practice and provide feedback on new approaches. Changes which do not address the organizational conditions within the school *as well as* alterations to the curriculum and teaching are quickly marginalized.

- The culture of the school is the key to successful school improvement. Although we have not begun to address the issue of school culture (this is the main task of Chapter 6), it is important to note at an early stage that a major issue for developing schools is the relationship between implementation of reform and school culture. The real agenda is not implementing single innovations but changing the culture of the school.

Chapter 3

Making Sense of Change

Innovation overload, reduced resources and the complexity of reform initiatives put great strains on schools' ability to respond to the overwhelming demands for change. Change itself is a complex phenomenon that one needs to make sense of before being able to take any control over the process. The task of this chapter is to attempt a more comprehensive definition of the concept of change and to describe a number of frameworks for viewing change in educational settings. But first, a definition of change itself.

Change tends to manifest itself in organizations in one of two forms: *incremental change*, a gradual, often subtle transition from one state to another; and *planned change*, which seeks to interrupt the natural development of events and, often on a given day, to break with previous practice to establish a new order. As well as presenting in two forms, change tends to arise from one of two sources: external and internal. *Internal change*, whether at individual or at system level, is often seen as 'natural' or 'organic' — like the growth of a child one becomes conscious of without often noticing it. By contrast, *external change* is much harder to assimilate — it is what others would do to us, to our school. As writers on change have been pointing out for many years now, resistance to such sudden alteration in circumstances is natural, even when it would seem to be for the better.

These two features of change, the sources and the style, interact to produce a basic typology (Figure 3.1). Obviously, the type of change has implications for implementation, particularly innovation (planned external) or purposive (planned internal) change. Planned educational change combines purposive change and innovation in an attempt to plan the development of the school, college or other educational institution consciously, often in response, it must be said, to external demands. Although it is these types of change which we address in this book, one would do well to remember that incremental change inches forward day by day, impossible to halt, and often, when we look back over a period of time, it surprises us by its progress.

We tend in this book to use the terms 'reform', 'change', 'planned change' and 'innovation' interchangeably; but despite this imprecision (which is for obvious stylistic reasons), it is important to remember that innovation, the adoption and use of specific educational ideas and practices, has a more precise meaning. School improvement, on the other hand, is not simply about innovation and purposive change, but also tends to incorporate an implementation strategy and a focus on the school as an organization. This results in a two-pronged approach that, ideally, not only helps to put the change or innovation in place, but also enhances the school's ability to manage change.

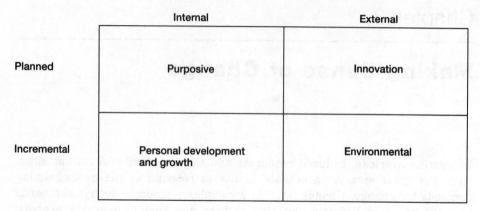

Figure 3.1 *A typology of change.*

In this book the emphasis is on planned educational change and school improvement; approaches to change over which the school has some control. In the rest of this chapter we attempt to make more sense of 'change' by:

- reviewing the history of the study of change;
- exploring the nature of educational change;
- presenting a variety of frameworks for thinking about change;
- describing three perspectives on planned change;
- relating aspects of the change process to school improvement.

THE STUDY OF CHANGE

It is surprising to realize, as Fullan (1991, p. 5) has also pointed out, how short is the history of serious investigation into the change process in schools. Over the past thirty years or so there have been four major phases in the study of planned educational change.

The first, which dates from the mid-1960s, was the emphasis on the *adoption of curriculum materials*. On both sides of the Atlantic the curriculum reform movement was intended to have a major impact on student achievement through the production and dissemination of exemplary curriculum materials. Although the materials were often of high quality, being produced by teams of designers, academics and psychologists, in the main they failed to have an impact on teaching. The reason is obvious with hindsight; teachers were not included in the production process and the INSET that accompanied the new curricula was often perfunctory and rudimentary. Teachers, of course, got their own back. The imaginative educational archaeologist will to this day find partly rifled packs of curriculum materials among the cobwebs at the back of stockrooms and store cupboards. Teachers took what they thought was of use from the materials and integrated them into their own teaching. The curriculum as an innovation, however, was consequently subverted.

Although this analysis applies more to North America than to the UK, the materials emanating from the Schools Council in the late 1960s (see Stenhouse, 1980, for a comprehensive account of these projects) cannot escape censure. Although the Schools Council curriculum projects involved teachers and some had attendant INSET schemes, they were still conceived within a top-down or 'centre-periphery' model of educational change. Few of these projects paid anything more than lip service to the essential connection between teaching style and curriculum development (Hopkins, 1987a).

The second phase, covering most of the 1970s, was essentially one of *documenting failure* — the failure of the curriculum reform movement to affect practice. It became increasingly apparent from this work that top-down models of change did not work, that teachers required inservice training to acquire new knowledge and skills, and that implementation does not occur sponta-neously as a result of legislative fiat. It was clear that implementation is an extremely complex and lengthy process that requires a sensitive combination of strategic planning, individual learning and commitment to succeed. Much was learned about implementation during this period, however, that was to lay the basis for future work. We have already noted the contribution of Fullan in this respect. His work was paralleled by UK curriculum developers and evaluators, particularly those connected with the numerous Schools Council curriculum projects of the time. The implications of these have been admirably and wittily summarized and conceptualized by Barry Macdonald and Rob Walker (1976) from the Centre of Applied Research in Education at the University of East Anglia, in their *Changing the Curriculum*.

The third phase, roughly from the late 1970s to the mid-1980s and building on previous experience, was a period of *success*. It was during this time that the first studies of school effectiveness were published (Rutter *et al.*, 1979; Reynolds, 1985), and that a consensus was established over the characteristics of effective schools (Purkey and Smith, 1983; Wilson and Corcoran, 1988). This is not meant to imply, however, that this line of inquiry is unproblematic; there is still much more work to be done, as Scheerens (1992) illustrates. It was also during this period that some major large-scale studies of school improvement projects were conducted (Crandall *et al.*, 1982, 1986; Huberman and Miles, 1984; Hargreaves, 1984; Rosenholtz, 1989; Louis and Miles, 1990). Much was conse-quently learned about the dynamics of the change process. The OECD International School Improvement Project (ISIP) was also at work at this time producing case studies of and developing strategies for school improvement (for an overview see van Velzen *et al.*, 1985; Hopkins, 1987b). A number of syntheses of this work have also appeared, of which the contributions of Fullan (1985) and Joyce and his colleagues (1983) are very important.

Although this creative period produced knowledge of increasing specificity about the change process and the factors influencing effective schooling, this is a necessary but not sufficient condition to improve the quality of education. As Fullan points out, clear descriptions of success are not tantamount to solving the management-of-change problem.

Managing change, the fourth phase, which we have recently entered, will prove to be the most difficult and, let us hope, most productive of all, as we struggle to relate strategies and research knowledge to the realities of schools in a pragmatic, systematic and sensitive way. There is now a move away from studying change as a phenomenon, and towards actually participating in school development. The best of the current work on educational change is coming from people who are studying change as they are engaged in bringing it about. Research knowledge and 'change theory' are being refined through action. Recent work on the Department of Education and Science (DES) School Development Plans project is an example of the application of school improvement knowledge to the 'real world' of schools in an attempt to develop practical strategies to empower schools (Hargreaves and Hopkins, 1991). Similarly the IQEA project described in Parts 3 and 4 of this book is an example of this way of working.

This historical review of studies of innovation and planned change is one way of organizing the literature. It is helpful in so far as it gives a perspective on one's own work, and information on who looked at what when. However, it tells us little about what educational change actually is; this is the task of the following section.

WHAT IS EDUCATIONAL CHANGE?

Having established a definition of change and traced some of the recent history of studies of innovation, we now need to consider in more depth the reality of innovation and planned change. An anecdote sets the scene. In the course of our work we often talk with educational policy makers (by this we mean anyone who formulates and disseminates educational ideas, be they politicians, civil servants, LEA officers, heads or coordinators) about changes they wish to make. They frequently talk about these changes in the most concrete of terms, as if the change were an artefact we can see, touch and feel. In these conversations we are often reminded of the story of the emperor's clothes. Being the people we are, we then want to ask them to let us see how their change works; to put the change artefact on to a trolley and wheel it into a school. When in our imagination they do this, something very odd happens to the change; it begins to lose its shape and definition. By the time it approaches the classroom door the change has virtually disappeared and when the trolley enters the classroom it has vanished altogether. The reason is, of course, that at the classroom level educational changes and innovations are rarely tangible objects; they are manifest only in the way that teachers and pupils interact. Unfortunately this perspective is all too often lost on policy makers and those imbued with a more instrumental and concrete view of innovation and change.

Change, if it is to mean anything at all, has to have an impact at the classroom level — on the hearts and minds of teachers and students. Without this reality we are, to use Charters and Jones's (1973) felicitous phrase, in danger of 'appraising non-events'. As we noted in the previous chapter, the reality of change is not about policies, although they do provide a framework for action, but about the *implementation* of policies; and that means how they are interpreted by students, teachers and schools. If we are to take the study of change seriously, by considering whether it has a positive impact on teachers and the progress of students, then we must realize in a deep way that educational

24

change is ultimately an individual achievement. This is, of course, a radical and threatening position to take. But the evidence and experience are accumulating at such a rate that we ignore these insights at our peril.

So what are the implications of all of this? Probably the most convincing response to this question is found in the vignettes and strategies of practical work in schools described in Parts 3 and 4 of the book. For the moment we want to argue our case through the use of theory and research. We begin with the 'implementation perspective' that suggests that much of the failure of curriculum innovation was the result of assuming that change was an event rather than a process. This led to an underestimation of the way in which the curriculum was negotiated and used in classrooms (Fullan and Pomfret, 1977).

The thrust of what we have been saying in the last few paragraphs is that implementation ultimately concerns changes in individual practice. Implementation is a multidimensional concept and involves changes at a number of different levels (Fullan and Park, 1981). It is likely that the implementation of a significant curriculum or organizational change will involve one or more of the following features:

- changes in the *structure and organization* of the school; for example, timetabling or the formation of new working groups;
- new or additional teaching *materials*; for example, worksheets or books;
- teachers acquiring new *knowledge*; for example, in working with information technology (IT);
- teachers adopting new *behaviours* in terms of teaching style; for example, the non-didactic or consultancy approach often associated with resource-based learning;
- changes in *beliefs or values* on the part of some teachers; for example, in the early days of the Technical and Vocational Education Initiative (TVEI) many teachers did not believe that the initiative was a good thing.

These aspects of change are regarded as necessary because together they represent the means of achieving a particular educational goal or set of goals (Fullan, 1991, p. 37). This perspective makes sense, however, only as long as the implementer is in charge of the change process, or if there are curriculum materials present in the first place. If the implementer is not in charge, and the materials are conspicuously lacking, as in many situations in England and Wales at present, then implementation becomes far more problematic. Educational change is, then, a complex phenomenon that involves a chain of events over time leading from policy, through the local context and the inter-pretation of policy, to classroom action before it can hope to have any impact on the achievement of students. This partially explains the differential impact of reform, because individual teachers move through this process at different rates. Interestingly, because commitment to specific reforms builds during implementation, different groups of teachers moving at different rates may

Table 3.1 *The implementation and quality of educational change*

Quality	High implementation	Low implementation
High	2	1
Low	4	3

Adapted from Fullan, 1991, p. 18.

have opposing attitudes to the usefulness of certain aspects of the national reform agenda within the same school.

One more point needs to be added here: we should not assume that all change is good. This is particularly the case in times of reform and innovation overload. Table 3.1 helps make the point.

For the sake of argument we have collapsed the previous discussion on change to a consideration of its usefulness along two dimensions. Has the change been implemented? Is the change of high quality? Again, for the sake of exposition the response can be yes or no. High or low quality; high or low levels of implementation. This gives us four types of possible outcome.

Type 1 changes are where the change is of high quality yet poorly implemented. This is a situation which we try to address in our work with schools. An example would be the introduction of Records of Achievement. Here, although the change was of good quality and regarded as highly desirable, it absorbed a great deal of time and often required alterations in teacher-student relationships. Because of this, Records of Achievement were in many schools often 'bolted on' and never fully implemented.

Type 2 change, where the innovation is of high quality and well implemented, is presumably the outcome that we are all looking for. A good example of that in the UK would be the introduction of GCSE, which, with its emphasis on course work and teacher assessment, replaced the far more narrow O-level examinations. Despite early turbulence, most teachers felt that the reform was 'right' and with an appropriate level of pressure it was well implemented.

Type 3 changes occur when the school and its teachers or students are discerning enough not to implement poor-quality changes. As we write, there is a powerful coalition growing in many schools between parents, governors, heads and teachers against the implementation of government plans for national testing. This resistance has resulted in a modification to the tests in certain subject areas. This is also a desired outcome of school improvement: where the school is powerful enough to resist unwanted and unwarranted change.

Type 4 change is the situation we most want to avoid, where there is a high level of implementation of a poor-quality change. An example of this can be found in the increase in 'setting' which has occurred in order to ease the implementation of the National Curriculum, especially in primary schools. Although it is well established that 'setting' has a negative impact on student achievement, it is an easy change to implement, and may ease some of the pressure of implementing the National Curriculum, at least in the short term.

Our most successful schools tend to operate mainly in areas 2 and 3. Unfortunately, in many schools type 1 and 4 changes are more commonly seen. The key question, of course, is how to help schools achieve the critical capability that enables them to live comfortably in areas 2 and 3. In the rest of this chapter we look at the answers that the research on innovation and planned change can provide.

ON WAYS OF THINKING ABOUT CHANGE

Knowledge expands at such a rate that we need some way of classifying it and reducing it to manageable proportions. We also need to conceive of knowledge in ways that make sense and lead to action. This is why people often think in terms of *models*, because they often provide helpful frameworks for action. There is also a more profound way of viewing knowledge, in terms of underlying *values or assumptions*. In this section we will explore further these two ways of thinking about change.

There are almost as many conceptions of the change process as there are writers on the subject, but despite this there are some broad areas of agreement. Hoyle's (1976) Open University unit, Strategies of Curriculum Change, for example, provides a helpful review of the differing interpretations and facets of the term 'change', and an introduction to various change models from a UK perspective.

Our brief review serves to give a 'feel' for the area. Bennis *et al.* (1969) were the first to describe systematically the fundamental strategies of change. They identified three broad groupings which are said to comprise the range of approaches to change:

- *Power-coercive* refers to an approach which is direct, legalistic and authoritarian, and where the flow of communication is one way, from the initiator to the practitioner.
- *Normative re-educative* strategies are directed at the attitudes, norms and opinions of a group of practitioners, the mode of approach usually being made through group work with an emphasis on two-way interpersonal communication.
- *Rational-empirical* refers to an approach based on expertise which is aimed at the reason or intellect of the practitioner. The medium used is usually the book, lecture or advertisement, and communication is largely one-way.

In their book *The Planning of Change*, Bennis *et al.* (1969) provided a detailed rationale for each approach and gave examples of strategies under each of these three headings. The purpose of describing these three strategies or models is not merely taxonomic, but also to enable people, once having diagnosed a situation, to select the most appropriate change strategy for that particular change or setting.

The Bennis *et al.* approach, therefore, is about ordering the knowledge base in order to give researchers and practitioners more control over the

Dimension 1: The three major systems

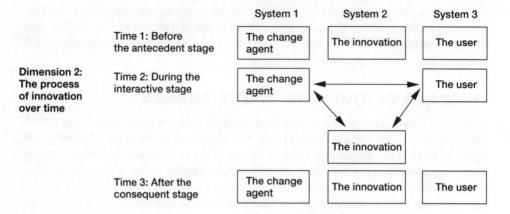

Figure 3.2 *A conceptual framework for the study of innovation (Bolam, 1975, pp. 274-5).*

process. Another interesting model that does just that was developed by Ray Bolam with his colleagues in Bristol during the mid-1970s while they were working on a succession of applied educational research projects. Bolam's conceptual framework for innovation provides a way of organizing a great deal of previous work, a way of thinking about the process of change, and an indication of how to go about doing it. It distinguishes between four major factors: the change agent, the innovation, the user system and the process of innovation over time. These four factors are presented (in Figure 3.2) as a two-dimensional conceptual framework. Bolam's framework, which merits closer attention, highlights the interactive nature of the innovation process, which is vitally important in any mature appreciation of how change comes about.

We have also found the distinction between 'adoptive' and 'adaptive' models of change helpful as a means of categorizing the literature (Hopkins, 1984). The *adoptive* approach to change tends to disregard the variables existing within the individual school environment. These strategies are preoccupied with a top-down approach to change: they assume that change is linear and motivated by an authority figure. These models are often based on the (correct) assumption that it is usually the case that external pressure provides the motivation for change. This linear approach to change has been described by Lippitt and his colleagues (1978, p. 24) in this way:

> The aim [is] to get the client to change in certain specified ways, to adopt certain practices, [and to] use certain technological devices. All are oriented towards the development of knowledge, by researchers, which could be of benefit to potential users if put into practice. Thus the central question voiced by all three models is, 'Given that researchers have developed some new device, mechanism, process or procedure, how can potential users be convinced to put it into practice?'

Table 3.2 *Guba and Clark's (1965) RD&D model (quoted in Hoyle, 1976, p. 40)*

Method	Purpose
Research	To advance knowledge
Invention	To innovate
Design	To systematize the components of the innovation
Dissemination	To inform
Demonstration	To build conviction
Trial	To test
Installation	To operationalize
Institutionalization	To establish as an integral component of the system

The best known of these approaches is probably the Research, Development and Dissemination (RD&D) model of educational change. As we have said, this is a top-down, or more accurately a centre-periphery, model of change that was developed to assist the implementation of centralized curriculum innovation in the mid-1960s and later. The ideas underlying the model are well known, but the most sophisticated description of the model has been given by Guba and Clark (1965). Their classification is seen in Table 3.2.

This model, or variations of it, follows an almost irresistible logic. It represents the strategy used by most centralized curriculum development agencies, and by the same token policy makers, in implementing their 'products' or policies. It is recognizable as an 'ideal type' of approach, used in the UK, for example, by the Schools Council in the late 1960s and 1970s, and more recently by the National Curriculum Council (NCC). Ironically, as we have already intimated, this approach to educational change has not proved very successful. Although this fact is now widely recognized by researchers and practitioners, it is still the preferred approach of policy makers and politicians — a situation unlikely to change in the near future.

There are other approaches to educational change that are more sensitive to the situation of the individual school and local context. They are appreciative of the environment in which they intervene, and demonstrate a concern for developing a capacity for change within the school situation rather than the adoption *per se* of the specific approach. These have been described as *adaptive* models of change (Lippitt *et al.*, 1978). Interestingly, even Guba and Clark (1975) have publicly abandoned their advocacy for the RD&D approach, and ten years later proposed a more adaptive or cultural conceptualization of change.

If we stay with curriculum change for the moment, then a well-developed model which illustrates the adaptive approach has been provided by Malcolm Skilbeck's (1984) articulation of school-based curriculum development. Skilbeck outlines a five-stage model for this: situational analysis; goal formulation; programme building; interpretation and implementation; and monitoring, feedback assessment and reconstruction. Although there is a logical order to these stages, there may be sound reasons for intervening first at any one of them. Skilbeck also admits that, despite the technical appeal of such a model, teachers do not in fact proceed in such a linear fashion. His view is that the model should encourage groups of teachers involved in curriculum development to take into account different aspects of the process, to see it as an organic whole, and to work in a moderately systematic way.

School-based curriculum development is an appealing concept. Skilbeck's description, however, has a historical ring to it, especially to those of us enmeshed in the challenges of centrally imposed curricula and innovation overload. Certainly the model as it stands needs modifying to fit current circumstances. What, however, is interesting about moves to a National Curriculum is that, ironically, they are putting more pressure on schools to develop their own version of a curriculum as a response to and elaboration of highly specific national criteria. As is illustrated by the work on the DES 'School Development Plans' project (Hargreaves and Hopkins, 1991), by Denis Lawton's (1989) analysis of the teacher's and school's response to the National Curriculum, and even by the NCC's (1990) guidance on the 'Whole Curriculum', successful schools will be increasingly developing their own curriculum to reflect their own aspirations and the needs of their own pupils within the context of national criteria. This is where an adaptive model of curriculum change such as Skilbeck's could prove very helpful.

The distinction between adoptive and adaptive models of change is, of course, overly simplistic. At best these should be regarded as 'ideal type' and be open to modification. Mature responses to prescriptions of this type have been provided by Ronald Havelock, and by Gene Hall and Susan Loucks.

Havelock's (1975) linkage model embraces both adoptive and adaptive models of change, albeit at a structural level, and provides a more realistic approach to school autonomy in times of centralized change. He envisages a linkage process that mediates between RD&D agencies and the school. In the UK the best examples of these linking organizations would be teacher centres or LEA curriculum agencies. At present, such external support in the UK is in a hiatus. This, however, as we see in Chapter 5, is no reason to underestimate the importance of this function in facilitating the change process in schools.

The Levels of Use (LOU) instrument and the Concerns Based Adoption Model (CBAM) were originally developed by Hall and Loucks (1977, 1978) as a means of evaluating the level of implementation of a change in curriculum or teaching practice, and assessing the concerns of teachers as they move through the innovation process. These approaches were technically valid and extremely useful as evaluation tools. In this respect they fell into the 'adoption' category, as they had a specific and instrumental purpose. In later work (e.g. Loucks-Horsley and Hergert, 1985; Hall and Hord, 1987) these approaches have been used with great success, in a more adaptive way, in school-based development programmes. This is a good example of a well-developed and reliable approach to school development.

Beside the descriptions of specific approaches, what we are now beginning to see in these classifications of change strategies is not only ways of making change happen, but values about how change should be accomplished. Views on the complexity of change are value laden. The world view of those committed to change by adoption, for example, is most probably very different from that of those committed to an adaptive approach. To highlight this point, we provide examples of the value positions underpinning curriculum

Table 3.3 *Two contrasting views of curriculum implementation*

As instrumental action	As practical action
With the researcher as the locus implies the following:	**With the teacher as the locus implies the following:**
Doing curriculum implementation is installing curriculum X.	Within this framework, to do curriculum implementation is to come to a deep understanding of curriculum X and to transform it based on the appropriateness to the situation.
The interest of the teacher is in placing curriculum X in a classroom or school faithfully and efficiently.	The implementer's interest is in the transformation of curriculum X within the situation based on disclosed underlying assumptions and conditions that make the transformation possible.
The implied view of curriculum is that of a commodity to be dispensed by teachers and consumed by students.	The implied view of curriculum X is that it is an object to be interpreted and critically reflected upon in an on-going transformation of curriculum and self.
The implied view of the good teacher is one who installs curriculum X efficiently and faithfully.	The implied view of the teacher is that of an actor who acts with and upon curriculum X as he/she reflects upon his/her own assumptions underlying action.
To explain 'implementation' within this framework is to give a cause–effect relationship.	Within this framework, to explain implementation is to trace it to underlying unreflected aspects which upon disclosure imply transformative action.
The implementer's subjectivity is irrelevant as implementing curriculum X is seen as an objective process.	The implementer's central activity is reflection upon his/her subjectively based action with and upon curriculum X.
The implied underlying relationship between theory and practice is one in which to implement is to put into practice curriculum-as-plan (that is, to apply to a practical situation an ideal construct).	The implied form of theory/practice relationship is that theory and practice are in dialectic relationship. To implement within this framework is to reflect critically upon the relationship between curriculum-as-plan and curriculum-in-use.
The typical approach to implementation studies is through examination of the degree of fidelity of the installed curriculum compared with the master curriculum.	To evaluate implementation within this framework is to examine the quality of the activity of discovering underlying assumptions, interests, values, motives, perspectives, root metaphors and implications for action to improve the human condition.

Adapted from Aoki (1984, pp. 112–13 and 116–17).

implementation which have been graphically contrasted by Ted Aoki (1984). He summarizes two polarized approaches to implementation: implementation as instrumental action as compared with practical action (Table 3.3). What Aoki is demonstrating so vividly here is the importance of people's values or view of the world in determining their approach to educational change or innovation. We see clearly in this example some of the reasons why a more instrumental approach to change has not always been overwhelmingly successful. These, of course, are the same values as underpin the adoption approaches to change we have just described, and Barth's 'school improvement by lists' approach described in Chapter 1. There are, however, other similar, but more accessible, frameworks for clarifying the values underlying our approaches to change, as we see in the following section.

THREE PERSPECTIVES ON PLANNED CHANGE

Some years ago Ernest House (1979) wrote a 'state-of-the-art' paper on curriculum innovation. The organizing framework that he used in it contained three perspectives on educational change: the technological, the political and the cultural.

The *technological* perspective is best illustrated by the RD&D model, and has all the characteristics of the adoption approach to change we have already described. It has been, and continues to be, used by those concerned with centralized approaches to curriculum and educational change such as we have already described. In many countries, despite the apparent moves towards decentralization, the dominant *modus operandi* has been, as we have seen, technological.

The perspective assumes a rational view of the world. Yet as Jerry Patterson and his colleagues (1986) hint in the title of their book, *Productive School Systems for a Non-rational World*, things are not always like that. This is not to imply that schools are irrational or do not make sense, but rather that they are complex organizations operating in a disorderly environment. Although we live in a non-rational world, most educational policy assumes a rational logic: if A happens then B will follow. When the 'if-then' logic does not work, it is common to resort to 'if only' statements. If only X had not happened, then B would have occurred. The problem with 'if-then and if only' thinking is twofold: (1) it only rarely mirrors reality, and (2) it encourages individuals to externalize blame and not take action themselves. Be this as it may, the technological approach continues to be the dominant perspective, and by trying to pretend otherwise one also falls into the 'if only' trap. The approach, as we have already said, is logical, it makes sense; our approach to school improvement would be unrealistic unless it also embraced this perspective.

The *political* perspective emphasizes that educational change inevitably involves conflict. Change by its very nature involves certain individuals and groups doing new things which inevitably disturb the status quo. What for some is improvement may for others, initially at least, appear at best irrelevant and in some cases foolish. In many schools it is fairly easy to predict the reactions of certain groups and individuals. Often senior management in school will try different strategies to get the various groups and significant individuals to support their proposals. Michael Huberman (1992, p. 17) understands this situation well:

> What typically happens is that there are usually dozens of bargains being struck along the way. Try out this programme and we'll get

some interesting materials and training. Let the principal have her visibility from this new project and she'll let us modify it to suit our purposes or our constraints. Tell the inspector that we'll go ahead if he agrees to suspend the standardized tests in the experimental classes for two years. Tell the teachers that we'll set up a facility for immigrant children if they'll accept to raise the class size so we can release staff for this project.

These bargains, moreover, are usually *implicit* ones. All sides know one another well enough to get the right signals, and know that making such agreements explicit is asking for trouble if they fall into the wrong hands. And *because* these negotiations are handled implicitly, we might make the mistake of assuming that implementation is a straightforward affair of setting things right, introducing promising new practices, meeting new or old objectives more efficiently. In fact, it is no more straightforward than in other micro-political arenas of social life. Simply, we in the educational business have something like a moral mandate to under-emphasize, at least in public, the more distasteful aspects of social behaviour. So when we talk about educational change, or even execute it, we may paper over the more irrational, conflictual, subtly authoritarian aspects of its execution. We are guilty of rhetorical angelism.

The micro-political aspects of educational change have received a great deal of attention recently from British commentators. Educational sociologists like Eric Hoyle (1986), Stephen Ball (1987), Andy Hargreaves (1986) and Peter Woods (1986) have, in a series of book, and papers, illustrated aspects of the phenomenon. Studies in this area have introduced a number of very helpful concepts. The mid-1970s Rand study on educational change in the USA, mentioned in Chapter 2, introduced the notion of 'mutual adaption' whereby the successful implementation of national initiatives was characterized by both the school *and* the innovation changing through a process of mutual adaption. A similar concept, that of 'curriculum negotiation', was introduced by Barry Macdonald and Rob Walker (1976) in their study of curriculum innovation in England. They maintain that basic conflicts in values are camouflaged by a common rhetoric to which all subscribe. Their context is that of the Schools Council and similar centralized curriculum projects. Here, the gap between project intent and classroom practice is the consequence of trade-offs in meaning that are negotiated between developers and teachers on the one hand, and developers and academic critics on the other. Their argument is that with academics they negotiate an ideal version of the project, and with teachers a watered-down version that is 'do-able' in practice. Although the situation is different now (no one cares what academics think any more), the micro-political trade-offs survive, whatever the context.

The *cultural* perspective, in studies of educational change at least, is concerned with the social setting in which innovation intervenes. It demonstrates a commitment to the everyday reality, the cultural norms that are disturbed when innovation threatens. It is the antithesis of the adoptive models we reviewed earlier, and shares many of the values of the adaptive approach we described at the same time. We refer here also to Sarason (1982), where the problem of change is treated as essentially a cultural one.

There is a strong research tradition in the UK of in-depth studies that throw some light upon the impact of culture in schools and classrooms. Many of these studies take a sociological perspective and most involve ethnographic approaches to inquiry. Some of these studies help us to understand the way structures influence culture (see Chapter 6) within a school (e.g. Ball, 1981; Woods, 1979), whereas others focus on the sub-cultures of particular student groups (e.g. Hargreaves, 1967; Willis, 1977). Much of this literature is rich with accounts that reveal the complexities of school life, including the ways in which the culture of an organization impacts upon individual teachers and the way they go about their tasks.

A relevant example of a study that provides insights as to how school culture influences the destination of an innovation is provided by Keddie (1971). She collected data in the humanities department of a secondary school during the introduction of a new inquiry-based course. The course used 'key lessons' to introduce topics, followed by a workcard system that was intended to allow students to work at their own pace. Much of Keddie's research provides insights into the micro-political processes that occurred during the process of curriculum innovation. However, the data also suggest ways in which the expectations and norms of teachers influence the treatment of particular groups of students. She makes us aware of the ways in which the culture of a given workplace influences the behaviour of teachers, and leads to the curriculum innovation taking particular forms. Indeed Keddie concludes that innovations in schools are unlikely to be of a very radical kind unless they produce fundamental changes in the ways in which teachers perceive their tasks.

We have other excellent examples of British work in this 'cultural' tradition. The work of Jean Rudduck, who, more than anyone else, has followed in the tradition of Lawrence Stenhouse, has exemplified a commitment to appreciating culture as a social phenomenon. Stenhouse (quoted in House, 1979, p. 8) defined culture as 'a complex of shared understandings which serve as a medium through which individualized human minds interact'. Rudduck (1991) amplifies this definition through a series of research projects that embrace the 'cultural' perspective, including that of pupils. Jennifer Nias, Geoff Southworth and their colleagues have, in their long-term research into primary schools, given a great deal of texture to the perspective (e.g. Nias et al., 1989). Nias (1989, p. 143), besides complaining that the term 'culture' is applied with 'a wilful lack of precision' to schools, maintains on the basis of her and her colleagues' work that a school's culture does not have an existence independent of those who participate in it. The cultural phenomenon, as we shall see in the chapters that follow, deserves more attention.

This trinity of perspectives, besides being a helpful way of organizing the research literature, seems also to have a degree of universal applicability. In Table 3.4 we have summarized the three perspectives and compared them to some of the other interpretations of change reviewed in this chapter. Each

Table 3.4 *A comparison of perspectives on change and innovation*

Perspective	House	Bennis et al.	Fullan and Pomfret	Bolam
Technological	Innovation	Rational-empirical	Fidelity	Innovation
Political	Innovation in context	Power-coercive	Mutual adaptation	Change agent
Cultural	Context	Normative-rational	Process studies	User

of these perspectives affords a unique insight into the process of change. The important point is that no one perspective has a monopoly of the truth. It is through a holistic overview of all three that one is able to grasp the reality of *all* those involved in the process of change.

A striking example of this point is provided by the conclusions of a recent study of curriculum innovation and change. On the basis of two qualitative studies of innovation involving seventeen schools, Corbett and Rossman (1989, pp. 187-8) concluded that successful change requires the simultaneous use of multiple perspectives. Every school contains those susceptible to each of these perspectives. Focusing on all three 'increases the pool of potential implementors'. Their study goes further than that in detailing the contribution each perspective contributes to the innovation process:

> First, certain antecedent conditions set the stage for how well or poorly a change project will go. Manipulating these to support innovative efforts creates an organization capable of intentionally changing whenever a worthwhile opportunity presents itself.
>
> Second, several intervening variables can be very powerful components of a change strategy. The three pivotal leverage points in the network seem to be: the encouragement/assistance, trial run and judgement of fit loop in the technical path; altering rules and procedures to accommodate change in the political path; and encouraging acceptance of new norms in the cultural path. The common denominators among the three were that at least some technical information was shared and systematic discussion of the information and trial runs of the new practices took place.
>
> Essentially, then, implementation is greater in social, supportive settings than in isolated environments ... Forcing teachers to implement directly as the result of a change in rules or procedures creates problems later.

The point that we are trying to emphasize is that each of these perspectives provides us with a valuable lens through which to view the change process. And each is important in its own right. Looking at a specific problem, at a particular point in time, may emphasize one view at the expense of another; but in the long run, all are equally valuable. In order to hammer the point home further and to provide descriptions of substantive points we wish to develop later, these three perspectives combine in the following section to give further insights into the process of change.

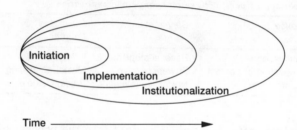

Figure 3.3 *The three overlapping phases of the change process (Miles et al., 1987).*

THE PROCESS OF CHANGE AND SCHOOL IMPROVEMENT

Although we deal with school improvement in detail in Chapter 5, there are three further issues from the literature on planned change that are crucial to our formulation of school improvement strategies. They cut across the three perspectives discussed in the previous section, each issue containing elements of the other. These three issues relate to the unfolding of the change process over time, the importance of student outcomes, and the meaning individuals make of the change process.

The first is the way in which the change process *unfolds*. As Miles (1986) and Fullan (1991) have demonstrated, the change process is not linear, but consists of a series of three stages that merge into each other. Although these phases often coexist in practice, there are some advantages in describing them separately; particularly in terms of what happens during them, and what behaviours within each phase make for success. The process is generally considered to consist of three overlapping phases: initiation, implementation, and institutionalization (Figure 3.3).

Although implementation has received the most attention historically, this has most probably been disadvantageous to the process as a whole. Emphasizing initiation and implementation at the expense of institutionalization leads to a short-term view of innovation, and encourages the faddism we discussed in Chapter 2. Consequently, it is probably more helpful to think of the three phases as a series of overlapping circles, as in Figure 3.3, rather than a straight line.

The *initiation* phase is about deciding to embark on innovation, and developing commitment towards the process. The key activities in the initiation phase are the decision to begin the innovation, and a review of the school's current state as regards it. There are, however, a number of factors associated with initiation that will influence whether the change gets started in the first place. We have already noted many of these in passing; they are issues such as the existence of and access to innovations, pressures from within and without the school, availability of resources and consultancy support, and the quality of the school's internal conditions and organization. Fullan (1991, p. 50) describes them in detail and emphasizes that it is not simply the existence of these factors but their combinations that are important.

Matthew Miles (1986) has made an analysis of the various stages of school improvement: here is a summary of his list of factors that make for successful initiation:

- an innovation tied to a *local agenda* and high-profile *local need*;
- a clear, *well-structured* approach to change;
- an active *advocate* or champion who understands the innovation and supports it;
- *active initiation* to start the innovation (top-down is all right under certain conditions);
- *good-quality* innovation.

Implementation is, as we have said, the phase of the process which has received the most attention. It is the phase of attempted use of the innovation. We have already referred to many of the factors influencing implementation, such as the characteristics of the change, the internal conditions of the school and the pressure and support from the outside. We have also discussed the various assumptions underlying the implementation process. It is during this phase that skills and understanding are being acquired, some success is being achieved, and responsibility is delegated to working groups of teachers. It is often helpful to regard implementation as being of two types: pre-implementation and implementation. Many innovations founder at the pre-implementation stage because not enough initial support has been generated.

The key activities occurring during implementation are the carrying out of action plans, the developing and sustaining of commitment, the checking of progress and the overcoming of problems. The key factors making for success at this stage, according to Miles (1986), are:

- clear responsibility for orchestration/coordination (head, coordinator, external consultant);
- shared control over implementation (top-down is *not* all right); good cross-hierarchical work and relations; empowerment of both individuals and the school;
- a mix of pressure, an insistence on 'doing it right', and support;
- adequate and sustained staff development and inservice support (an external or internal coordinator, or a combination that builds personal and organizational capacity);
- rewards for teachers early in the process (empowerment, collegiality, meeting needs, classroom help, load reduction, supply cover, expenses resources).

Institutionalization is the phase when innovation and change stop being regarded as something new and become part of the school's usual way of doing things. Until recently it was assumed that this happened automatically. This is despite the evidence that innovations associated with many centralized initiatives tend to fade away after the initial wave of enthusiasm, or after a key actor leaves, or when the funding ceases. The move from implementation to institutionalization, however, often involves the transformation of a pilot project to a school-wide initiative, often without the advantage of the previously available funding. It is change of a new order. In these cases there tends to be widespread use of the change by staff, its impact is seen on classroom practice, and by that time the whole process is not regarded as being unusual. As the researchers who worked on the Dissemination Efforts Supporting School Improvement (DESSI) study remarked (Huberman and Crandall, quoted in Miles, 1983, p. 14):

> In the chronicle of research on dissemination and use of educational practices, we first put our chips on adoption [i.e. initiation], then on implementation. It turns out that these investments are lost without deliberate attention to the institutional steps that lock an innovation into the local setting. New practices that get built in to the training, regulatory, staffing and budgetary cycle survive; others don't. Innovations are highly perishable goods. Taking institutionalisation for granted — assuming somewhat ... magically that it will happen by itself, or will necessarily result from a technically mastered, ... demonstrably effective project — is naive and usually self-defeating.

Key activities at this stage, according to Miles (1986), are:

- an emphasis on *embedding* the change within the school's structures, its organization and resources;
- the elimination of *competing or contradictory practices*;
- strong and purposeful *links to other change efforts*, the curriculum and classroom teaching;
- *widespread use* in the school and local area;
- an adequate *bank of local facilitators* — advisory teachers for skills training.

The failure of many efforts towards change to progress beyond early implementation is partially explained by the lack of realization on the part of those involved that the above activities are necessary. They have also failed to understand that each of these phases has different characteristics that require different strategies if success is to be achieved.

The second and related issue is the importance of *process* leading to *outcomes*. The logic of the approach is as follows: we begin with some educational goal, which leads to some form of innovation. The impact and outcomes of the innovation are dependent on the nature of the initiation decisions (both within and outside the school), the factors affecting implementation, the implementation strategy and the degree to which institutionalization is achieved; all of which are embedded in, and dependent on, the culture of the school. The important point is that all of this effort should have some impact on student learning. Unfortunately many school improvement efforts have neglected this 'bottom line' by underemphasizing the 'end of the chain'.

Despite the evident truth of this point, it is unfortunately one that has been implicitly neglected in many educational change efforts. Michael Huberman (1992, p. 11) summarizes the issue nicely:

> [We need] to draw on studies that can actually demonstrate the causal relationship between adoption > implementation > enhanced technical capacity > revised institutional arrangements > measurable impacts on pupils in line with the 'thrust' of the innovation. Without that causal chain, we shall have no 'social technology' of implementation. Nor shall we be able to talk of 'school improvement' with a straight face. And by not addressing the impact on pupils, we will have indulged in some magical thinking as before: that adoption meant implementation ... that implementation meant institutionalization ... that enhanced teacher capacity means enhanced pupil achievement or development.
> ... if changes in organizational and instructional practices are not followed down to the level of effects on pupils, we will have to admit more openly that we are essentially investing in staff development rather than in the improvement of pupils' abilities.

This is why we take the issue of student outcomes so seriously in our own school improvement work.

The third issue relates to the *meaning* that individuals give to their involvement in the change process. This perspective needs to underpin all the rational and political conceptions of change reviewed in this chapter. Fullan (1991, p. 32) reminds us that real change, 'whether desired or not, represents a serious personal and collective experience characterized by ambivalence and uncertainty' for the individual involved. If the result of this engagement is to be empowerment and fulfilment, then such a judgement can only be made with hindsight. There is no such certainty as one works through the process that meaning will be achieved.

As is seen later, the existing internal conditions within the school will make success or failure more or less likely. The reason we need organizational settings in schools which support teachers and students in the process of change is that the experience of change is individually threatening and disconcerting. These settings should be organized around the realization that change is a process whereby individuals alter their ways of thinking and doing. There are a number of implications that stem from this (Fullan, 1985, p. 396):

- change takes place over time;
- change initially involves anxiety and uncertainty;
- technical and psychological support is crucial;

- the learning of new skills is incremental and developmental;
- organizational conditions within and in relation to the school make it more or less likely that school improvement will occur;
- successful change involves pressure and support within a collaborative setting.

MESSAGES

In concluding this chapter, which has contained many different themes and cut across boundaries between rational change strategies and the subjective meaning of change, we need a summary that unites these dichotomous perspectives. The following 'messages about change' attempt to capture some of the ambivalence, ironies, paradoxes and uncertainty of making progress in difficult times. Taken together they provide the basis for creating a 'mind set' about change (see Fullan, 1991, pp. 105-7). Individually these suggestions are of little help: even when taken together they do not tell us how to proceed; but they do suggest a way of thinking about change that perhaps provides us with the basis of the new paradigm we discussed earlier. As a whole these assumptions help us to think creatively, proactively and realistically about change and provide us with the essential foundation for the more practical advice that follows.

- *Change takes place over time.* Assume that effective change takes time. Unrealistic or undefined time-lines fail to recognize that implementation occurs developmentally. Persistence is a critical attribute of successful change. It is helpful to view change as a journey that has the present situation as a starting point, but no clear destination. This having been said, there are still some predictable staging posts along the way and different skills and approaches are needed to ensure success at different times.

- *Embrace multiple perspectives.* Because different perspectives on change are often in conflict they provide complementary forms of understanding and routes for action. Technical approaches are useful for planning, for example, but micro-political views give deeper understanding.

- *Be self-conscious about the process of change.* No amount of research knowledge will ever make it totally clear what to do. But those who do not think about change or attempt to conceptualize it do not do it very well. Teachers know a great deal about change in students, but rarely is this understanding translated to adult or organizational learning. The insights about change that all teachers have are an untapped resource.

- *Assume resistance.* Conflict and disagreement are not only inevitable but fundamental to successful planned change. Rational models of change underestimate resistance or treat it as a problem. Resistance is normal; collaboration is about utilizing conflict.

- *Invest in teachers and schools*. All successful change requires an individual response. Often the experience of change is individually threatening and disconcerting, which is why we need organizational settings in schools which support teachers and students in the process of change. These settings need first to be organized around the realization that change is a process whereby individuals alter their ways of thinking and doing. But teachers and schools are not the same and one needs to pay regard to these differences.

Chapter 4

School and Classroom Effectiveness

It is now over fifteen years since Ron Edmonds asked his felicitous question: 'How many effective schools would you have to see to be persuaded of the educability of all children?'. He continued: 'We already know more than we need to do that. Whether or not we do it, must depend on how we feel about the fact that we haven't so far.' This well-known quotation from the person generally credited with being the founding father of school effectiveness research sets the scene for this chapter. Unfortunately, although we now know a lot more about school and classroom effectiveness than was known when Edmonds wrote, student achievement still lags far behind society's expectations. This is a great pity, because the research knowledge about the characteristics of those schools and classrooms 'whose pupils progress further than might be expected from considerations of intake' (Mortimore, 1991, p. 216) is among the most robust that we have in our quest for educational reform: *and* it is directly connected with the progress and academic attainment of students.

One of the major problems with research-based knowledge in general, and the research on school and classroom effectiveness in particular, is that because it has become an area of inquiry in its own right, it has been kept distinct from knowledge about *how* schools improve. The tendency to compartmentalize knowledge is a major stumbling block to progress, and consequently this knowledge has not affected practice as much as it should. We are therefore concerned not so much with the nature of school and classroom effectiveness knowledge *per se*, but more with its implications for school improvement and how it can be applied in schools (Reynolds *et al.*, 1993). Having said that, in this chapter we consider school and classroom effectiveness knowledge independently from school improvement before, in later chapters, attempting to draw them together. We do this because at times the knowledge base is complex and needs careful articulation before we can begin to transcend it. This is particularly the case with the school effectiveness research, where the degree of methodological sophistication has increased dramatically of late. We tend to ignore these considerations here, preferring to concentrate more on the knowledge emerging from this research tradition. The interested reader will, however, find plentiful discussion of these issues in the references we cite in the following pages.

Our analysis of the research on school and classroom effectiveness is fairly traditional in so far as our interpretation respects the conventional wisdom in the area. It is important that we do this because this knowledge is empirically the most valid in the whole area of educational change. It must therefore be taken seriously. The effective school correlates provide, as Miles (1992, p. 12) has recently noted, 'a legitimated list of markers or criteria for a desired state of organisational being — a vision, in current parlance ... [which] is a crucial element of any deliberate change strategy.' As such it provides a foundation on which to base our school improvement work. In future chapters, however, we tend not to refer much to 'the school effectiveness research', preferring to integrate these insights into schools and classrooms into what we later call a 'holistic' approach to school improvement.

In this chapter we discuss:

- school effectiveness;
- classroom effectiveness;
- teacher development;
- creating effective schools and classrooms.

SCHOOL EFFECTIVENESS

Over the past fifteen years or so, a vast amount of evidence to support the common-sense notion that the internal features of individual schools can make a difference to pupil progress has been accumulated. Surprisingly, this conviction has not always been the accepted wisdom. Until quite recently the ability of schools to make a difference to student learning was widely doubted. The research on 'effective schools', however, consistently demonstrates correlations between student achievement on tests of basic skills, and a stable set of school organization and process characteristics, commonly known as 'correlates'. So great has been the impact of the research over the past decade and a half, however, that a recent commentator has claimed that 'the effective schools movement "blew up" the foundations of traditional schooling' (quoted in Murphy, 1992a, p. 91).

Even as late as the 1960s and 1970s, well-known studies and 'blue riband' reports, many of which influenced national policies, looked to influences other than the school as predictors of a student's academic performance. The family, in particular, was regarded as being far more important. The Coleman (1966) study in the USA and the Plowden Report (1967) in Britain were highly influential both publicly and politically, and both strongly maintained that the home influence outweighed that of the school. In a similar but more populist vein, Basil Bernstein (1970), in a widely quoted article, claimed that 'education cannot compensate for society'. Other views were also advanced. At around the same time, in a highly controversial paper, Arthur Jensen (1969) reasserted the claim that hereditary influences were pre-eminent, while Bowles and Gintis (1976), in their equally controversial (for very different reasons) critique *Schooling in Capitalist America*, claimed that educational inequalities are rooted in the basic sub-cultures and social biases of our economy. The one thing that these widely divergent views on what accounted for pupil progress had in common was that they all vastly underestimated the influence of the school. By the late 1970s the prevailing view began to change in the face of an emerging consensus that *schools do make a difference*.

In the USA this was largely due to the advocacy of Edmonds, who did much of the early work on effective school correlates. Edmonds' commitment to reducing racial inequality in inner-city American schools and his original 'five-factor theory' are well known. Edmonds' (1978) list of the effective school correlates is as follows:

1 Emphasis on student acquisition of basic skills.

2 High expectations for students.

3 Strong administrative leadership.

4 Frequent monitoring of student progress.

5 Orderly climate conducive to learning.

The first major study conducted in the UK was that of Michael Rutter and his colleagues (1979), who compared the 'effectiveness' of ten secondary schools in south London on a range of student outcome measures. The 'effective schools' described in their book were characterized by factors 'as varied as the degree of academic emphasis, teacher actions in lessons, the availability of incentives and rewards, good conditions for pupils, and the extent to which children are able to take responsibility' (Rutter *et al.*, 1979, p. 178). It was this constellation of factors that Rutter and his colleagues later referred to as the school's 'ethos'. They further claimed (Rutter *et al.*, 1979, p. 179) that the characteristics of schools as social institutions *combine* to create a particular ethos, or set of values, attitudes and behaviours which are representative of the school as a whole.

So by the beginning of the 1980s, at a time when the cold winds of account-ability were beginning to blow through most Western educational systems, there came striking evidence that at last schools had something to be held accountable for. The effective schools research makes it very clear that it defines 'effectiveness' in terms of the differences in student outcomes (on a variety of measures, not simply standardized tests of basic skills) that schools achieve after full account has been taken of the pupil's prior learning history and family background at the time he or she enters the school. In terms of the contemporary debate over league tables, this is the 'value added' to a pupil over and above what ability and socio-economic status would naturally bring him or her. This is not to say, of course, that an individual's learning history and family background are not important. It is to say, however, that schools can also con-tribute *differentially* to pupil achievement. The school a child goes to *does* matter.

Not only did the early 'effective schools' research conclude that schools do make a difference, but there was also agreement on two further issues. First, the differences in outcome were systematically related to variations in the school's climate, culture or ethos. Second, the school's culture was amenable to alteration by concerted action on the part of the school staff. Although this is not an easy task, the evidence suggested that teachers and schools had more control than they might have imagined over their ability to change their present situation.

This summary of the early effective schools research begs as many questions as it answers. It may be appropriate therefore in exploring the intricacies of this knowledge base to follow the example of Dave Reynolds in his authoritative review of the research (Reynolds, 1992), by setting ourselves a series of questions to answer.

How much difference does a school make?

This first question is the obvious one. Not surprisingly, the various research studies differ, but more recent studies support earlier claims of larger effects. Reynolds (1992, p. 3), on the basis of John Gray's (1981) early work, suggests that as a rule of thumb 'the competitive edge' possessed by the most effective fifth of state secondary schools, as compared with the least effective fifth, was equivalent to one and a half of the old O-level public examinations per child. That order of magnitude, and greater, is commonly found in the more recent studies (e.g. Reynolds *et al.*, 1987; Nuttall *et al.*, 1989; Smith and Tomlinson, 1989; Gray *et al.*, 1990; Cuttance, 1992). Mortimore and his colleagues (1988) also report substantial school effects, not upon attainment at a point in time, but upon progress over time, where, in the case of mathematics for example, the influence of the school was ten times more important than that of the home. But the effect is not simply related to examination results, as the Rutter study illustrated; the impact of the school is also on behaviour, delinquency and attendance.

What makes this difference?

We have already noted the features of effective schools as outlined by Edmonds and Rutter. By and large, subsequent research supported these findings. There is broad agreement that the following eight criteria are representative of the *organization factors* characteristic of effective schools (e.g. Purkey and Smith, 1983):

1 Curriculum-focused school leadership.
2 Supportive climate within the school.
3 Emphasis on curriculum and teaching.
4 Clear goals and high expectations for students.
5 A system for monitoring performance and achievement.
6 On-going staff development and inservice.
7 Parental involvement and support.
8 LEA and external support.

These factors do not, however, address the dynamics of schools as organizations. There appear to be four additional factors which infuse some meaning and life into the process of improvement within the school. These so-called *process factors* provide the means of achieving the organizational factors; they lubricate the system and 'fuel the dynamics of interaction' (Fullan, 1985, p. 400). They have been described by Fullan (1985, p. 400) as follows:

1 A feel for the process of leadership; this is difficult to characterize because the complexity of factors involved tends to deny rational planning. A useful analogy would be that organizations are to be sailed rather than driven.

2 A guiding value system; this refers to a consensus on high expectations, explicit goals, clear rules, a genuine caring about individuals, etc.

3 Intense interaction and communication; this refers to simultaneous support and pressure at both horizontal and vertical levels within the school.

4 Collaborative planning and implementation; this needs to occur both within the school and externally, particularly in the local education authority.

A particularly well-designed and well-executed British study was carried out by Peter Mortimore and his colleagues in the Inner London Education Authority (ILEA) during the mid-1980s. Known as the 'Junior School Effectiveness Study', this was the most detailed study of the primary school milieu ever undertaken. It involved fifty randomly selected London primary schools and some two thousand pupils. The study was published as a book (Mortimore *et al.*, 1988), which complemented the Rutter study of secondary schools.

The researchers identified twelve key factors of 'junior school effectiveness'. This list of effectiveness factors is perhaps as good as any at illustrating the richness and detail of the knowledge base. It is as follows (adapted from Mortimore *et al.*, 1988, pp. 250-6):

1 *Purposeful leadership of the staff by the headteacher.* Key aspects: effective headteachers are sufficiently involved in and knowledgeable about what goes on in classrooms and about the progress of individual pupils. Although they do not interfere constantly, they are not afraid to assert their leadership.

2 *The involvement of the deputy head.* Key aspects: a certain amount of delegation by the head and the sharing of responsibilities promote effectiveness.

3 *The involvement of teachers.* Key aspects: active involvement in curriculum planning, developing curriculum guidelines, and participation in decision making on school policy.

4 *Consistency among teachers.* Key aspects: continuity in teaching staff and consistency of teacher approach are important.

5 *Structured sessions.* Key aspects: teachers organize a framework within which pupils can work, encourage a degree of independence, and allow some freedom within this structure.

6 *Intellectually challenging teaching.* Key aspects: higher-order questions and statements are used, pupils are encouraged to use their creative imagination and powers of problem solving, teachers

have an enthusiastic approach, and there are high expectations of pupils.

7 *Work-centred environment.* Key aspects: much content-related work and feedback, relatively little time spent on routine matters, a low level of noise, and not an excessive amount of pupil movement.

8 *Limited focus within lessons.* Key aspects: a focus upon only one curriculum area during a lesson.

9 *Maximum communication between teachers and pupils.* Key aspects: a flexible approach, blending individual, class and group interaction as appropriate, including class discussion.

10 *Record keeping.* Key aspects: record keeping linked to planning and assessment by both head and teachers.

11 *Parental involvement.* Key aspects: help in classrooms and on educational visits, attendance at meetings to discuss children's progress, parents' reading to their children and access to books at home, informal open-door policy rather than parent-teacher associations.

12 *Positive climate.* Key aspects: more emphasis on praise and reward than on punishment and control, enthusiastic attitude of teachers, involvement of staff and children in a range of out-of-classroom activities.

The response to our initial two questions has been based on knowledge emerging from tightly designed quantitative research studies. It is interesting to note, therefore, that Her Majesty's Inspectors of Schools (HMI), who work within a very different tradition, came to similar conclusions in their *Ten Good Schools*, published in 1977. To HMI the 'good school' is one that can demonstrate 'quality in its aims, in oversight of pupils, in curriculum design, in standards of teaching and academic achievements and in its links with the local community. What they all have in common is effective leadership and a "climate" that is conducive to growth' (DES, 1977, p. 36).

A more recent HMI survey (HMI, 1988), which was based on the evidence of thousands of inspections throughout England and Wales, concluded that 'effective' schools displayed twelve characteristics. Although their list sounds like a counsel of perfection, it does correlate fairly well with the more 'scientific' research findings. For example, HMI claim that effective schools have or exhibit: good leadership; clear aims; high academic standards; good relationships with pupils; a coherent curriculum; concern for pupils' development; well-qualified staff; suitable and respected working accommodation; good relationships with the community; and a capacity to manage change.

Do schools have the same effect upon different aspects of pupil development?

The early work on school effectiveness, such as Rutter's, suggested that schools were equally effective across a range of outcomes. More recent research, however, suggests that schools may be differentially effective in different areas (Reynolds, 1992, p. 5). This is not just the case between academic and social outcomes, but also within academic studies. Mortimore *et al.* (1988), for example, reported substantial variations between oracy (heavily school-influenced) and reading skills (less heavily school-influenced).

Are schools consistently 'effective' or 'ineffective' over time?

Once again, early studies suggested stability in outcomes over a period of years. More recent studies shed some doubt on that conclusion. Desmond Nuttall and his colleagues (1989), in their research on the effectiveness of ILEA schools, found marked difference in school performance during the period 1985-87. The effectiveness of individual schools was not very stable over the three-year period. They conclude that their analysis 'gives rise to a note of caution about any study of school effectiveness that relies on measures of outcome in just a single year, or of just a single cohort of students' (Nuttall *et al.*, 1989, p. 775).

Are schools equally effective for all pupils?

New analytical techniques have enabled more detailed investigation of the differential impact of school effectiveness on sub-groups. Nuttall and his colleagues (1989), in their research on the effectiveness of ILEA schools, for example, showed large differences for different types of pupil in the relative effectiveness of schools in London. The ILEA research suggests that the difference in experience between able and less able pupils varies markedly between school and school. The performance of schools also varied in the ways they impacted upon boys and girls, and in their effects upon students from different ethnic groups. Some schools narrowed the gap between these different groups over time and other schools widened them in both instances (Reynolds, 1992, p. 7).

In their research report (ILEA, 1990, pp. 20, 21), Nuttall and his colleagues note that some schools were more effective in raising the achievement of students with high attainment at entry than that of those with low attainment, that others showed the reverse effect, but that it was rare for a school to be particularly effective across the ability range. They also found that some schools were more effective in raising the achievements of one or more ethnic minority groups in comparison with those of pupils from England, Scotland and Wales, and that in others the latter group of pupils does better than ethnic minority students.

The ILEA team (1990, p. 19) claim on the basis of this evidence that:

> it is not appropriate to talk of *the* effectiveness of a single school, as though effectiveness was measured on a single dimension and as though the school was equally effective for all groups of pupils. Rather one must investigate the differential effectiveness of schools.

We should add, however, that although Nuttall and his colleagues cite other research (notably the Junior School Study, which was also conducted in the ILEA) to support their claim of the existence of differential school effectiveness, other researchers are more sceptical. Gray *et al.* (1990), for example, found little evidence of the differential effectiveness in their study of schools in a wide range of LEAs. On this issue, as well as a number of others in school effectiveness research, the jury, as Reynolds (1992, p. 8) notes, is still out.

Does school effectiveness research have all the answers?

Despite some inevitable contradictions, it may appear from this review of the school effectiveness research that our quest for the Holy Grail of educational reform is already at an end, and that the knowledge generated by those working within the effective schools tradition provides us with the answer to the challenge of raising student achievement. Unfortunately, this is not the case. Besides the problems and gaps in the knowledge base that we have already seen, there are four limitations in particular that need to be addressed.

The first is a conceptual problem. It is obvious from the lists we have cited that the correlates are often of a different order: 'strong leadership', for example, is a very different phenomenon from 'a school's guiding value system'. Similarly, the distinction between 'organizational' and 'process' factors is not clear cut; for example, 'climate' and 'leadership' appear under both headings. In any case, what do the terms mean in practice? 'Emphasis on curriculum and teaching' is hardly an operational definition. There needs to be much more conceptual work done on the effective schools criteria before they can provide an unambiguous guide for action.

A second problem is more empirical than conceptual. Scheerens (1992, p. 84) has subjected individual correlates to empirical investigation. The result of his analysis suggests that some widely quoted correlates, such as context and external support, either have very low support or are hypothetical. Scheerens only finds unequivocal support for 'structured teaching' and 'time on task'.

Third, the criteria for school effectiveness tend to be treated individually. The nature of the research designs in most of these studies results in a list of individual factors, rather than a holistic picture of school culture. When studies of this genre do talk of school 'ethos' or culture, it is usually as a result of some *ex post facto* conceptualization. Yet all we know about school development suggests that it is the *combination* of factors that has the impact on pupil progress.

The fourth problem is the way in which those outside the school use this research knowledge. Lists of school effectiveness correlates which are backed by research evidence can be very appealing to policy makers. Many states in the USA, for example, now have 'effective schools' legislation, and the correlates are also creeping into the specification of schemes for inspection in the UK. This is a consequence of the naive tendency of educational administrators, in their search for simple solutions to complex problems, to regard research evidence and test scores as a panacea for their pressing educational concerns. As Larry Cuban (1983) points out, too narrow an interpretation of the school effectiveness criteria leads to an increase in standardization, a narrowing of the educational agenda, and a removal of the obligation to improve from schools that have good examination results. Cuban (1983, p. 696) argues that the question should really be: 'How can the broader more complex and less easily measured goals of schooling be achieved as we improve test scores?' The current changes in the policy for the inspection of schools, and the publication of non-adjusted 'league tables', make it unlikely that this question will be addressed at least at the national level in the UK in the foreseeable future.

Despite this, the contribution of the effective school research to improving the quality of education for all pupils is indeed highly significant. It provides strong evidence that individual schools can make a difference for their pupils, and this is a major achievement. Yet we are left with a feeling that this form of research has run its course. In some ways there is little more that it can tell us. The recent, highly sophisticated studies only serve to contradict each other, as the multilevel modelling techniques more and more accurately analyse less and less useful data. Different groups of researchers increasingly vie with each other for their version of the truth, their formula for analysis, and so on. It is also becoming apparent that what is essentially an Anglo-Saxon research tradition does not travel that well to other cultures. These concerns are not ours alone. Peter Mortimore (1991), in recently assessing the current 'state of the art' of the school effectiveness research, asked the question, 'Which way at the crossroads?'

What is the legacy of the effective schools movement?

It is time for school effectiveness researchers to move beyond the narrow interpretation of effectiveness characteristics, and take a broader view of what the tradition can offer the wider educational community. Joseph Murphy (1992a, b) has recently formulated this issue in a very helpful way. Murphy (1992a, p. 93) begins by arguing that the correlates are simply the means to an end — student learning. From that perspective it is not the correlates themselves that are important, but rather the principles that support them. Indeed the correlates may look very different in the future; they certainly change in differing contexts at present, although the concept of effectiveness remains the same. It was this line of argument that encouraged Murphy to look at the 'real legacy of the effective school movement'. He identified four aspects to the legacy (Murphy, 1992a, pp. 94-6):

- *The educability of learners.* At the heart of the effective schools movement is an attack on the prevailing notion of the distribution of achievement according to a normal curve. There is a clear demonstration that all students can learn. The single most important contribution of the effective schools movement is that it helped push the dominant behavioural psychological model of learning off centre stage in schools throughout the world.

- *A focus on outcomes.* For a variety of reasons educators tend to avoid serious inspection of the educational process. Effective school advocates, however, argued persuasively that rigorous assessments of schooling were needed and that one could judge the quality of education only by examining student outcomes, especially indices of learning. Equally important, they defined success not in absolute terms, but as the value added to what students brought to the educational process.

- *Taking responsibility for students.* The third major contribution of the effective schools movement is its attack on the practice of blaming the victim for the shortcomings of the school itself. The movement has been insistent that the school community take a fair share of the responsibility for what happens to the youth in its care.

- *Attention to consistency throughout the school community.* Murphy summarized the loosely linked organizational character of schools by defining them as a collection of individual entrepreneurs (teachers) surrounded by a common parking lot, or as a group of classrooms held together by a common heating system! One of the most powerful and enduring lessons from all the research on effective schools is that the better schools are more tightly linked — structurally, symbolically and culturally — than the less effective ones. They operate more as an organic whole and less as a loose collection of disparate sub-systems. An overarching sense of consistency and coordination is a key element that cuts across the effectiveness correlates and permeates our better schools. It represents a major contribution of the effective schools literature to our understanding of school improvement.

The legacy of the effective schools movement as outlined by Murphy is leading us away from effective schools research *per se* into the territory of school improvement. This is the direction that we believe the research should take. Before considering in later chapters what such a synthesis would look like, we must achieve a little more clarity on one aspect of these characteristics — the nature of effective teaching.

CLASSROOM EFFECTIVENESS

One of the criticisms of school improvement efforts in general is that they are not substantive: that they focus on process at the expense of content. If this is true then it is a serious error; the quality of what is taught, in terms of the curriculum, is obviously related to what students learn and achieve, and therefore should be of great concern to school improvers. The nature of the curriculum is, however, beyond the scope of this book. This is not because we regard curriculum as unimportant. Rather, it is because at a time of nationally imposed curriculum guidelines, the discussion of curriculum content would inevitably be too specific in terms of subject content for a book written for a wide educational audience. Such particularities require a book in themselves. We should, however, note that a characteristic of the successful schools is the ability to evaluate and discriminate between a variety of curriculum content.

There is another aspect to this question of substance on which we have more to say. As important as *what* students learn is *how* they learn. Teaching is the other side of the 'substance' coin. We focus on teaching here because it seems to us that in the UK, it is often the case that discussion of teaching strategies take second place to debates about curriculum content. This is unfortunate for at least two reasons. First, in a situation where curricula are being increasingly imposed by central authorities, there is still the opportunity for teachers to be creative in their use of teaching strategies. Second, it is now evident that the content of a lesson notwithstanding, the use of appropriate teaching strategies can dramatically increase student achievement. A major goal for school improvement therefore is to help teachers become so professionally flexible that they can select, from a repertoire of possibilities, the teaching approach most suited to a particular content area and their students' ages, interests and aptitudes.

We believe that evidence from research on teaching can help teachers become more creative in their search for increased effectiveness. One of the characteristics of successful schools is that teachers talk about teaching. To assist in this they should turn to the literature and resources on teaching to help focus these discussions and enable them to become more specific and informed. But such research and strategies should not be regarded as panaceas to be followed slavishly. Research knowledge and the various specifications of teaching can have many limitations, especially if they are adopted uncritically. In terms of school improvement, such knowledge only becomes useful when it is subjected to the discipline of practice through the exercise of the teacher's professional judgement. For, as Lawrence Stenhouse (1975, p. 142) said in a slightly different context, such proposals are not to be regarded 'as an unqualified recommendation, but rather as a provisional specification claiming no more than to be worth putting to the test of practice. Such proposals claim to be intelligent rather than correct.' We find that teachers in successful schools take individual and collective responsibility for basing their teaching on the best knowledge and practice available. But they then take those ideas and strategies and critically reflect on them through practice in their own and each other's classrooms.

The reasons that we wish to emphasize teaching so strongly are twofold. First, teaching is the skill that makes teachers and schools unique, that sets us as educators apart from other professions — teaching is our thing! Second, of all the variables under our control teaching has the most demonstrable impact upon student learning. Indeed we have already noted Scheerens' (1992) claim that of all the school effectiveness characteristics it is those that relate to teaching that have the most empirical support.

We must, of course, continually bear in mind that scores in examinations and on tests are not the only student outcomes that are of interest. Some teaching approaches, if carefully selected, can influence a range of outcomes in both the cognitive and affective domains. In this sense we are searching for approaches that are effective in achieving high academic standards while, at the same time, developing aspects of personal and social development.

As we found with our review of evidence about effective schools, there is a reasonable degree of consensus about the features of effective teaching (e.g. Bennett, 1991; Bickel and Bickel, 1986; Brophy, 1983; Rosenshine, 1983; Wang, 1991; Walberg, 1990). While there are inevitably differences of emphasis and detail between findings, the overall consistency across so many studies gives reason for optimism. Furthermore, the extent of the research, carried out in so many different contexts and in such a variety of ways, compensates for methodological weaknesses in particular studies.

A useful synthesis of the findings of this research is provided by Porter and Brophy (1988). They suggest that this provides a picture of effective teachers as semi-autonomous professionals who:

- are clear about their instructional goals;
- are knowledgeable about their content and the strategies for teaching it;
- communicate to their students what is expected of them — and why;
- make expert use of existing teaching materials in order to devote more time to practices that enrich and clarify the content;
- are knowledgeable about their students, adapting teaching to their needs and anticipating misconceptions in their existing knowledge;
- teach students 'meta-cognitive strategies' and give them opportunities to master them;
- address higher- as well as lower-level cognitive objectives;
- monitor students' understanding by offering regular, appropriate feedback;
- integrate their teaching with that in other subject areas;
- accept responsibility for student outcomes;
- are thoughtful and reflective about their practice.

In order to provide an introduction to the vast research evidence about effectiveness in teaching we have chosen to adopt an organizing format based upon different perspectives. Our knowledge of the available literature suggests the existence of three broad ways of looking at classroom practice. These are as follows:

- *Models of teaching*. Here approaches to teaching are defined in terms of distinct approaches, including operational specifications of what these involve.
- *Skills*. This approach views teaching as a complex task that can be analysed in order to examine individual elements.
- *Artistry*. From this perspective teaching is seen as being a highly creative activity involving the use of repertoires of responses

53

gained through experience and refined in response to new situations.

While we will use this typology to organize our review of evidence we must emphasize that it involves what we believe to be rather crude distinctions. We are aware, also, that sometimes those who feel a particular affinity for one or other of the three positions may reject the value of the other two. For our own part, however, we will argue that evidence drawn from studies arising from all three of these orientations provide resources and insights that can be of value in our search for quality in teaching.

Models of teaching

The most extensive work on models of teaching has been carried out by Bruce Joyce and his colleagues (e.g. Joyce *et al.*, 1992; Joyce and Showers, 1991). They define a series of models of teaching designed to bring about particular kinds of learning and to help students become more effective learners. They argue that educators need to be able to identify these models and to select the ones that they should master in order to increase their competence. To learn to use these teaching strategies comfortably and effectively requires much study and practice, but by concentrating on one or two at a time repertoires can be expanded quite easily (Joyce and Showers, 1991, p. 9).

Models of teaching, it is argued, are really models of learning. As we help students acquire information, ideas, skills, values, ways of thinking and means of expressing themselves, we are also teaching them how to learn. In fact, the most important long-term outcome may be the students' increased capabilities to learn more easily and effectively in the future both because of the knowledge and skill they have acquired, and because they have mastered learning processes. How teaching is conducted has a large impact on students' abilities to educate themselves. Successful teachers are not simply charismatic, persuasive and expert presenters. Rather, they present powerful cognitive and social tasks to their students and teach them how to make productive use of them. For example, learning to lecture clearly and knowledgeably is highly desirable, but it is the learner who does the learning and successful lecturers teach students how to use the information in the talk and how to make it their own. Effective learners draw information, ideas and wisdom from their teachers and use learning resources effectively. Thus, a major role in teaching is to create powerful learners (see Joyce and Showers, 1991, pp. 9-10).

Joyce and his colleagues (1987) use the concept of 'effect size' to describe the impact of any given change in practice and to predict what might be accomplished by its use. Effect size, they argue, permits an assessment of how much teaching practices affect the outcomes to which they are directed. The approach involves comparisons of progress between experimental and control groups. In addition to giving a measure of the impact overall of particular teaching models, this approach helps determine whether the intervention has different effects for all students or just for some.

Using this idea of effect size, Joyce and his colleagues (e.g. Joyce *et al.*,

1987, p. 13) claim that research conducted during the past ten years yields impressive evidence for the effectiveness of a variety of innovative teaching practices:

- *Cooperative learning approaches*, representing social models of teaching, yield effect sizes from modest to high. The more complex the outcomes — higher-order thinking, problem solving, social skills and attitudes — the greater are the effects.

- *Information-processing models*, especially the use of advance organizers and mnemonics, yield modest to substantial effect sizes; and the effects are long-lasting.

- *Synectics and non-directive teaching* increase student creativity and enhance self-concept as well as effecting student achievement in such basic areas as recall of information.

- *Direct instruction* such as DISTAR, an example of the behavioural family of models, yields modest effect sizes in achievement and, further, influences aptitude to learn.

- When these models and strategies are combined, they have even greater potential for improving student learning.

Despite what appears to be weighty evidence, the idea of 'models of teaching' does not seem to be attractive to all teachers, particularly those in the UK. Highly prescriptive approaches in particular (for example, direct instruction) have been found to be distinctly unacceptable. While this is perhaps understandable, it is to be regretted if teachers become cut off from ideas that could stimulate a reconsideration of particular aspects of their existing practice. Perhaps it would be more helpful to see models of teaching as being specifications that have arisen as a result of the work of master teachers (which they are), rather than the product of an academic imagination (which they are not). This does not mean that any specification provides an instant answer that can be adopted by anyone. Rather, they offer accounts of how particular teachers, or groups of teachers, have refined approaches that seemed to be beneficial under certain conditions. In saying this, we are reminded of Dewey (1929), who, when talking about outstanding teachers, observed that 'the successes of such individuals tend to be born and to die with them; beneficial consequences extend only to those pupils who have personal contact with such gifted teachers'. He continued, 'the only way by which we can prevent such waste in the future is by methods which enable us to make an analysis of what the gifted teacher does intuitively, so that something accruing from his work can be communicated to others'.

It must also be stressed that the idea of teaching models need not adopt a prescriptive form to be followed in a step-by-step manner. In the UK we have a tradition, mainly the preserve of the erstwhile Schools Council curriculum projects, of linking curriculum materials to teaching styles (Stenhouse, 1980; Hopkins, 1987a). The History 13-16 and Science 5-13 curriculum projects, in particular, espoused a radical form of pedagogy to support their curriculum materials. Both of these teaching styles could be said to be discovery/inquiry led.

The Schools Council curriculum that is perhaps best known, and most highly regarded, for launching into what had been uncharted waters was Stenhouse's (1970, 1975, 1983) Humanities Curriculum Project (HCP). In this curriculum project, discussion was the main mode of inquiry and the teacher acted as a neutral chairperson. Discussion was informed and disciplined by evidence, such as items from history, journalism and literature. This particular curriculum project, as is apparent, placed new kinds of demand on both teachers and pupils (Rudduck, 1984, p. 57). For example:

New skills for most teachers:

- discussion rather than instruction;
- teacher as neutral chairperson;
- teacher talk reduced to about 15 per cent of the total talking done in the classroom;
- teacher handling material from different disciplines;
- new modes of assessment.

New skills for most pupils:

- discussion, not argument or debate;
- listening to, and talking to, each other, not just the teacher;
- taking initiatives in contributing — not being cued by the teacher.

The important point about the Humanities Curriculum was that it was specific rather than prescriptive. It encouraged teachers to experiment with the specificity rather than be bound by the prescription. When viewed through this particular lens, centrally imposed curricula are in danger of becoming prescriptive blueprints that tend to inhibit autonomy in teaching and learning. On the other hand, the process model of curriculum, as described by Stenhouse (1975), is liberating or emancipatory because it encourages independence of thought and argument on the part of the pupil, and experimentation and the use of judgement on the part of the teacher. When teachers adopt this experimental approach to their teaching they are taking on an educational idea, cast in the form of a curriculum proposal, and testing it out within their classrooms. It is in this sense that we advocate the use of 'teaching models' as a strategy for school improvement.

Skills

Clearly there is an overlap between the idea of models of teaching and those that see teaching as being the application of a range of distinct skills. However, the skills approach provides a wealth of evidence and ideas that can be used to encourage teachers to reflect upon their existing practice. Furthermore, our experience is that a consideration of particular aspects of teaching (for example, questioning, use of praise) tends to be an attractive idea for many teachers.

There is an extensive research literature on teaching effects. This indicates that there are consistently high levels of correlation between student achievement scores and classroom processes (Brophy and Good, 1986). This is very complex territory, the intricacies of which are beyond the scope of this chapter. One general conclusion, however, stands out: 'The most consistently replicated findings link achievement to the quantity and pacing of instruction' (Brophy and Good, 1986, p. 360). That having been said, it is naive to assume that the amount of time spent teaching is in itself a sufficient condition for student achievement.

The literature on teaching effects is replete with the cues and tactics necessary for effective teaching. For example, Doyle (1987, p. 95) argues that classroom studies of teaching effects have generally supported a direct and structured approach to instruction. That is, students usually achieve more when a teacher:

- emphasizes academic goals, makes them explicit, and expects students to be able to master the curriculum;
- carefully organizes and sequences curriculum experiences;
- clearly explains and illustrates what students are to learn;
- frequently asks direct and specific questions to monitor students' progress and check their understanding;
- provides students with ample opportunity to practise, gives prompts and feedback to ensure success, corrects mistakes, and allows students to use a skill until it is over-learned or automatic;
- reviews regularly and holds students accountable for work.

From this perspective, a teacher promotes student learning by being active in planning and organizing his or her teaching, explaining to students what they are to learn, arranging occasions for guided practice, monitoring progress, providing feedback, and otherwise helping students understand and accomplish work.

Jere Brophy (1983) has also reviewed the research on teaching behaviours most closely associated with student achievement gains. He comes to the following conclusions:

- *Content coverage*. Students learn more when their teachers cover more material.
- *Time allocated to instruction*. Students learn more when teachers allocate available class time to academic activities.
- *Engaged time*. Students learn more when they are on task a high proportion of class time.
- *Consistent success*. Students learn more when their success rates (responses to questions, answers to written work at desk) are high.
- *Active teaching*. Student learn more in classes where their teachers spend most of their time actively teaching them rather than having students work on their own without direct teacher supervision.

- *Structuring information.* Students learn more when teachers structure information using such techniques as advance organizers, reviewing objectives, outlining content, signalling transitions between lesson parts, drawing attention to main ideas, and reviewing main ideas. Clarity of presentation and enthusiasm in presenting material are also associated with achievement gains.

- *Effective questioning.* Students learn more when questions are asked frequently and are relatively easy. Waiting for responses, acknowledging correct answers, and sticking with students who give partial or incorrect answers to give them a chance to improve their answers are all associated with achievement gain.

The work of Neville Bennett and his colleagues has, over many years, focused on the area of task setting in classrooms (e.g. Bennett *et al.*, 1984). He takes the view that the activities of learners during classroom activities are critical to their cognitive development. This being the case, it is necessary to seek an understanding of children's performances on their tasks and the appropriateness of task demands for individual learners. Consequently, Bennett has carried out a series of studies to observe the tasks teachers assign, how and why they assign them, how and why pupils interpret and work on them, and how and why teachers respond to pupils' work (e.g. Bennett, 1991). The findings of this research provide a useful resource for helping teachers review the ways in which they cater for and respond to individual students within their classes.

At the heart of the teacher's work, of course, is the whole area of classroom management. If classrooms are to be places where students can feel safe to concentrate on the tasks that are set, teachers have to be skilled in organizing and managing large groups of people within a relatively confined space. During staff development sessions in schools we find it helpful to encourage teachers to look at some of the specific issues involved and the skills that are required. In this context we use short summaries of research evidence to stimulate discussion between groups of colleagues. Useful sources of appropriate reading matter include Good and Brophy (1987), Kyriacou (1986, 1991) and some of the other studies reported earlier in this section. In using this kind of approach our aim is not to present research evidence as being the source of instant solutions to the practical problems faced by teachers. Rather we see it as a means of stimulating discussion of existing thinking on practice for the purpose of encouraging professional development.

Artistry

Our third approach to the study of teaching is of a different order from the first two. Here there is a recognition that teaching involves creativity and is carried out in a highly personalized way. While this need not deny the potential value of considering particular models of teaching or examining the impact of specific skills, it draws attention to the fact that once in the classroom each teacher has the sole responsibility for creating the conditions within which each student can experience success. This must involve a degree of previous planning, but it also requires a capacity to improvise. Even the best-defined lesson plan has to be adapted to take account of unforeseen happenings. Indeed the artistry of a very successful teacher involves this ability to engage with, and turn to advantage, events and responses that could not have been anticipated.

It is much more difficult to report research evidence that arises from this frame of reference. The evidence does not lend itself readily to specifications or lists of features. Yet this perspective on teachers' work is one that is immediately recognized by practitioners and, indeed, others in the wider community. It is not uncommon for teachers to be told by friends from outside the profession of 'the teacher who made a difference'. The personality and flair of the individual teacher is increasingly receiving belated attention. For example, one of John Gray's (1990) three performance indicators of an 'effective' school is the proportion of pupils who 'have a good or "vital" relationship with one or more teachers'. This good or vital relationship is a fundamentally important aspect of the teaching process.

The idea of artistry in teaching is well summed up by Lou Rubin (1985, p. v) when he comments:

> There is a striking quality to fine classrooms. Students are caught up
> in learning; excitement abounds; and playfulness and seriousness
> blend easily because the purposes are clear, the goals sensible, and an
> unmistakeable feeling of well-being prevails.
>
> Artist teachers achieve these qualities by knowing both their
> subject matter and their students; by guiding the learning with deft
> control — a control that itself is born out of perception, intuition, and
> creative impulse.

One way in which teachers can be helped to think about their own artistry is by reading accounts of how other teachers work and their impact upon students. Fortunately, there is an extensive range of such accounts available, some written by researchers as a result of their observations in classrooms, and others written by teachers themselves. For example, in-depth studies of particular primary-school classrooms are provided by Armstrong (1980), Holt (1964), Louden (1991) and Rowland (1984). While there are fewer in-depth studies of secondary-school classrooms, interesting accounts of classroom events are reported in a number of wider-ranging research studies. For example, Hargreaves' (1982) observations of life in the classrooms of comprehensive schools are very evocative, as is Woods's (1980) account of why pupils choose to behave differently with different teachers. In another study carried out in secondary schools, Hull (1985) describes the problems of communication and understanding which can arise between teachers and learners.

In encouraging teachers to think about their own ways of working, it may be helpful to provide some format for structuring this process. Pollard and Tann (1987) give a framework for exploring classroom processes and looking for ways to enhance provision for all pupils. This can be particularly useful at the stage of identifying areas for investigation as it contains checklists for use in classroom observation and inquiry.

Similarly, Ainscow and Tweddle (1988) provide a framework that has been found to be useful as teachers seek to review their practice. Their focus is the question, 'How can all pupils be helped to succeed in the classroom?' They call their approach 'classroom evaluation' in order to emphasize the importance of gathering information about how pupils respond to the curriculum as it is enacted. Their suggested focus for classroom evaluation is those areas of decision making over which teachers have a significant influence. Broadly speaking, these areas are as follows:

- Are objectives being achieved?
- Are tasks and activities being completed?
- Do classroom arrangements make effective use of available resources?

Also, since unintended outcomes are seen as being very important, a further question is added:

- What else is happening?

The intention is that these four questions should provide an overall agenda within which teachers can reflect upon the encounters in which they are engaged, and the difficulties they face. In this respect the feedback from students is seen as an important source of understanding as to how classroom conditions can be improved.

TEACHER DEVELOPMENT

Our review of thinking and research about effective teaching has, we hope, provided a summary of useful sources for further consideration. It has also indicated how different perspectives on teaching can be used to inform the development of practice. This is important since we see the issue of teacher development as being at the heart of school improvement efforts.

We use the term 'teacher development' deliberately, as opposed to the more familiar 'in-service training'. This is our attempt to conceptualize an approach to the improvement of practice that is analogous to the one we would recommend in connection with the learning of children. Just as successful classrooms provide conditions that support and encourage all children's learning, so a successful approach to teacher development must address contextual matters in order to create the conditions that facilitate the learning of adults. This is what connects the two literatures reported in the chapter. Successful schools are successful in so far as they facilitate the learning of both students and teachers.

The research evidence that is available on the effectiveness of teacher development initiatives is far from encouraging. Despite all the effort and resources that have been utilized, the impact of such programmes in terms of improvements in teaching and better learning outcomes for pupils is rather disappointing (Fullan, 1991; Joyce and Showers, 1988). What is the explanation for this sad state of affairs? What is the nature of the mistakes that have been made?

As a result of his review of available research evidence, Fullan (1991, p. 316) provides the following summary of the reasons for the failure of in-service education:

- One-shot workshops are widespread but are ineffective.
- Topics are frequently selected by people other than those for whom the in-service is provided.
- Follow-up support for ideas and practices introduced during in-service programmes occurs in only a very small minority of cases.
- Follow-up evaluation occurs infrequently.
- In-service programmes rarely address the individual needs and concerns of participants.
- The majority of programmes involve teachers from many different schools and/or school districts, but there is no recognition of the differential impact of positive and negative factors within the system to which they must return.
- There is a profound lack of any conceptual basis in the planning and implementation of in-service programmes that would ensure their effectiveness.

From this analysis we have a picture of in-service initiatives that are poorly conceptualized, insensitive to the concerns of individual participants, and, perhaps critically, make little effort to help participants relate their learning experiences to their usual workplace conditions.

Recognizing the strength of these arguments, successful schools build infrastructures for teacher development within their day-to-day arrangements. Such infrastructures involve portions of the school week being devoted to staff development activities such as curriculum development and implementation, discussion of teaching approaches, regular observation sessions and on-site coaching. Integral to these activities is a commitment to reviewing one's performance as a prelude to development.

Bruce Joyce and Beverly Showers' (1988) work on staff development, in particular their peer-coaching strategy, has in recent years transformed thinking about staff development (Joyce et al., 1989). Joyce and Showers (1980, p. 380) identified a number of key training components which when used in combination have much greater power than when they are used alone. The major components are:

- presentation of theory or description of skill or strategy;
- modelling or demonstration of skills or models of teaching;
- practice in simulated and classroom settings;
- structured and open-ended feedback (provision of information about performance);
- coaching for application (hands-on, in-classroom assistance with the transfer of skills and strategies to the classroom).

A final important point needs to be made. Central to any successful approach for teacher development is the need for reflection on experience. Here the work of Donald Schon (1983, 1987) concerning professional development has been particularly important and helpful. Schon stresses the importance of what he calls professional artistry as a basis for the improvement of practice. His analysis leads him to be highly critical of existing approaches to professional development in a number of fields, including that of teacher education. The central problem, he argues, lies in the doctrine of technical rationality that dominates thinking within the professions. Embedded in technical rationality is the assumption that a profession is an occupational group whose practice is grounded in knowledge derived from scientific research. As a result, professional competence is seen as the skilful application of theoretical knowledge to the instrumental problems of practice. Within such a view of practice, artistry has little place.

Schon argues that such a view of professional knowledge and practice is inadequate in a number of ways. In terms of our concern here, he suggests that although technical rationality portrays professional competence as a technical problem-solving competence, the problems of the real world do not present themselves as given. Rather, they are messy, indeterminate and problematic situations that arise often because of conflicting values. Such problems cannot be resolved by the use of techniques derived from theoretical research, but call for what Schon calls 'artful competence'. This is a process of clarification of a problematic situation that enables practitioners to redefine their problems in terms of both the ends to be achieved and the means for their achievement. As a result of his analysis, Schon argues that the technical rational model should be replaced by an emphasis on what he calls reflective inquiry. This leads him to seek approaches to professional development that encourage practitioners to reflect upon taken-for-granted knowledge that is implicit in their actions.

We tend to agree with Shulman (1988) when he argues that Schon may be creating a false dichotomy in making his distinction between technical rationality and reflective inquiry. We do believe, however, that reflection is essential to the improvement of teaching. It is through a commitment to reflection that the resources for learning outlined in this chapter can be best utilized.

CREATING EFFECTIVE SCHOOLS AND CLASSROOMS

In linking effective schools and classrooms we need to be concerned with social processes as a means of facilitating professional development and learning. As we have already seen, effective schools seem to be characterized by a culture of collaboration leading to a shared consensus (Fullan *et al.*, 1990). In this respect they have accepted the argument of Handy and Aitken (1986, p. 64), who maintain that: 'Groups allow individuals to reach beyond themselves, to be part of something that none of them would have attained on their own and to discover ways of working with others to mutual benefit.' Consequently, in establishing policies for teacher development there is a need to emphasize the importance of collaboration as a means by which one can learn through experience. In making this point we are persuaded to misquote T. S. Eliot and ensure that in having the experience we do not miss the meaning.

We find this more dynamic way of viewing effective schools and classrooms most encouraging. One of our main concerns with both of these literatures is that they appear static. They emerge from research methodologies committed to portraying organizational variables *at a point* in time, rather than *over* time. Given this, it seems to us that one of the major difficulties in implementing the effective schools and classrooms research is the way in which the knowledge is presented and used, particularly as the outcomes of the research are often portrayed in the form of lists, the limitations of which we have already seen.

Knowledge of the type discussed so far in this chapter is not a panacea; at best it is informed advice that schools may wish to test out in their own settings. The knowledge is there to inform, not control, practice. We therefore use such lists and summaries of school and classroom effectiveness characteristics in our own work as a starting point for thinking about the school as an environment where young people learn. There are two research studies that we find especially helpful in this regard.

Although there is clarity and consensus in this research as to the effective school correlates, there is generally little discussion about the nature of the process that leads to effectiveness. Dan Levine (1992), however, has made a particular study of this aspect of the effective schools research. He has generated a list of ten guidelines that can assist in this endeavour. We have summarized them as follows:

1 Substantial staff development time must be provided; at least in part, during the teacher's regular workday.

2 Groups of staff engaged in effective schools projects must not wait very long before beginning to address issues involving improving the quality of teaching.

3 Conversely, staff embarking in an effective schools project must avoid getting bogged down in elaborate schemes to train all staff in the details of a particular teaching technique or approach at the beginning of the project.

4 Priorities for development must be sharply focused and few in number, in order to avoid teacher and school overload.

5 The success of changes in teaching practice is also dependent on parallel changes in the conditions within the school that support it.

6 Significant support (for example, consultancy or advisory teachers) must be made available to staff participating in effective schools projects.

7 Effective schools projects should be 'data driven' in the sense that appropriate information from evaluation should guide participants in preparing and carrying out plans for improvement.

8 Effective schools projects must avoid reliance on bureaucratic

implementation stressing forms, check-lists and 'quick-fix' remedies rigidly applied in participating schools and classrooms.

9 Effective schools projects should seek out and consider using materials, methods and approaches that have been successful elsewhere.

10 The success of an effective schools project depends on a judicious mixture of autonomy within the school and a measure of directiveness from outside.

In this analysis Levine is moving beyond school effectiveness research *per se* to encompass research on classroom practices and to link them both with school improvement strategies. This, in our opinion, is how it should be.

Another research study has, in a similar way, moved beyond traditional school effectiveness research to encompass improvement strategies at the level of both the classroom and the school. As part of their longitudinal study of school effectiveness in Louisiana, Sam Stringfield and Charles Teddlie (1988, 1991) identified sixteen schools that were either highly effective or highly ineffective over a period of time — that is, the students in these schools continued to perform either significantly above or below expectation based on previous learning history and family background. Seven observers then spent over 700 hours observing in classrooms and over 1,000 hours on data gathering in the schools. Neither the participants in the schools observed, nor the visiting teams of researchers, knew which schools were high- or low-achieving. Despite this, the observers held educated guesses about the schools, and all were correct in their attribution of positive and negative outlier status. The analysis of field notes and extensive interviews with the researchers indicated that they made their judgements on the basis of broad themes and striking individual events at three levels: school/principal, classroom and student. These 'data categories' provide very helpful insights into what accounts for successful and unsuccessful schools (Table 4.1). We have retained the word 'principal', for which the UK equivalent is 'head'.

The work of Levine and, especially, Stringfield and Teddlie is concerned with creating effective schools and classrooms. It is also implicitly concerned with school improvement. Recent work has been exploring the ways in which school effectiveness researchers and school improvement practitioners can work more fruitfully together, and there is now a series of suggestions about how this confluence can be achieved (Reynolds *et al.*, 1993). The basis of the argument is that each speciality could contribute greatly to the academic and practical needs of the other. To take school improvement first, school improvers need to have knowledge about those factors within schools and within classrooms that may be manipulated or changed to produce higher-quality schooling: school effectiveness researchers can provide that knowledge. Correspondingly, at their simplest level, school improvement strategies provide the ultimate test for many of the theories posited by the school effectiveness research. It is with this collaborative aspiration that we have described the characteristics of effective schools and classrooms in this chapter.

Table 4.1 *Factors observed to differentiate effective and ineffective schools*

Level	Stable high-achieving school	Stable low-achieving school
Student	High to moderate time on task*	Low or uneven time on task; students 'escape' from class and reduce academic time
	School makes academic sense to students	School is intellectual anarchy
Classroom	Planned academic push*	Classes progress at leisurely pace
	Teachers articulate academic plans	Minimal to no planning — 'following the curriculum'; 'going through the motions'
	High to moderate interactive teaching — 'Get the show on the road', and so on*	Low or uneven interactive teaching rates
	Teachers seek new instructional techniques	Teachers teach in isolation
	Varied curriculum	Many 'ditto sheets' and workbooks
School and principal	Friendly, serious academic atmosphere* — 'We're here to teach, students are here to learn'	Occasionally friendly, never academically focused — 'If kids had a better attitude, we could teach'
	Respect for academic time*	Lack of primary academic focus
	Accurate schedules	Schedules overestimate instructional time — 'extended break', etc.
	Resource (special needs) classes well coordinated	Resources (especially for special needs pupils) working at cross-purposes
	Principals know curricula and instructional details, often mention specifics	Principals rarely discuss academic specifics
	Principals seek and integrate new intellectual experiences for schools	Principals define their work bureaucratically
	Principals actively recruit new teachers*	Principals passively accept new teachers
	Focused, often school-wide staff development	Diffuse staff development
	Principals move ineffective teachers out*	Principals rarely observe classes — 'All our teachers are good'
	Student-focused, academically oriented library*	Rarely used or non-academic library
	Prominently posted academic 'honour roll'*	No school academic rewards

*Applies especially to the four schools that the observers felt were deliberately attempting to 'improve' themselves.
Adapted from Stringfield and Teddlie (1991, p. 362).

MESSAGES

We have been concerned in this chapter to describe aspects of the effective school and classroom. We have concentrated on the organizational characteristics supportive of student achievement and have noted that existing structures can be modified. We have also focused on the nature of effective teaching, because of the links between teaching and student achievement. In trying to bring this discussion together we draw out the following messages:

- *Student outcomes are the fundamental goal for educational reform.* It is incontrovertible that the reason for engaging in innovation and planned change is to enhance the progress of students. Monitor this assertion carefully, and if the links of the chain become too extended then quickly move to refocus on the real reason we are doing all of this. This suggests a broader definition of outcome than student scores on achievement tests, even though for some schools these may be pre-eminent. We are concerned with those educational goals that reflect the particular mission of a school, and represent what the school itself regards as desirable. The important point is that all of this development should focus on and have some impact on student learning.

- *The characteristics of the effective school are open to modification by the staff of the school.* The research on 'effective schools' suggests that certain internal conditions are typical in schools that achieve higher levels of outcomes for their students. The literature is also in agreement on two further issues: first, that these differences in outcome are systematically related to variations in the school's climate, culture or ethos; second, that the school's culture is amenable to alteration by concerted action on the part of the school staff. Although this alteration is not an easy task, the evidence suggests that teachers and schools have more control than they may have imagined over their ability to change their present situation.

- *Teaching and learning are the prime focus of school improvement efforts.* Despite curricula being increasingly imposed by central authorities, there is still the opportunity for teachers to exercise discretion in the use of teaching strategies. It is now evident that, the content of a lesson notwithstanding, the use of appropriate teaching strategies can dramatically increase student achievement. A major goal for school improvement therefore is for teachers who are so professionally flexible that they can select, from a repertoire of models, the teaching approach most suited to a particular content area and their students' age and ability.

- *The two key elements of staff development are the workshop and the workplace.* The workshop, which is equivalent to the best practice on the traditional INSET course, is where teachers gain understanding, see demonstrations of the teaching strategy they may wish to acquire, and have the opportunity to practise them in a non-threatening environment. If, however, they wish to transfer those skills back into the workplace — the classroom and school — support on the job is required. This implies changes to the ways in which staff development is organized in schools. In particular this means the opportunity for immediate and sustained practice, collaboration and peer coaching, and studying development and implementation.

- *Use school and classroom effectiveness knowledge for the purpose of school development.* School effectiveness research has given us clear indications of what effective school cultures look like; and the same research tradition has been very specific in detailing those teaching strategies that lead to increased student achievement. Yet knowledge, without the process to put it into practice, is of little use. Similarly, strategies for school improvement that focus solely on whole-school processes without much substantive content, or those that address single curriculum innovations or isolated teaching practices rather than whole-school developments, are doomed to tinkering. In short, we need to see school development whole; to see what these cultures, strategies and processes actually look like within schools. When we do this we begin to meet the real challenge of educational reform.

Chapter 5

Approaches to School Improvement

We have defined school improvement as an approach to educational change that has the twin purposes of enhancing student achievement and strengthening the school's capacity for managing change. Those who work in the field of school improvement, in the sense that we are using the term, actively seek to collaborate with schools in finding ways of enhancing student outcomes through specific changes in teaching approaches and the curriculum, and through strengthening the school's organizational ability to support the work of teachers. School improvement cannot therefore be simply equated with educational change in general. Many externally (and some internally) imposed innovations do not improve student outcomes, and most appear to neglect the importance of the culture and organization of the school as key factors in sustaining teacher and school development.

It is the more extensive definition of school improvement as an alternative approach to educational change that we will elaborate during this chapter. We do this by reviewing and trying to make sense of a variety of efforts to bring about and support school improvement. In particular we:

- expand the definition of school improvement;
- classify the range of school improvement efforts;
- evaluate the effectiveness of various school improvement approaches;
- describe ways in which school improvement can be supported.

DEFINING SCHOOL IMPROVEMENT

School improvement approaches to educational change of the type that we are concerned with in this chapter embody the long-term goal of moving towards the 'ideal type' of 'self-renewing school'. This obviously implies a very different way of thinking about change as compared with the ubiquitous top-down approach discussed in Chapter 2. When the school is regarded as the centre of change, then strategies for change need to take this new perspective into account. This approach is exemplified in the work of the OECD-sponsored International School Improvement Project (ISIP) and the knowledge that emanated from it (van Velzen et al., 1985; Hopkins, 1987b, 1990a). School improvement was defined in the ISIP as: 'a systematic, sustained effort aimed at change in learning conditions and other related internal conditions in one or more schools, with the ultimate aim of accomplishing educational goals more effectively' (van Velzen et al., 1985, p. 48). School improvement as an approach to educational change therefore rests on a number of assumptions:

- *The school as the centre of change.* This means that external reforms need to be sensitive to the situation in individual schools, rather than assuming that all schools are the same. It also implies that school improvement efforts need to adopt a 'classroom-exceeding' perspective, without ignoring the classroom.

- *A systematic approach to change.* School improvement is a carefully planned and managed process that takes place over a period of several years.

- *The 'internal conditions' of schools as a key focus for change.* These include not only the teaching-learning activities used in the school, but also the schools' procedures, role allocation and resource use that support the teaching-learning process.

- *Accomplishing educational goals more effectively.* Educational goals reflect the particular mission of a school, and represent what the school itself regards as desirable. This suggests a broader definition of outcome than student scores on achievement tests, even though for some schools these may be pre-eminent. Schools also serve the more general developmental needs of students, the professional development of teachers and the needs of its community.

- *A multi-level perspective.* Although the school is the centre of change it does not act alone. The school is embedded in an educational system that has to work collaboratively or symbiotically if the highest degrees of quality are to be achieved. This means that the roles of teachers, heads, governors, parents, support people (advisers, higher education, consultants, etc.) and local authorities should be defined, harnessed and committed to the process of school improvement.

- *Integrative implementation strategies.* This implies a linkage between top-down and bottom-up; though remember of course that both approaches can apply at a number of different levels in the system. Ideally, top-down provides policy aims, an overall strategy, and operational plans; this is complemented by a bottom-up response involving diagnosis, priority goal setting, and implementation. The former provides the framework, resources and a menu of alternatives; the latter, energy and school-based implementation.

- *The drive towards institutionalization.* Change is only successful when it has become part of the natural behaviour of teachers in the school. Implementation by itself is not enough.

It is this philosophy and approach that underpinned the ISIP and laid the basis for further thinking and action.

ON CLASSIFYING SCHOOL IMPROVEMENT EFFORTS

Such definitions and assumptions are helpful in understanding the principles underlying the approach, but what does school improvement look like in practice? There is no one place to start with school improvement. It basically depends on the aspirations and experience of the school and the individuals involved. As we have seen, though, there are not only some principles to guide us but also some proven approaches. It is difficult, however, to analyse the range of school improvement efforts because of their different foci and underlying philosophies. In thinking about school improvement efforts we find it helpful to characterize the various approaches in two broad categories, both of which have a contribution to make: those approaches that provide us with the *ingredients* of school improvement — that is, tell us the essential elements; and those that give us *recipes* — that is, tell us how to go about it. Within the 'ingredients' approach are two main strands. The first is research-based knowledge about the characteristics that define school improvement, the *table d'hôte* menu; the other is more of a compilation or *à la carte* menu of school improvement strategies. The 'recipe' approach is more strategic, but even here there is wide variation between what we have called the mechanistic and the organic strategies. The mechanistic or step-by-step approach provides us with guidelines as what to do; the organic approach suggests principles within which schools are likely to flourish. If we pursue this way of thinking it is possible to classify school improvement approaches (Table 5.1). In the table we have given one example of each approach, which we will briefly describe below to give a sense of the range of school improvement efforts.

Table 5.1. *Classifying school improvement efforts*

Approach	Strategy	Example
Ingredients	Table d'hôte	Improving the urban high school
	A la carte	The doors to school improvement
Recipe	Mechanistic	The self-managing school
	Organic	School development planning

Improving the urban high school

An example of the research-based 'ingredients' or *table d'hôte* approach to school improvement is Karen Seashore Louis and Matthew Miles's (1990) study on improving the urban high school. The book describes in depth school improvement efforts in five large American urban high schools. In contrast to studies of effective schools and effective teaching, this sets itself the task of answering the question, 'How do we get there?'. The authors had five major findings concerning what it takes to improve big-city schools:

1   *School-LEA relationships.* They found that these worked best when the LEA provided support and direction, and the school had a great deal of autonomy in choosing goals and strategies. Effective working relationships were the key.

2 They found that an *evolutionary approach to planning* 'works best, with plenty of early action (small-scale wins) to create energy and support learning'. They also claim that 'planning is the first point where empowerment takes hold' (p. 292). This factor relates specifically to the theme of this book.

3 The importance of *'shared images* of what the school should become' (p. 293). The importance of generating ownership of the school's vision and aims and their reflection in the priorities of the plan is crucial. This factor, too, resonates with themes in this book.

4 They also mention *resources* as a key variable. They call 'for a broad based view of resources' (p. 294) in support of the school's vision. They emphasize the linking of developmental priorities to a cool appraisal of the resource implications.

5 Finally, they refer to *'problem coping'*. They found that 'problems during school improvement efforts are multiple, pervasive, and often nearly intractable. But dealing with them actively, promptly, and with some depth is the single biggest determinant of program success' (p. 295). 'Depth', they emphasize, is not about 'fire-fighting', but (to use our language) about dealing directly with the school's management arrangements.

There are now a number of studies which proffer similar advice to that of Louis and Miles. For example, Miles together with Michael Huberman (Huberman and Miles, 1984) reported on school improvement efforts in twelve American schools. This study highlights a series of dilemmas for schools attempting to improve themselves: for example, how far does a school adapt an innovation to its own purposes before losing the integrity of the approach? How does a school balance stability and change? How does a local school district balance centralization with local autonomy? The best of this research is insightful and has the ring of truth to it.

The doors to school improvement

The strategic dimension is highly visible in Bruce Joyce's (1991) review of a series of individual approaches, which he describes as being 'doors' which can open or unlock the process of school improvement. Joyce concludes that each approach emphasizes different aspects of school culture at the outset — in other words, they provide a range of ways of 'getting into' school improvement. Each door opens a passageway into the culture of the school. His review reveals five major emphases (Joyce, 1991, p. 59):

1 *Collegiality*. Collaborative and professional relations are developed within a school staff and between their surrounding communities.

2 *Research*. A school staff studies research findings about, for example, effective school and teaching practices, or the process of change.

3 *Action research*. Teachers collect and analyse information and data about their classrooms and schools, and their students' progress.

4 *Curriculum initiatives*. Changes are introduced within subject areas or, as in the case of the computer, across curriculum areas.

5 *Teaching strategies*. Teachers discuss, observe and acquire a range of teaching skills and strategies.

He argues that all these emphases can eventually change the culture of the school substantially. If we look carefully at each door to school improvement, we can discover where each is likely to lead, how the passageways are connected, what proponents of any one approach can borrow from the others, and the costs and benefits of opening any one (or any combination) first. Joyce argues that single approaches are unlikely to be as powerful an agent for school improvement as a synthesis. He says somewhat wryly that while a school is making up its mind about which door to open first, it should be collecting information about itself and trying to acquire an extra teaching strategy or two! His point is well taken: move into action while decision making, and make school improvement everyone's business.

There are a number of familiar doors that we have passed through during the recent history of educational change in the UK, some of which are similar to those identified by Joyce. We regard his list as being illustrative rather than exclusive (despite our attempt at translating from the American). Finding time to study research findings is not a luxury most school staff can afford nowadays. There has, however, been a great emphasis on curriculum change as a source of school improvement. There is also a strong action research tradition in the UK, which has led to countless very successful small-scale improvement projects.

A much-opened door in UK schools in the early 1980s, as we have already seen, was the one named 'school self-evaluation'. The Schools Council 'Guidelines for Internal Review and Development' (GRIDS) project, for example, was designed to help teachers review and develop the curriculum and organization of their school (Abbott *et al.*, 1988). During the early to mid-1980s, school self-evaluation established itself as a major strategy for managing the change process (Bollington and Hopkins, 1989). Unfortunately, the empirical support for its effectiveness as a school improvement strategy is at best ambivalent (e.g. Clift *et al.*, 1987). For most schools it proved easier to identify priorities for future development than to implement selected targets within a specific time frame. Because of this, and a failure to implement the total process — for example, training for feedback and follow-up — school self-evaluation, despite its popularity, has had limited impact on the daily life of many schools. It is a good example of a 'one-club' school improvement strategy.

The implicit assumption made by Joyce is that behind the door is a series of interconnecting pathways that lead inexorably to school improvement. Unfortunately this is not always so. Because of their singular nature, most school improvement strategies, as we have seen, fail to a greater or lesser degree to affect the culture of the school. They tend to focus on individual changes, and individual teachers and classrooms, rather than how these changes can fit in with and adapt the organization and ethos of the school. As a consequence, when the door is opened it leads only into a cul-de-sac. This partly accounts for the uneven effect of most of our educational reforms.

To continue in this vein for a moment, it seems logical that if we are to overcome the problems of educational change already described, we need to find some way of integrating organizational and curriculum change within a coherent strategy. We need to find ways of opening the doors to school improvement simultaneously or consecutively and of linking together the pathways behind them.

The self-managing school

The 'self-managing school' approach to school improvement, as we have already noted, was developed in the mid-1980s, by Brian Caldwell and Jim Spinks (1988) in Tasmania, Australia, as a response to a policy for devolved management and budgets for schools. This approach has been widely disseminated, adapted and emulated in many other school systems, particularly in Canada and the UK. The popularity of this approach was due to two factors: first the increasing financial devolution to schools in developed countries; and second the transferability of the self-managing school model. With the rapid implementation of local management of schools or site-based management in the late 1980s, many schools and school districts or LEAs found the step-by-step approach proposed by the self-managing school model very attractive.

The 'collaborative school management cycle' provides the basis of the approach. The management cycle has six phases:

1 Goal setting and need identification.
2 Policy making, with policies consisting of purposes and broad guidelines.
3 Planning of programmes.
4 Preparation and approval of programme budgets.
5 Implementing.
6 Evaluating.

Although this is a fairly commonplace cycle of activity Caldwell and Spinks (1988, pp. 22-4) claim that its special contribution is based on three characteristics:

1 The clear and unambiguous specification of those phases which are the responsibility of the policy-making group in the school (policy group) and of other phases which are the concerns of groups responsible for implementing policy (programme teams).
2 A definition of policy which goes beyond a statement of general purpose but is not so detailed as to specify action.
3 The organization of planning activities around programmes which correspond to the normal patterns of work in the school.

Through their book *The Self-managing School* (1988) and their workshops, Caldwell and Spinks have popularized the approach. Certain aspects of the model, in particular the use of 'one-page policies', are now found in many schools. The clearer links between policy and budgets in some schools is also a result of their advocacy. Both the book and their workshop materials set out the approach in a logical and sequential manner that make it readily accessible.

We are using the self-managing school as an example of a mechanistic approach to school improvement. We use the term 'mechanistic' not in a pejorative but in a technical sense. Burns and Stalker (1961) deal with the conditions necessary for renewal and change in organizations. They contrast two opposite types of administrative systems — the mechanistic and the organic. Their definition of mechanistic systems is close to the description we have just given of the self-managing school approach, in particular the specialized differentiation of functional tasks, the precise definition of methods and so on. Although there is by no means an exact fit between the two, the self-managing school approach is well categorized as mechanistic according to the definition of Burns and Stalker.

If we now broaden the discussion a little and regard the self-managing school as an example of a wider phenomenon, we can begin to understand more clearly why such approaches to local management are proving difficult to implement. Burns and Stalker regard mechanistic approaches as ideally suited for stable conditions; that is, when the organization is not subject to many pressures towards change. Unfortunately, by definition most schools *do* find themselves under pressure to change when they adopt approaches like the self-managing school. The superficial attractiveness of a step-by-step approach which is easy to understand in theory does in practice tend towards inflexibility during times of change. This is not to criticize the self-managing school or similar approaches; the discussion does serve, however, to highlight the point that different models serve different purposes at different times. At times of great change, it is argued (at least by Burns and Stalker), more responsive approaches are required.

School development planning

By way of contrast to the self-managing school we now provide an example of an organic approach to school improvement, one that in Burns and Stalker's view is more suitable for a changing environment. Development planning, as this approach is commonly called ('school growth plans' is another popular term for similar activities), provides a generic and paradigmatic illustration of a school improvement strategy, combining as it does selected curriculum change with modifications to the school's management arrangements or organization. It is a strategy that is becoming increasingly widespread in British schools as teachers and school leaders struggle to take control of the process of change. The DES project on school development plans (SDP), for example, was an attempt to develop a strategy that would, among other things, help governors, heads and staff to change the culture of their school (Hargreaves *et al.*, 1989; Hargreaves and Hopkins, 1991).

Development planning, besides helping the school organize what it is already doing and what it needs to do in a more purposeful and coherent way, is about helping schools manage innovation and change successfully. The distinctive feature of a development plan is that it brings together, in an overall plan, national and local policies and initiatives, the school's aims and values, its existing achievements and its needs for development. By coordinating aspects of planning which are otherwise separate, the school acquires a shared sense of direction and is able to control and manage more easily the tasks of development and change. A development plan is easily described. Priorities for development are selected and planned in detail for one year and are supported by action plans or working documents for staff. The priorities for later years are sketched in outline to provide the longer-term programme (Hargreaves et al., 1989, p. 4).

Not all schools find development planning easy. Schools face a double problem: they cannot remain as they now are if they are to implement recent reforms, but at the same time they also need to maintain some continuity between their present and their previous practices. There is therefore for most schools a tension between development (change) and maintenance (stability and continuity). The problem is that schools tend to generate organizational structures that predispose them towards one or the other. Schools (or parts of schools) at the development extreme may be so over-confident of their innovative capacities that they take on too much too quickly. Schools at the maintenance extreme may either see little purpose in reform or have a poor record in managing innovation. Schools that can balance the demands of development and maintenance will find it most easy to engage in development planning.

The term 'management arrangements' is used by Hargreaves and Hopkins (1991) to describe the organizational culture of the school. Their descriptions of the three basic aspects or dimensions of the management arrangements are drawn from schools where development planning is most successful. They may be used as a guide for a school to review the character and quality of its management arrangements. They are also consistent with the descriptions of the effective school given earlier. Space unfortunately precludes all but a cursory description:

- There are *frameworks* which guide the actions of all who are involved in the school. Examples of frameworks are the school's aims and policies, and the systems for decision making and consultation. Without clear frameworks, the school would soon lapse into confusion and conflict.

- The management arrangements clarify *roles and responsibilities*. All who are involved in the school need to have a shared understanding of their respective roles and of who is taking responsibility for what. Well-designed frameworks are useless without clear roles and responsibilities.

- The management arrangements promote ways in which the people involved can *work together* so that each person finds his or her particular role enjoyable and rewarding, and at the same time the

75

aims of the school as a whole can be achieved successfully. While the head undoubtedly plays the key role, management and the arrangements to support it are a collective activity and responsibility. (Hargreaves and Hopkins, 1991, p. 43)

In the light of its review, a school may select changes to its management arrangements as a priority in the plan.

In selecting and sequencing priorities for a development plan there is also another distinction to be borne in mind. Development planning involves two kinds of change: *root innovations*, which generate a base, and *branch innovations*, which can be sustained on that base. Strong roots to support the curriculum and teaching aspects of the development plan are provided by, for example, a well-developed staff development policy, or a history of collaborative work among the staff and with the school's partners. When such roots are lacking, there is a danger that some of the planned branch innovations will wither and die (Hargreaves and Hopkins, 1991).

Because the management arrangements serve as a root to so many innovations, adjustments to them will be a strong candidate for an early priority in many schools. Recognizing that the appropriate management arrangements will evolve progressively to support new roles and relationships is itself a step in changing the culture of the school.

School development planning is but one example of a contemporary genre of organic approaches to school improvement. We have already noted the 'School Growth Plan' approach developed in Toronto, Canada (Stoll and Fink, 1992). The IMTEC approach to institutional development developed in Norway (Dalin *et al.*, 1993), and certain approaches to 'restructuring' in the USA (e.g. Elmore, 1990; Murphy, 1991), are also taking a more fundamental approach to educational reform by transforming the organization of the school in the quest for enhanced student achievement. Another example of a more organic approach is found in the various school improvement networks that are based on a particular philosophy or set of principles. They are a sort of school improvement club where the rules of admission define a generalized approach to development work in schools. The Comer School Development Programme (Comer, 1988), the Coalition of Essential Schools based at Brown University, which has evolved on the basis of the ideas of Theodore Sizer (Sizer, 1989), and the League of Professional Schools at the University of Georgia, which is led by Carl Glickman (Glickman, 1990), are all fine examples of this approach to school improvement. The 'Improving the Quality of Education for All' (IQEA) project based at Cambridge, which we describe in Parts 3 and 4 of the book, is another well-developed example of this type (Ainscow and Hopkins, 1992).

THE EFFECTIVENESS OF SCHOOL IMPROVEMENT INITIATIVES

In the previous sections we have classified a range of school improvement initiatives and given a variety of examples. We have not as yet, however, considered the effectiveness of various school improvement initiatives in enhancing the performance of students. Unfortunately and surprisingly, there have been few large-scale efforts at evaluating the effectiveness of school improvement. The two best known are both American. The Rand Study (e.g. Berman and McLaughlin, 1978), which was carried out in the mid-1970s, has recently been reanalysed (McLaughlin, 1990). We have also noted in passing the DESSI study carried out in the early 1980s (e.g. Crandall *et al.*, 1982). Although both of these studies have increased our knowledge about school improvement in general, evaluations of specific approaches to school improvement are still in short supply. Consequently, in practice much is taken on faith. When a school either by itself, or at the behest of or in collaboration with the LEA, decides to engage in a school improvement initiative, what does it do? Does it buy in a package? Does it attempt school-wide reforms? Does it join a school improvement club? In the interests of student learning, which works best?

This is the question that Sam Stringfield (Stringfield, 1993) and his colleagues (Stringfield *et al.*, 1992) have recently been trying to answer. Over the past few years they have been engaged in a massive research project undertaken for the US Department of Education, where they have been evaluating examples of these three types of innovations, all of which are or could be funded under federal Chapter 1 legislation. Chapter 1 is a $6,700-million annual supplement for those schools serving large numbers of economically and educationally disadvantaged children. This is big money, and the US government is concerned to ensure that it is spending it wisely in so far as the initiatives funded under Chapter 1 are actually having a positive impact on this particular group of young people.

The details of Stringfield's research are not applicable to the UK situation, but the general findings certainly are. He and his colleagues are investigating ten programmes that fall into three types. As will be seen, their 'types' are similar to our categories. As they reviewed the range of school improvement initiatives open to schools, they classified them as follows:

1 *Adjunct or 'add-on'* innovations that a school adopts ready-made for specific purposes; for example, a new reading course.

2 *School-wide projects* that a school invents itself and works on as a whole school, rather than on a single-classroom basis. Examples of this approach to school improvement would be a decision to move to mixed-ability teaching, or the integration of students with special learning needs into the regular class programme.

3 *Philosophical or research-based projects* where a school joins a school improvement project that is informed by a particular educational philosophy, or is based on an approach that builds on specific research-based knowledge. This is a phenomenon less well known in the UK than in North America, but the 'free school' movement in the early to mid-1970s had a common philosophic base, as do Montessori schools.

'Add-on' programmes that they are studying include a reading programme, computer-assisted learning, peer tutoring and extended day/extended year approaches. These programmes have two primary advantages. First, they do not require changing the whole school; for example, special teachers can be hired, and equipment and materials purchased. Second, they can be targeted at particular groups of students. These advantages can, however, also be disadvantages. The programmes tend to lack integration, and 'pull-outs' can be disruptive to the class as a whole and the individual students involved. Many of these programmes create bitterness among staff, who are jealous of what they see as special treatment for colleagues involved in such programmes. They certainly do not encourage a learning community among staff, and in general the programme may not fit with the overall curriculum of the school.

School-wide projects by their nature are individualistic, but Stringfield and his colleagues have seen some striking similarities across the cases they studied. Three almost universal features are reduced class size, increased frequency and quality of staff development, and increased availability of books and materials. The big advantage of these programmes is that they are seen to be responding to needs of staff and students, and consequently generate high levels of 'ownership'. They do, however, seem to lack vision, for students and the curriculum; they also seem to be insufficiently stretching or demanding of staff. There appears to be an assumption that smaller class sizes and better materials will somehow do the trick. There is little 'dreaming' in these schools or discussion about what they could become.

Philosophy or research-based projects share a number of common and unique features. All are university based, are reform or development oriented, have highly sophisticated rationales which include a 'vision' of what the school could be like, and provide consultancy support. The advantages mirror these characteristics: there is a clear vision, and high-quality support, strategies and materials. When there is a strong curriculum and teaching element to these programmes they do seem to have significant impact. There are also concomitant disadvantages. If the fit between the programme philosophy and the school culture is not good, then chaos almost always results. They are usually expensive, and if not all staff 'buy in' then disunity results.

Although this research is on-going, there are already some striking conclusions to be drawn from their investigations. We list ten insights drawn from their work which are already well substantiated:

1 All the programmes have some aspect which might be useful to particular schools.

2 However, specific programmes are often chosen with little consideration of alternatives or of specific strengths and needs.

3 Strategies aimed at whole schools are more likely to change students' whole days.

4 Additional funding facilitates implementation.

5 Staff development throughout the length of the initiative is the vital ingredient for successful implementation. This is particularly the case with externally developed innovations.

6 Active leadership is critical.

7 Schools experiencing the greatest difficulties with implementation display other problems.

8 Powerful contextual variables differentially affect implementation; in particular, when the fit between programme and school is poor, implementation is poor.

9 Each programme has its own, often unstated, necessary preconditions for successful implementation.

10 Almost all the programmes continue to evolve.

There are a number of implications from this work for those who choose school improvement options, and for those who support schools in so doing. The first is that some form of evaluation, review or needs assessment should proceed selection of the innovation. These decisions need to be made rationally on the basis of evidence. In these cases, and in our own experience, this preliminary process is often neglected. A connected point is that in virtually all these cases the innovation was chosen with little regard to local conditions. Too often, according to Stringfield (1993, p. 6), 'schools grasp at the first "program" to come by, in the hope that it would "solve our [unstated] problems"'.

This work also confirms our own emphasis on the vital importance of continuing staff development and the modification of workplace conditions to support the innovation. As we continue to argue, and will see graphically in the following section, unless these conditions are attended to, then sustained school improvement will remain elusive. Stringfield (1993, p. 7) argues a similar point. He claims that a basic level of school effectiveness is necessary to implement any programme. We agree, but do not exclude schools that cannot reach the starting post. The conditions for this basic level of effectiveness have to be worked on first. This is why we argue in the following section that schools that do not reach this basic level of effectiveness require dedicated and sustained support early in the process.

Finally, Stringfield (1993, p. 7) implies that external development is likely to have more impact on student achievement than school-wide programmes. He argues that externally developed programmes usually have proven track records and relieve teachers from the responsibility of 'building the airplane in flight'. They allow teachers time for implementation and for adapting the innovation to local conditions. This conclusion is highly consistent with other large-scale evaluations of school improvement efforts (Crandall *et al.*, 1986; McLaughlin, 1990). This is *not* to say that teachers have no role to play in the development process, and should have innovations imposed on them from the outside. It is to say, however, that they should first make a thorough evaluation of their needs, then review available resources to see if there is anything already produced that fits. Assuming (as in most cases) there is, then these innovations should be subject to staff development, and experimentation by teachers as they adapt them to their classrooms and local situation. This process is very similar to the situation that led Stenhouse (1975) to develop his concept of 'teacher as researcher'.

This discussion about alternative approaches to school improvement programmes is leading us into a broader discussion of the process of change. The nature of the programme is important, but so too is the process by which it is put into practice. This is why we have argued and will continue to argue for more 'organic' approaches to school improvement. Often schools, as we have already noted, need support to get started and to sustain development. A discussion of how schools can be supported in the process of school improvement provides the focus for the following section.

SUPPORTING SCHOOL IMPROVEMENT

The quest for school improvement is not restricted to the territory of the school: no school is an island. Despite the decentralizing emphasis found in most Western countries today, school improvement is not a function of isolation or competition. The Dutch, whose work presaged the ISIP, captured this sense nicely in the phrase 'the relatively autonomous school'. More recently commentators have talked about the school as the *centre*, rather than the unit, of change. This is an important distinction, because despite contemporary political pressure, recent research points to effective schools existing within a climate of mutual collaboration with outside agencies. For this reason we despair at the erosion of the LEA in England and Wales, not so much because we are great supporters of the LEA, but because no school can go it alone. We need to search for more effective ways of supporting schools within a context of decentralization.

It is only recently that research has been reported on the school-LEA or school-district interface (we will use the terms 'LEA', 'district' and 'local' level interchangeably). One of the earlier papers was by Purkey and Smith (1985), who had already written influentially on school effectiveness. Their prescription for district-school effectiveness is contained in four general policy recommendations:

1　Take the school as the focus of change.
2　Review the school situation.
3　Provide resources, consultancy support and staff development, and encourage collaboration.
4　Establish appropriate shelter conditions at the local or district level.

This sensible but general advice was corroborated by subsequent studies, experience and common sense. But at times when the relationship between schools and their immediate external environment is changing, we need more detailed guidelines on what support is needed for successful school improvement. We begin this task by describing a successful case of local authority-school collaboration, the principles of which have a potential application to the contemporary scene in the UK. On the basis of this and other experiences we draw up some guidelines for school-district collaboration.

The example is from London and describes an attempt to improve schools on the basis of school evaluations conducted by local inspectors. Until recently, the traditional pattern in English schools was for visits of usually a week by teams of inspectors who then produced reports, which of late were published. However, this information was rarely used systematically for school improvement purposes. This was the situation in the ILEA (which became another victim of the educational reforms in England and Wales during the 1980s). The ILEA's penultimate chief inspector clearly regarded this situation as unsatisfactory. Despite the thoroughness of the inspections, his judgement was that (Hargreaves, 1990, pp. 18-9):

> there remained the important task of how these schools might be improved to narrow the gap between the best and the worst. It was evident that such schools needed sustained help and support, yet inspectors had insufficient time at their disposal to work intensively with them.
>
> The solution was a team of inspectors who would be freed from all normal duties to devote all their time to school improvement. This became known as the IBIS or Inspectors Based in Schools scheme. In the secondary phase a team of twelve inspectors undertook this task, beginning in autumn 1986. Entry to the school was for the most part amicably negotiated between the inspectorate and the head. The team introduced themselves at a staff meeting, explained the team's approach and answered questions. The life of the school and lessons were observed by the team, who also interviewed all the staff as well as some pupils and parents. The team then withdrew for a few days to write a diagnostic report, which was presented to the staff as a series of discussion documents. Following a full discussion with the staff, the team remained in the school for a further four weeks or so to engage in the developmental work arising out of the diagnostic reports and the discussion of them. At the end of this phase, the team wrote its final report for the school's governors and this covered both the school's strengths and weaknesses (which is somewhat like an inspection report) and the action being taken in the developmental phase to remedy the weaknesses (normally not part of an inspection report).

This more strategic approach to inspection and support derives from a recognition that change is a relatively long-term process which cannot be done quickly or easily and that a carefully formulated, step-by-step approach is to be preferred. This will require an alignment between the LEA's or district's strategy for support and the school's slowly emerging strategy for its own development. In later work Hargreaves suggested that strategic alignment of this kind is likely to involve (Hargreaves and Hopkins, 1991, p. 106):

- *external support* that provides needed knowledge of curriculum or teaching strategies, effective staff development and critical friendship;
- *external pressure*, without which the school may not move from its stable pattern of self-maintenance — for example, an inspection,

expressions of parental dissatisfaction, or even visits of a consultant to check on progress;

- *internal pressure* — the recognition by all of the advantages of development to the school itself, and the need to meet deadlines and the expectations of colleagues;

- *internal support* — the release of self-help and self-directing energy which allows the school to break free from too great a dependence on external support.

External support of this kind not only enhances the partnership between the school and its local authority or support agency, but also promotes the concept and practice of the 'relatively autonomous school', which is essential in an era of decentralization. This example involves a strong lead from the LEA, by taking a positive approach to inspection, often by using a school improvement strategy such as the school's development plan. On all the evidence so far, this appears to be the only form of partnership which can help those schools that are under-performing to become more successful.

The example of local support for school improvement that we have just described shares a number of characteristics with others that we have reviewed (Hopkins, 1994). All of these other examples were of strong proactive intervention and support from the outside, which was tempered by a concern for the nature of the individual school. In each case the commitment initially came from the local level in the form of a policy change and redeployment of personnel, as well as fairly significant resource (re)allocation. The other key characteristic was the clear focus on teaching and learning. There was a similar emphasis on the internal conditions of schools. This was the result of a real-ization that, in some cases, sustained classroom change will not occur without a radical transformation in the organization and workplace conditions of the school. Two other features of these other cases are worth mentioning: first, the emphasis on involving a range of partners in school improvement; and second, the extent to which in one way or another these approaches were data driven.

This general picture is corroborated by other studies. Michael Fullan's review of change processes and strategies at the local level (Fullan, 1985) is helpfully detailed and specific. His empirical study of school districts in Ontario contributes a number of insights (Fullan *et al.*, 1986, pp. 325, 327):

Neither grass-roots nor top-down approaches work by themselves. Central co-ordination, pressure, and development is essential, but so is corresponding school-based development on the part of principals and teachers as implementation decision makers. The solution is neither more nor less centralization, but rather it lies in the area of increased interaction and negotiation between schools and area or central offices, and investment in the development of capacities at both levels. The process is probably more powerful if it is initiated from the centre because the centre has more scope, resources, and, consequently, potentially more influence. Once started, equal attention must be given to development at both levels and to their co-ordination.

> ... once school-level development occurs, as it must if
> improvements are to be made, the school gradually takes on more
> initiative in not only identifying needed implementation resources, but
> also in selecting priorities. While the district may set up ways to
> enable and ensure that schools are focusing on implementation, we
> should not be mistaken about what is happening. It is a process of
> empowering the school and community and of committing district
> resources to follow through on implementation requests arising from
> school-level planning.

Karen Seashore Louis and Matthew Miles (1990, p. 291) come to a similar
conclusion:

> District offices will have to learn to rely more on their working
> relationships with schools to steer a course through the turbulent
> waters, and less on rules and mandates. When there is pressure, it
> had better be accompanied by plenty of support. Schools have to have
> room, a good deal of local decision power, and help with the problems
> they face. That means a well-coupled relationship, not a distant one.

What all these examples illustrate is a symbiotic relationship between
school and local level that is at the same time 'loose' and 'tight'. Besides being
a felicitous phrase, 'loose-tight' coupling can, as we have seen, take many
forms. It also depends on what one is 'loose-tight' about. The 'tighter' a school
or school district is about goals for example, the 'looser' it can be about means.
This to us is the preferred balance, because it gives the school or working group
a great deal of freedom in and control over implementation. As a head of a large
and successful secondary school said to us recently, 'When there is reasonable
degree of consensus over values, then decision making is not much of a
problem.' When there is looseness over goals or values, however, one has to
be tighter over means. This situation often leads to extremely bureaucratic and
de-powering organizational structures.

What this discussion suggests is that the most productive and challenging
form of school-LEA relationship is not just 'loose-tight', but one where there
is also a high degree of both pressure and support operating at all levels. As
has been seen in this section, there is now a considerable body of research-
based knowledge that can help with designing school improvement initiatives
at the school-local level. Once again we need to issue the familiar health warning: not all of this advice will apply to every school or situation, but much of
it is by now well enough tested to warrant serious consideration.

MESSAGES

The history of educational innovation is littered with the skeletons of innovations and changes whose implementers failed to recognize that successful
school improvement efforts are characterized by a dual emphasis on enhancing
the school's capacity for change and implementing specific reforms — both of
which have as their ultimate goal an increase in student achievement. The

skeletons are usually the remains of single innovations, which may have been school wide in so far as they aimed to affect all students, but were not school deep because they ignored the process of change and the culture of the school. It is now well established that unless innovations take account of these two conditions their impact will be short lived. There appear to be a number of problems with such contemporary efforts at school improvement:

- focusing on single innovations;
- the imposition of externally validated models;
- the failure to impact at the classroom level;
- the ignoring of the culture of the school.

In these approaches there is often too much concern with process as against substance. As a result, school improvement, as we have noted before, can become a grand-sounding name for low-level staff development. To be successful, innovations need to be set within strategies that incorporate fundamental and lasting organizational change. Strategies are needed that directly address the culture of the school, and this is what *successful* school improvement is all about. Unfortunately the term 'school improvement' is most often used in the more common-sense and less precise meaning, and this lack of precision has resulted in school-based approaches that are superficial and simplistic, but costly in terms of raised expectations and wasted resources.

Although the term 'school improvement', even in its technical sense, is in common usage, few commentators have fully explored the potential of this approach as an alternative means of educational change. Most have been content to use the term as a collective name for a variety of strategies for innovation and change that pay some attention to the organizational context in which they intervene. The more rigorous definition that we prefer requires a broader and more sophisticated view of the concept. In a sense, it requires us to 'see school improvement whole'.

In summary, we regard school improvement as:

- a vehicle for planned educational change; but we also realize that educational change is necessary for school improvement;
- particularly appropriate during times of centralized initiatives and innovation overload when there are competing reforms to implement;
- usually involving some form of external support;
- having a dual emphasis on strategies for strengthening the school's capacity for managing change;
- raising student achievement (broadly defined);
- specifically focusing on the teaching-learning process.

Chapter 6

Towards the Moving School

In the preceding four chapters we have talked a great deal about schools: about the external pressure on them for change, about ways of thinking about change, about the research knowledge that makes for an effective school, and about strategies for school improvement. All this discussion, although necessary and important in its own terms, has had a somewhat abstract quality to it. We now wish to look more closely at what an effective or (to use our preferred word) *successful* school looks like from the inside. It is very hard to capture such a complex and multifaceted image in words, but there are a number of phrases that we have borrowed from others that describe what it feels like to be part of a successful school. Susan Rosenholtz (1989), for example, writes of the 'learning enriched school', where the excitement and motivation of learning is a full part of the daily lives of both students and teachers.

This is a similar thought to the one that inspired Roland Barth (1990) to describe the assumptions that we quoted early in Chapter 1, under which schools can be improved *from within*. Central to Barth's argument is that schools, or the community of learners within them, need to discover what the conditions that elicit and support human learning are, and then to provide those conditions within them. He continues (Barth, 1990, p. 45):

> Whereas many attempts to improve schools dwell on monitoring adult behaviour, on controlling students, on the assurance of student achievement, and on the visible attainment of prescribed skills, the central question for a community of learners is not, 'What should students, teachers, and principals know and do, and how do we get them to know and do it?' Instead the underlying question is, 'Under what conditions will principal and student and teacher become serious, committed, sustained, lifelong, cooperative learners?'

One of the difficulties of reviews such as we have conducted in the previous chapters is that they lead us to consider each of these key issues in isolation. There is a tendency to discuss the ingredients of school improvement without mentioning, or at times avoiding, the recipe. As a consequence the culture of the school, although alluded to throughout, has escaped being pinned down. Yet it is the culture of the school that enables the conditions referred to by Rosenholtz and Barth to flourish. Unless we address the issue of school culture in a direct way there is little chance that school improvement will be achieved. As we shall see, it is culture that sustains Rosenholtz's 'learning enriched school'. Similarly, taking Barth's (1990, p. 45) assumptions seriously 'leads to some fresh thinking about the culture of schools and about what people do in them'.

Yet it is difficult to do this fresh thinking when most of the reviews and research are atomistic rather than holistic. Not only is there a semantic difficulty, but the words and definitions people use often betray more substantial differences. Those who write from the school effectiveness research perspective tend to underplay culture, at best regarding it as a constellation of effectiveness factors. Those writing in the change literature tend to regard culture as a tool to be manipulated as part of a macro-strategy, whereas school improvers regard it as part of the environment within which one has to work. Culture is, of course, all of these things, but viewing it in just one way gives us an impoverished view and tends to restrict the way we respond to it. This situation is compounded when we inevitably write about culture as a stable phenomenon. It is not. A school's culture is dynamic and constantly evolving despite the dominant perception of stability.

The difficulty in coming to terms with the notion of culture has resulted in the somewhat abstract quality of the writing about schools that we alluded to above and reviewed in the preceding three chapters. The problematic nature of 'culture', however, is no reason for not discussing it. Our definition of culture may be inadequate and incomplete — it is certainly interim. But it is only through grappling with the concept both theoretically and practically that one can achieve any purchase on its power to affect school improvement. This is particularly the case with school improvement strategies, which are continually interacting with school culture in a way that affects both. Some may say that we have not dealt with culture at all yet in the book; others that culture is the only issue that we have dealt with. This is part of the problem, because culture can at one and the same time be both a leading and a following variable.

We have found that it helps to use a range of 'frames' to understand culture and its relationship with school improvement. It is these frames and their relationship to school improvement that we deal with in this chapter. In particular we discuss:

- the nature of structure and culture in school improvement;
- four expressions of school culture that are descriptive as well as action oriented;
- the ideal notion of a collaborative culture;
- the links between a collaborative culture and school improvement.

CULTURE AND STRUCTURE IN SCHOOL IMPROVEMENT

Although everyone appears to agree that the 'culture of the school' holds the key to improving the quality of student learning, there is a great deal of confusion about what the word actually means and what the concept looks like in practice. The common view that the culture of the school is best thought of as the procedures, norms, expectations and values of its members does not take us very far. Nor do the popular phrases that describe the culture of the school as 'the way we get things done around here' or 'what keeps the herd moving west' (Deal and Kennedy, 1983, p. 4) advance our understanding in a profound way. At best they provide a cosy image that everyone is comfortable with; more often they act as a cover for the sloppy thinking of which we are all at times guilty. Slogans such as this provide an excuse for not engaging in the difficult and painful conceptual work that is required to gain some clarity on this important concept.

We have found it helpful in our own work to heed the sociologists' distinction between structure and culture. Ignoring this important distinction is, in our opinion, one of the main reasons for the confusion that reigns in our discussions of culture and its impact on schools. Structure and culture are, of course, interdependent, and the relationship between them is dialectical. Structure influences culture, but it works the other way around too. Structures are often regarded as the more basic and profound, in that they generate cultures which not only allow the structures to 'work' but also justify or legitimate them. On the other hand, changes in culture — that is, value systems and beliefs — can change underlying structures. So, for example, the decline in religious beliefs (a change in culture) has led to a modification or diminution of the role the church plays in society and politics (a change in structure). The two go hand in hand and are mutually reinforcing. At a practical level, however, it is often easier to change structures than cultures. But if one changes structures too radically, without paying attention to the underlying culture, then one may get the appearance of change (change in structure), but not the reality of change (change in culture). Similarly, it is difficult to sustain changes in culture, perhaps inspired by a charismatic leader, without some concomitant change in structure to support the ideas about curriculum or instructional innovation.

In a paper on restructuring, Andy Hargreaves put the distinction in this way (n.d., p. 28):

> it is not possible to establish productive school cultures without prior changes being effected in school structures that increase the opportunities for meaningful working relationships and collegial support between teachers. The importance of the structural option of restructuring, therefore, may be less in terms of its direct impact on curriculum, assessment, ability grouping and the like, than in terms of how it creates improved opportunities for teachers to work together on a continuing basis.

In terms of school improvement we believe that we need to direct equal attention to both structure and culture, and to be alert to the effect one has on the other. It may be helpful if we describe in a little more detail what we mean by both these terms.

In much of our recent work we have been preoccupied with the internal conditions of schools that support development. This much is apparent from the definitions we have already given of school improvement. Much of this has focused on the structural aspects of schools. In the work on development planning, for example, the term 'management arrangements' was used to emphasize that the content of management is a set of arrangements which are *chosen* by the school to help it conduct its affairs and realize its aims (Hargreaves and Hopkins, 1991, Chapter 3). There is a wide variety of possible arrangements, which can be changed or adapted according to circumstances and preferences, and we doubt whether there is an ideal set, a recipe, which all schools should follow. There are, however, some dimensions shared by all management arrangements, whatever the particular set that is chosen by any individual school. As was seen in Chapter 5, there appear to be three main dimensions common to all sets of management arrangements: *frameworks*, *roles and responsibilities*, and *ways of working*. In terms of this discussion, *frameworks* provide the structures within which action for change takes place; *roles and responsibilities* comprise elements of both structure and culture; while *ways of working* are mainly cultural.

There are also a number of recent national innovations that are content free and offer the potential for forming an infrastructure supportive of change at the school level. Although innovations such as self-evaluation, development planning, changes in staff development policy and practice, and teacher appraisal have a carefully specified process or structure, the substance of each — that is, what they are used for — is for the teacher and school to decide. In combination, these strategies can form an infrastructure at the school level that facilitates the implementation of specific curriculum changes or teaching methods that have a direct impact on student achievement.

In our search for adequate and conceptually clear definitions of culture we were struck by the clarity with which Edgar Schein has discussed the concept. In his book *Organizational Culture and Leadership* (1985, p. 6), he gives some common meanings of the word 'culture' (the examples are ours):

- *observed behavioural regularities* when teachers interact in a staff room — the language they use and the rituals they establish;
- the *norms* that evolve in working groups of teachers in terms of lesson planning or monitoring the progress of students;
- the *dominant values* espoused by a school, its aims or 'mission statement';
- the *philosophy* that, for example, guides the dominant approach to teaching and learning of particular subjects in a school;
- the *rules of the game* that new teachers have to learn in order to get along in the school or their department;
- the *feeling or climate* that is conveyed by the entrance hall to a school, or the way in which students' work is or is not displayed.

Schein (1985, p. 6) continues:

All these meanings, and many others, do, in my view, *reflect* the organization's culture, but none of them *is* the essence of culture. I will argue that the term 'culture' should be reserved for the deeper level of *basic assumptions* and *beliefs* that are shared by members of an organization, that operate unconsciously, and that define in a basic 'taken-for-granted' fashion an organization's view of itself and its environment.

We find Schein's distinction between the various interpretations of culture very convincing and feel that his definition of culture fits well with our own conceptualization; it is also widely applicable to a variety of organizational settings.

We hope that this discussion of structure and culture has been sufficiently detailed to give a clearer picture of the difference between them, and some understanding of their dialectical relationship. As we shall see in the examples in Chapter 14, the interaction between structure and culture gives school leaders and staff members a great deal of control over the types of school culture they inhabit. Cultures are not fixed, immutable and inert, but created by their participants; or, if not created, are 'open to modification', to use Rutter's phrase (Rutter *et al.*, 1979, p. 178). We agree with Nias (1989) and Pollard (1985) that cultures are actively constructed by their participants and are therefore political and dynamic. Nias (1989, p. 145) quotes Pollard's notion of an 'institutional bias' that is a type of 'generally shared knowledge' about school practices and the assumptions that underlie them. Although imprecise and elusive, this tacit agreement deeply affects classroom and staffroom processes throughout the whole school. Indeed, we now have evidence to suggest that the quality of the school culture is related not only to enhanced teacher performance in the classroom, but also to higher levels of teacher self-esteem (Evans and Hopkins, 1988; Hopkins, 1990b).

Achieving the correct balance between structure and culture is a sophisticated but necessary achievement if schools are to sustain their improvement efforts over time. Unfortunately we know as yet very little about how in practice each affects the other, and what one has to do to affect either. This disjuncture between structure and culture also goes some way, we believe, towards explaining the phenomenon noted by Heckman (1987, p. 68) of schools that are renewing at the organizational but not at the classroom level. It also begins to explain why, as we see in the following section, different schools exhibit different cultures.

FOUR EXPRESSIONS OF SCHOOL CULTURE

We have already used the phrase 'leaning enriched' to describe our ideal type of school. It is taken from Susan Rosenholtz's (1989) book *Teachers' Workplace*, where she argues that the social organization of the school directly affects the commitment of teachers and the achievement of students. We like her phrase because it captures for us the vital characteristic of the successful school — it is a place where *both students and teachers learn*. In her book Rosenholtz distinguishes between two stereotypical schools: the 'moving' school and the 'stuck' school. We find the image suggested by these words appealing too; we use the phrase 'moving school' in the title of this chapter to describe the experiences of many of the schools that we are working with.

Rosenholtz found in her research, perhaps unsurprisingly, that the moving schools produced much higher outcomes for students than those pupils in the so-called stuck schools. They were better places for teachers to work in, too. In the following extract, Rosenholtz (1989, pp. 209-10) graphically contrasts the differences in teacher commitment in the moving and stuck schools:

> Even in an era of political tribulation, moving schools were uplifted like iron fragments to a giant magnet. Here teachers frequently experienced the edifying sensation of hopes fulfilled as they invented new school futures. They were like Geiger counters calibrated to precious values, their commitment beating stronger and faster in the rich, rarefied atmosphere of their workplace ...
>
> In the main, teachers from stuck schools looked through the wrong end of the telescope. They seemed interested in freedom *from*; they thought little of freedom *to*. The range of teacher unfreedoms was wide, subtle, and often alarming. Boredom, punitiveness, and self defensiveness were unfreedoms. Feeling helpless and unable to cope was a state of unfreedom ... As a form of freedom teachers often absented themselves in one-day breaks, much to the detriment of their school and students.

From our reading of Rosenholtz's work we have produced a contrasting set of characteristics of these two types of schools (Table 6.1). Although we find Rosenholtz's description of these two school cultures convincing, our experience also suggests that the schools we usually work with are not like that at all! We rarely find genuinely moving or stuck schools; most fall some way in between these ideal types.

Table 6.1 *Rosenholtz's (1989) school work cultures*

Stuck	Moving
Low consensus	High consensus
Teacher uncertainty	Teacher certainty
Low commitment	High commitment
Isolation	Cohesiveness
Individualized	Collaborative
Learning impoverished	Learning enriched

In thinking about these matters we have found it helpful to link the descriptions of school effectiveness to a notion of movement in those schools that are actively improving. Put another way, we relate effectiveness to school outcomes, and improvement to the degree of 'dynamism' of school processes. Although each of these dimensions is on a continuum, when they are contrasted we see four expressions of school culture (Figure 6.1). The words we have chosen to describe these expressions of school culture are related to our metaphor of school improvement as a journey. In our discussion of these four types, we also relate them to the way in which they balance maintenance and development activities.

Stuck schools are often failing schools. Conditions are poor, teaching is an isolated activity, and a sense of mediocrity and powerlessness pervades. Expectations from all around are very low, and external conditions are blamed

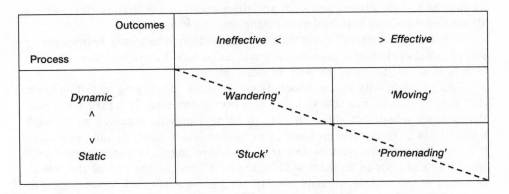

Outcomes Process	Ineffective <	> Effective
Dynamic ∧ ∨ Static	'Wandering'	'Moving'
	'Stuck'	'Promenading'

Figure 6.1 *Four expressions of school culture.*

for the situation. One typically hears phrases like, 'There's not much we can do with these kids', 'We've tried change before, but it doesn't work.' The notion of culture is relatively unheard of, and even if it is known it is regarded as something that is given and cannot be changed. As the school is buffeted by the winds of change, it responds capriciously if at all. There is little appreciation of the difference between development and maintenance, and in many ways the school could be regarded as being inactive.

The *wandering school* has experienced and is experiencing too much innovation. These schools have all the appearance, but little of the reality, of change, and staff quickly become exhausted and fragmented. Overall there is movement going on but it lacks a settled route or a clear destination. Sometimes this involves a lack of agreement about purpose, with groups or individuals pursuing their own aims. These activities, however, may lead to some valuable developments. More often than not the cry, 'We've tried many new things, but nothing gets finished' is heard. This is the school that is committed to development at the expense of maintenance and could be categorized as 'hyperactive'.

The *promenading* school often seems to be living on its past achievements, which may well have been impressive. It does not move fast or far, and when it does this may be for display rather than exercise. Promenading schools are often traditional schools with a stable staff that have enjoyed success in more stable times but are currently reluctant to change. One often hears from staff that they 'are pretty pleased with the way things are ... there is no real reason to change'. These are in fact very difficult schools to change. They usually attract pupils with successful learning histories, and although they score well in the league tables, their level of value added is often very low. Maintenance is all, development is regarded as being quirky; 'under-active' is the adjective that comes to mind.

The *moving* school is an ideal type of 'active' school which has achieved a healthy blend of change and stability, and balanced development and maintenance. Internally the school is relatively calm as it adapts successfully to an often rapidly changing environment. It adapts its structures in line with its culture and traditions, and staff are often heard to say that 'we try to keep abreast of developments and everything under review'.

What we find useful about this schema is that it not only helps classify school cultures, but also provides a guide as to how to work with them. The matrix is action oriented as well as descriptive.

The problem with stuck schools is not so much identifying or telling them that they are stuck, but how to help them become moving. It is rarely the case that a stuck school can move directly to being a moving school. Usually such a school has to pass through some intermediate stage first. In our experience it either becomes over-active and tries to do too much, or concentrates on a few areas and tries to do them well before rejuvenating the rest of the school. In terms of the matrix, schools usually need to pass through a wandering or promenading phase before becoming moving.

Which phase they go through is dependent on their previous history and organizational background. Diagnosis is necessary to tell this. The matrix can also be of some assistance here by using the diagonal line on it as a rule of thumb. Below the line, schools need to work more on their internal conditions to put themselves in a position to carry out successful development work. Above the line, the balance should be more on the side of the identified priorities, although work on the conditions should not be neglected. Stuck schools generally require work on their internal conditions before they can move more positively to identifying and resolving curriculum priorities. Working with schools in the other two phases, however, implies different strategies. Put simply, promenading schools need more movement, wandering schools more focus.

We have talked a great deal about school cultures at the expense of sub-cultures. Although we would be among the first to admit that schools are not unitary organizational phenomena, and that there are within them more or less dynamic or effective individuals, groups or departments, these four expressions of a school's culture represent the 'dominant' culture within the school.

We should also note that in times of great change, school cultures and structures are continually adapting. This is not to say that there is great introspection and turmoil in the schools where this is happening. In fact the opposite is almost always the case: if the structure/culture balance is appropriate, stability should result. What is of great importance, however, is that the structures and culture are not regarded as being cast in stone, but evolve gradually in line with each other as they too adapt to changing circumstance.

In Chapter 14 we will be looking at how these various types of school cultures can be supported and possibly changed. For the moment we wish to stay with our ideal type of the moving school, which in the main balances change and stability, development and maintenance, structure and culture.

COLLABORATIVE CULTURES

The striking characteristic of the 'moving' school is that it has a culture that sustains quality teaching. It is this key idea that we wish to explore in the rest of this chapter. Although there are many other features of successful schools that we have already discussed in research terms, and will see in more practical terms later on, it is this condition that we feel is paramount. Put another way, successful schools consciously develop organizational cultures that are supportive of the teaching process. The type of culture that characterizes such schools has received much attention of late from educational researchers. Most of these commentators refer to these schools as having a *collaborative culture*.

As Rosenholtz says (1985, p. 351), 'the most effective schools do not isolate teachers but instead encourage professional dialogue and collaboration'. Nias and her colleagues (1989) talk also of collaborative cultures and claim that they are characterized by their ability simultaneously to value groups and individuals. Judith Warren Little (1990) has reviewed many forms of teacher collaboration. She claims that 'joint work', where teachers work together on substantive tasks — for example, paired teaching, action research, school-based curriculum development — lays the basis for the form of collaboration most likely to lead to significant progress for pupils. This implies strong interdependence, shared responsibility and collective commitment. This does not mean, however, that every collaborative culture is identical. Although they may have similar characteristics, each collaborative culture is an individual achievement for that school.

Andy Hargreaves has done more than most to clarify the cultural aspects of teaching (see, for example, Hargreaves, 1991, 1992, 1993). His work also strongly supports the notion of collaborative cultures as being an essential building block for school improvement. The following four contrasting cultures of teaching are drawn from a range of his work:

- *Fragmented individualism* occurs where the teacher is isolated, is protected from outside interference, and at times takes refuge behind the 'sanctity of the classroom door'. It reinforces uncertainty and insulates the teacher from positive feedback and support.

- *Balkanization* describes a teacher culture 'made up of separate and sometimes competing groups jockeying for position and supremacy like loosely connected independent city states ... The existence of such groups often reflects and reinforces very different group outlooks on learning, teaching styles, discipline and curriculum' (Fullan and Hargreaves, 1992, pp. 71, 72).

- *Contrived collegiality* occurs where the forms of collaboration are determined by administrators, not teachers. As a result they are usually 'regulated, compulsory, implementation oriented, fixed in time and space, and predictable'. As this form of collaboration is imposed from above, it discourages true collegiality through the desire for power (Fullan and Hargreaves, 1992, p. 68).

- *Collaborative cultures*, by way of contrast, facilitate teacher development through mutual support, joint work and a broad agreement on educational values. Within schools that possess collaborative cultures 'the individual and the group are inherently and simultaneously valued' (Fullan and Hargreaves, 1992, p. 67).

Fullan and Hargreaves (1992) outline in a very practical way how collaborative cultures can be achieved and the problems of individualism, balkanization and contrived collegiality avoided. In an elaboration of his concept of collaborative cultures, Hargreaves (1991, pp. 53-4) describes them as being:

- *spontaneous*. They emerge primarily from the teachers themselves as a social group. They may be administratively supported and facilitated ... ultimately, however, collaborative working relationships evolve from and are sustained through the teaching community itself.

- *voluntary*. Collaborative work relations arise ... from their perceived value among teachers that derives from experience, inclination, or noncoercive persuasion that working together is both enjoyable and productive.

- *development oriented*. In collaborative cultures, teachers work together primarily to develop initiatives of their own, or to work on externally supported or mandated initiatives to which they themselves have a commitment. In collaborative cultures, teachers most often establish the tasks and purposes for working together, rather than meet to implement the purposes of others. Teachers here are people who initiate change as much as, or more than, they react to it. When they have to respond to external mandates, they do so selectively, drawing on their professional confidence and discretionary judgment as a community.

- *pervasive across time and space*. In collaborative cultures, working together is not often a scheduled activity ... much of the way teachers work together is in almost unnoticed, brief yet frequent, informal encounters. This may take the form of such actions as passing words and glances, praises and thanks, offers to exchange classes in tough times, suggestions about new ideas, informal discussions about new units, sharing problems, or meeting parents together. Collaborative cultures are, in this sense, not clearly or closely regulated. They are constitutive of the very way that the teacher's working life operates in the school.

- *unpredictable*. Because, in collaborative cultures, teachers have discretion and control over what will be developed, the outcomes of collaboration are often uncertain and not easily predicted. ... In general, therefore, collaborative cultures are incompatible with school systems in which decisions about curriculum and evaluation are highly centralized. The difficulty for administrators seeking to help develop collaborative cultures may therefore be a difficulty not so much of human relations but of political control.

For us, one of the most evocative and resonant descriptions of a collaborative culture is given by Judith Little (1981, quoted in Fullan, 1991, p. 78):

> School improvement is most surely and thoroughly achieved when:
>
> Teachers engage in frequent, continuous and increasingly concrete and precise *talk* about teaching practice (as distinct from teacher characteristics and failings, the social lives of teachers, the foibles and failures of students and their families, and the unfortunate demands of society on the school). By such talk, teachers build up a shared language adequate to the complexity of teaching, capable of distinguishing one practice and its virtue from another.
>
> Teachers and administrators frequently *observe* each other teaching, and provide each other with useful (if potentially frightening) evaluations of their teaching. Only such observation and feedback can provide shared *referents* for the shared language of teaching, and both demand and provide the precision and concreteness which makes the talk about teaching useful.
>
> Teachers and administrators *plan, design, research, evaluate and prepare teaching materials together*. The most prescient observations remain academic ('just theory') without the machinery to act on them. By joint work on materials, teachers and administrators share the considerable burden of development required by long-term improvement, confirm their emerging understanding of their approach, and make rising standards for their work attainable by them and by their students.
>
> Teachers and administrators *teach each other* the practice of teaching.

COLLABORATIVE CULTURES AND THE LOGIC OF SCHOOL IMPROVEMENT

Having made the argument about the importance of establishing collaborative cultures in schools as clearly as we can, we now have to make the link back to school improvement. In this chapter we have already given some hints about how collaborative cultures can be achieved, but now is the time to become far more explicit.

What is striking about these descriptions of collaborative cultures is not only their power to create rich and meaningful learning environments for teachers and students, but also, in line with the arguments of this chapter, how far these cultures are established and maintained through structures that are deliberately created and modified within the school. Collaborative cultures do not emerge by chance; they are the result of deliberate actions which are based on some understanding, often intuitive, of the conditions that support the work of teachers and students.

This is the crucial point. Although these descriptions of collaborative cultures are helpful in identifying the phenomenon, they are misleading in terms of what a school has to do to achieve it. They place far too much emphasis on collaboration as a goal, rather than on the identification of *real*

95

tasks on which teachers can collaborate. Linking this back to the previous discussion in this chapter, it is through work on structures that cultures are modified. Structures can be worked on directly; cultures can only be affected indirectly. One also moves from the stuck school to the moving school, and through the intermediate phases, not by directly creating collaborative cultures but by engaging in appropriate real tasks that teachers can work on collaboratively. In the stuck school it will be working on the internal conditions of the school; in the wandering school it will be achieving clarity and focus on its priorities; and in the promenading school it will be adjusting the balance between development and maintenance activities. We can only move from one phase to another when a school has identified where it is going next. And although there will always have to be work on priorities and conditions, the balance will vary from school to school at different points in time.

It is often helpful to portray the separate elements of the moving school in the way that we have just done. But a caveat has to be entered here. School improvement is about fusion rather than fission. We need to retain a vision of the whole while attending to individual elements. Bearing this caution in mind, now is the time to ask the crucial question: 'What link is there between collaborative cultures, school improvement and student achievement?' The simple answer is that school improvement strategies can and do create the conditions for student achievement, but by themselves have little direct impact on the progress of pupils.

Experience, as well as the available research, suggests that the more systematic approaches to teaching provide the link to enhanced student performance. This raises the obvious question, 'If teaching methodology has such a proven impact on student achievement, why bother with establishing the conditions in the first place?' The answer is equally simple and pragmatic: changes in teaching behaviour cannot be acquired or sustained without in some cases dramatic, and in every case some, modification to the school-level conditions that support it. Development planning, has the power, for example, particularly when linked to other strategies such as staff development and teacher appraisal, to create the conditions within which more specific changes will take root and flourish. Enhanced student achievement is therefore the result of a constellation of factors interacting in subtle but self-conscious and meaningful ways that create collaborative school cultures in which both teachers and students learn and grow.

Our experience suggests that school improvement works best when a clear and practical focus for development is linked to simultaneous work on the internal conditions within the school. Such school improvement efforts appear to include three elements:

1 Reconstructing externally imposed education reform in the form of school *priorities*.

2 Creating *internal conditions* that will sustain and manage change in schools.

3 Embedding these priorities and conditions with an overall *strategy*.

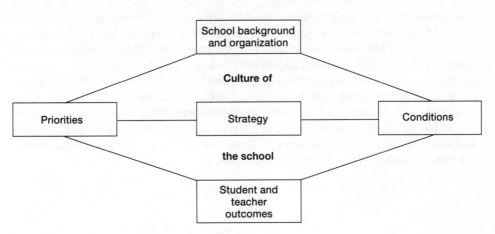

Figure 6.2 *A framework for school improvement.*

The school's *priorities* are normally some aspect of curriculum, assessment or classroom process which the school has identified from the many changes that confront it. In this sense, the choice represents the school's interpretation of the current reform agenda.

It is essential that some aspect of the *internal conditions* within the school are worked on at the same time as the curriculum or other priorities the school has set itself. Without an equal focus on conditions, even priorities that meet the criteria outlined in the previous paragraph become marginalized.

The third element is the school improvement *strategy*, which attempts to achieve developmental priorities and, at the same time, establish appropriate conditions that support these improvements. The nature of this strategy, or combination of strategies, is peculiar to each school, in taking account of the priorities that have been agreed, the existing conditions and the resources that are available.

The conclusion we draw from this discussion is that student achievement is predicated on a combination of strategies which relates both to the substance of teaching and learning *and* to modifications to the internal conditions of the school. This in turn argues for a more holistic approach to school improvement that uses combinations of strategies as mediating variables to link priorities to conditions. We have summarized this logic of school improvement in a framework (Figure 6.2). The implementation of this work is achieved against the school's background and organization. If successful, this developmental activity both affects student outcomes and, over time, generates a collaborative school culture.

As is seen in Parts 3 and 4, we are finding some common patterns in our own school improvement work. Many of the schools we are working with use the school development plan as an overarching strategy that focuses innovative efforts, generates ownership and galvanizes support. The priorities tend to relate to teaching and classroom organization in a broad sense, rather than curriculum in the conventional sense. Many of our schools are using some form of classroom or paired observation to implement these priorities. The effectiveness of this approach is considerably enhanced when 'quality time' is provided on the timetable, and the observation is underpinned by an agreed specification of the teaching strategy to be employed. This specification provides a standard for the mutual observation, as well as a detailed outline of the nature of the developmental activity. Indeed, peer observation is proving to be a powerful means for establishing ownership, acquiring new teaching strategies and eventually transforming the culture of the school. It is in these ways that collaborative cultures supportive of effective teaching are created and student achievement enhanced. These, as we see in the rest of the book, are the characteristics of the moving school.

PART 3

PRACTICE

Chapter 7

Improving the Quality of Education for All

In Part 2 we provided an account of existing knowledge with respect to educational reform, the processes of change, school and classroom effectiveness, and approaches to school improvement. This led us to formulate a vision of the successful school and to suggest a framework explaining how improvement might be achieved.

Now, in this part, we turn our attention to the application of this knowledge base. Here we will be considering how schools might approach the task of improving the quality of education provided for *all* their pupils. In order to address this issue we will draw on the experience of colleagues in a number of schools that have been engaged in various school improvement activities.

Many of the examples we will be considering have arisen from our work in the 'Improving the Quality of Education for All' (IQEA) project. In Chapter 1 we explained that this initiative is the focus of much of our own current activity. In this chapter we provide an account of the early development of IQEA, including a description of its rationale. We take as a focus the quality of education for all pupils, as we do not believe that a school can be considered inclusive or effective if it is serving the needs of only some groups of pupils. We accept that outcomes will, of course, be different for different pupils, but believe a school must aspire to the best for each pupil. It is this aspiration, reinforced by the acceptance that schools are places where teachers learn too, which provides schools with the rationale and the will to resist externally imposed change, except in so far as such change can be harnessed to further the quality of education provided.

It is through considering how external change can be married to internal development that we have constructed our own framework for school improvement, a framework that we will use as a basis for discussion of important issues in educational change. It also leads us to describe a set of internal school conditions that seem to increase the school's capacity to engage in development initiatives without surrendering to external pressure. We then provide a summary of the practical arrangements and project guidelines. Finally, we outline the structure of the remainder of this part of the book.

IQEA REVISITED

As outlined in Chapter 1, over the past three years we have been working closely with a group of schools in the IQEA project. This process has involved both the schools and ourselves in a collaborative enterprise designed to strengthen their ability to manage change, to enhance the work of teachers, and ultimately to improve the outcomes, however broadly defined, of students. At a time of great change in the educational system, the schools we are working with are using the impetus of external reform for internal purpose; they are, we believe, examples of what Susan Rosenholtz (1989) called 'moving schools'. We have used the metaphor of a journey to describe our work in the project, and as we have travelled with the schools we have continued to reflect on our interactions, the progress made and the problems encountered; and, as is our habit, we have continued to write.

As we have journeyed we have also realized that what we are doing in the project is perhaps different from what is being done in other school improvement or change-oriented projects. What is distinctive about our work is that we support, intervene and research the journey of school improvement as we are making it. The twin agenda of assisting in and, at the same time, researching the process of change creates many tensions. Nevertheless we believe that the insights gained from this involvement outweigh the difficulties and justify the effort.

We have noted that IQEA works from an assumption that schools are most likely to strengthen their ability to provide enhanced outcomes for all pupils when they adopt ways of working that are consistent with their own aspirations as well as the current reform agenda. We have suggested that this involves building confidence and capacity within the school, rather than reliance on externally produced packages — although good ideas from the outside are never rejected out of hand.

Towards some principles for working with schools

From our previous experience and our understanding of the research literature (described in Part 2), we have taken the view that school improvement is most likely to be effective when viewed and pursued holistically. Too often in the past such initiatives have consisted of small-scale, discrete interventions aimed at introducing particular approaches or reforming single aspects of the school's organization. In our view such approaches underestimate the extent to which forces within the school interact with one another and, as a consequence, fail to establish a strategy that encourages those involved to utilize these connections to their advantage.

At the outset of IQEA we attempted to distil these ideas into a series of principles which seemed to us to capture the essence of the moving school. These principles provided us with a philosophical and practical starting point. Because it is our assumption that schools are most likely to provide quality education and enhanced outcomes for pupils when they adopt ways of working that are consistent with these principles, they were offered as the basis for collaboration with the IQEA project schools. In short, we were inviting the schools to identify and to work on their own projects and priorities, but to do so in a way which embodied a set of core values about school improvement. Originally, there were ten such principles, but during our period of working with the schools we have found ourselves reorganizing these into the following five statements. They represent both the expectation we had of the way project schools would pursue school improvement, and (we hope) an *aide-mémoire* to the schools about principles which are likely to foster enduring school improvement initiatives.

The five principles of IQEA are:

1 The vision of the school (the school-in-the-future) should be one to which all members of the school community have an opportunity to contribute, and most will seek to.

2 The school, because it has its vision, will see in external pressures for change important opportunities to secure its internal priorities.

3 The school will seek to create and maintain conditions in which all members of the school's community can learn successfully.

4 The school will seek to adopt and develop structures which encourage collaboration and lead to the empowerment of individuals and groups.

5 The school will seek to promote the view that the monitoring and evaluation of quality is a responsibility in which all members of staff share.

We feel that the operation of these principles creates synergism: together they are greater than the sum of their parts. They characterize an overall approach rather than prescribe a course of action. The intention is that they should inform the thinking and actions of teachers during school improvement efforts, and provide a touchstone for the strategies they devise and the behaviours they adopt.

Beyond this, as we have indicated, our intention in the IQEA project was to allow each school considerable autonomy to determine its own priorities for development and, indeed, its own methods for achieving these priorities. Central to this approach was the requirement that each participating school devise its own project rather than adopt a focus which we imposed on it. Our stipulation was that, in pursuing these individual initiatives, collaborating schools should try, at all times, to be consistent with the principles. Although, in this sense, we can characterize our involvement with IQEA schools as supporting the school in the pursuit of its own development priorities, the IQEA project as a whole also attempts to map our own learning from this involvement, and to spread this learning across the schools.

WORKING WITHIN A FRAMEWORK FOR SCHOOL IMPROVEMENT

Establishing a method of working with schools which was both flexible and focused was an issue which arose at the outset. The method adopted in the project was to support each school in relation to the specific objective selected, while feeding into all schools information about and perspectives on improvement strategies.

Keeping in mind this idea of a project made up of many individual school

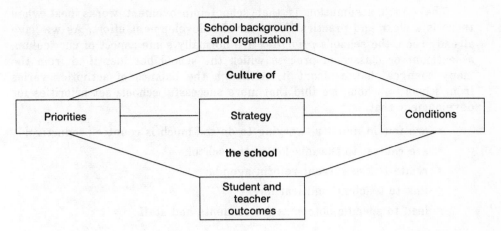

Figure 7.1 *A framework for school improvement.*

projects, we developed our own action framework, as was seen in Chapter 6. This framework provides the setting for a series of assumptions upon which the project is based (Figure 7.1). In describing these assumptions we relate them to the main components of the figure: outcomes for students and staff; school culture; the school's background and organization; the selected developmental priorities; the conditions necessary to support such changes; and the school improvement strategy.

The first assumption is that school improvement will result in enhanced *outcomes* for students and staff. We define 'outcomes' broadly, and they will obviously vary according to the focus of improvement effort. For students, they could be critical thinking, learning capacity, self-esteem and so on, as well as improved examination and test results. For staff, they could be increased collegiality, opportunities for professional learning and increased responsibility.

The second assumption is less obvious. School *culture* is the vital yet neglected dimension in the improvement process. It is, of course, a difficult concept to define. In general we see it as an amalgam of the values, norms and beliefs that characterize the way in which a group of people behave within a specific organizational setting. The types of school culture most supportive of school improvement efforts, and those that we are working towards in the project, are those that are collaborative, have high expectations for both students and staff, exhibit a consensus on values (or an ability to deal effectively with differences), support an orderly and secure environment, and encourage teachers to assume a variety of leadership roles.

The third assumption is that the school's *background* and *organization* are key factors in the school improvement process. Unfortunately most school improvement efforts view organizational factors, which are often the main inhibitors of change, as merely explanatory. It is also interesting to note that a school's organizational structure is inevitably a reflection of its values; so there is a strong, but not clearly understood, relationship between the school's organization and its culture.

The fourth assumption is that school improvement works best when there is a clear and practical focus for the development effort. As we have already seen, the school's *priorities* are normally some aspect of curriculum, assessment or classroom process which the school has identified from the many changes that confront it. Although the balance of activities varies from school to school, we find that more successful schools set priorities for development that:

- are few in number — trying to do too much is counter-productive;
- are central to the mission of the school;
- relate to the current reform agenda;
- link to teaching and learning;
- lead to specific outcomes for students and staff.

The fifth assumption is that the *conditions* for school improvement are worked on at the same time as the curriculum or other priorities the school has set itself. Conditions are the organizational features or management arrangements of a school. They are the frameworks, the roles and responsibilities, and the ways of working that enable a school to get work done. In this sense conditions are analogous to what sociologists call structures. As we argued in Chapter 6, without an equal focus on conditions, even priorities that meet the above criteria can quickly become marginalized. We have also found that when circumstances exist that are less supportive of change, it is necessary to concentrate much more in the initial stages on creating the internal conditions within the school which facilitate development, limiting work on the priorities until the conditions are in place.

The sixth assumption is that a school improvement *strategy* needs to be developed in order to link priorities to the conditions. These are the deliberate actions or sequence of actions taken by a school staff in order to implement identified curriculum or organizational priorities. The strategy will need to be more or less powerful depending on the relative strength of the other factors. In some cases, for example, the school's organizational structures have had to be altered as part of the development process. There is here an obvious overlap between strategies and conditions: a strategy becomes a condition when it stops being a means of achieving change and becomes part of the school's routine practices. This often creates confusion because the same activity can be both a strategy and a condition within the same school but at different times.

So what does this look like in practice? Although there are many faces to success, we have noted some patterns and trends which we believe can apply to other schools and other systems. Our theoretical arguments in Chapter 6 have found support in our work during the early phase of the project. Our experience to date continues to suggest that school improvement works best when a clear and practical focus for development is linked to simultaneous work on the internal conditions within the school. Such school improvement efforts appear to include the three elements previously described in Chapter 6: priorities, conditions and strategy.

Identifying priorities

Development planning is an important preliminary to school improvement. Whatever method or approach to development planning is adopted, the planning cycle is likely to involve the school in some form of audit, revealing current strengths and weaknesses, and to generate a number of priorities for action — often too many to work on. This means that decisions about priorities must be made, moving from the separate, perhaps even conflicting, priorities of individuals or groups to a systematically compiled set of priorities which represent the overall needs of a whole school community. Hargreaves and Hopkins (1991) have suggested that two principles should guide this process of choice among priorities:

> 1 *Manageability*: how much can we realistically hope to achieve?
>
> 2 *Coherence*: is there a sequence which will ease implementation?

To these principles we would add a third,

> 3 *Consonance*: the extent to which internally identified priorities coincide or overlap with external pressures for reform.

We believe that there is empirical evidence that those schools which recognize consonance, and therefore see externally generated change efforts as providing opportunities as well as (or instead of) problems, are better able to respond to external demands. We also believe that it is as important to be clear about what is not a priority as what is — otherwise it is possible to dissipate staff effort and enthusiasm across too many projects or in discussions about initiatives which we have neither the means nor the inclination to implement.

The IQEA schools were therefore encouraged to review, and in some cases to reconsider, their own priorities at the outset of the project. We were keen to ensure that each school participating in the project:

- had defined for itself the area or issue to be tackled;
- had ensured that this was not a 'new' or 'additional' activity undertaken simply because of involvement in the project, but a real issue, problem or opportunity which the school would need to work on anyway;
- had considered how this could be tackled in a way which developed the school and moved it some way towards the external requirements (stemming from national reforms) for quality improvement and assurance facing all schools;
- had communicated this to all staff in the school.

Developing the conditions

Our own experience of school structures leads us to believe that, though each school is unique, yet nevertheless schools share a number of properties (Miles, 1981, p. 43):

There are several theoretical and practical reasons for attending to schools' common properties.... a focus on common properties can help one see how such properties constrain and limit change efforts, as well as how they provide active driving and restraining forces.

We have described how our own collaboration with schools, particularly during the IQEA project, has led to a synthesizing of our understanding of the literature of school improvement with our experience of the practice of school improvement. We began by trying to establish what was common to the findings of school effectiveness studies. We also looked for evidence that schools could make sense of these findings, which were often expressed as principles rather than activities, and use them to generate school-level improvements. The rest of Part 3 will outline a number of examples of what this looks like in practice. However, when one engages with a particular school community there remains the problem of where and how to start.

We were keen to establish some method of auditing schools to find out whether or not these conditions were present, and so began by designing a 'conditions scale' rating questionnaire, which we could use to analyse staff views. The conditions scale was accordingly developed as an instrument rooted in the common properties of schools, one that enabled each school to identify its own readiness for action, by collating and analysing the views of staff members about the presence or absence of the conditions conducive to school improvement activity.

These conditions, around which we organize the rest of Part 3, have developed with the project, and, as previously acknowledged, represent our best estimate of what the important factors are at present, rather than a definitive statement. We believe that there is both research-based and empirical evidence to support the list and, though we recognize that any system for classifying variables must inevitably be arbitrary to a degree, we have found that mapping schools to find out whether or not these conditions are present forms a useful starting point.

Broadly stated, the conditions are:

- a commitment to staff development;
- practical efforts to involve staff, students and the community in school policies and decisions;
- transformational leadership;
- effective coordination strategies;
- proper attention to the potential benefits of inquiry and reflection;
- a commitment to collaborative planning activity.

Initially, an instrument was devised which allowed schools to assess their current position in relation to each of these conditions. This instrument helped, for example, to establish a common language to discuss school improvement strategies and barriers but did not start with the same set of conditions. We feel, however, that there remain important links between the principles we have articulated and the conditions we seek to promote. The early feedback from collaborating schools did convince us that some (relatively straight-forward) instrument, which could help schools to diagnose current strengths and weaknesses with regard to school improvement activity, would be welcome. In the light of this feedback and discussion with staff from project schools about their own readiness to engage in improvement activities, and how that might be assessed, the 'refined' version of the conditions as listed above was identified. Gradually, as we began to think about the wider generalizability of this approach, we began to wonder whether it might not be possible to devise an instrument with wide-ranging relevance to educational establishments.

Simultaneously, we were beginning to see that particular policies enjoyed different levels of success according to the school in which they were being implemented. This raised questions about the notion of school culture, and the impact (which we have noted above) of culture on behaviour and results. We were seeing differences in teacher behaviour which seemed culturally deter-mined, rather than responses to the specific demands being made on teachers. Thus, for example, a carefully thought out staff development programme was receiving poor teacher response in one school, while in another school teachers were finding useful aspects to even the most haphazard and disorganized professional development day. We needed, therefore, to find some way of coping with cultural differences in our approach. In particular, we wanted to be able to identify whether the success or failure of specific strategies for school improvement related to the strategy or to the school in which it was implemented. This is not a new problem, nor is it one we have been able to solve, but we have evolved a way of dealing with it which may help to delineate between culture and conditions within a school. This reflects Hargreaves' (1991) view (see Chapter 6) that a broadly collaborative culture is likely to be a better environment in which to introduce innovation, but also seeks to assess the *possibility* of collaboration in a school.

More generally, as Handy and Aitken (1986) have pointed out, a culture represents the 'total of the inherited ideas, beliefs, values and knowledge which constitute the shared bases of social action'. A culture is frequently revealed through the organization's structures and methods of communication. Schmuck and Runkel's (1985) notion that culture translates into a series of norms which 'hold together the organization's patterns of behaviour' (Schmuck and Runkel, 1985, p. 19) seemed a useful one, and we began to ask whether there were some norms in schools which would tell us something about a school's capacity to benefit from conditions such as appropriate leadership or systematic inquiry and reflection. Returning to the idea that it is the possibility of collaboration which is important, the question became whether we could identify norms which provide a basis for collaboration. Our under-standing of organization theory and experience of school organization led us to identify four areas where appropriate norms were likely to foster collaboration:

1 *Objectives:* norms relating to the purposes of the school, shared understanding of goals and priorities.

2 *Structures:* norms about the interrelationship between jobs, about responsibilities between jobs and obligations between job-holders.

3 *Roles:* norms about how a person in a particular position should perform (Schmuck and Runkel, 1985) or how two persons should interact and behave.

4 *Relationships:* norms about the levels of informal support colleagues expect from and give to one another.

The conditions scale has therefore been modified so that it is possible to analyse teacher attitudes towards these aspects of the school, as well as the original areas of interest. This has allowed the IQEA schools both to assess staff perceptions of the presence or absence of appropriate conditions, and to establish whether these important cultural norms had generally been clarified or not within the school community. (The conditions scale questionnaire can be found in the Appendix.)

Selecting a strategy

Reflecting our concern that schools constantly seek links that draw together external pressure for change and internal need for development, we take strategy to have both internal dimensions, which Quinn (1980, p. 5) defines as 'the pattern or plan that integrates an organisation's major goals, policies and action sequences', and external dimensions, which Asch and Bowman (1987, p. 36) define as 'the match an organisation makes between its own resources and the threats or risks or opportunities created by external environment'. In encouraging the IQEA schools to identify specific strategies to address their self-generated priorities, we hoped, as we have noted elsewhere, to help those schools to develop an understanding of the potency of the priority-strategy-conditions model in bringing about cultural change. Since cultural change will be necessary if the agenda for reform is to be carried forward in harmony with school improvement activities, then knowing how to bring about cultural change will become an increasingly important topic for school managers. We hoped therefore that the IQEA schools would be explicit about strategy, communicating and publishing strategy decisions, and evaluating and re-evaluating these decisions as part of an overall learning experience, which are important stepping-stones towards the moving school. Our reflections on this aspect of our work with schools, together with our preliminary thoughts on how this priority-strategy-conditions model might be further developed, are outlined in Chapter 14.

PRACTICAL ARRANGEMENTS

Any project carried in partnership with a number of schools requires a number of practical arrangements to be made. The arrangements which governed and supported the partnership between IQEA schools and the project team are briefly summarized here as:

- the IQEA contract;
- the cadre;
- development and support;
- evaluation.

The IQEA contract

It was seen as important from the outset that collaborating LEAs and project team members all demonstrate real commitment to the project. Consequently, a set of ground rules for commitments from participants was drawn up, as follows:

- The decision to participate in the project is made as a result of consultation among all staff in the school.
- Each school will designate a minimum of two members of staff as project coordinators (one of whom is the headteacher or deputy head), who attend days of training and support meetings (the group of coordinators is known as the 'project cadre').
- The whole school will allocate substantial staff development time to activities related to the project.
- At least 40 per cent of teachers (representing a cross-section of staff) will take part in specified staff development activities related to the project.
- At least 40 per cent of teachers (representing a cross-section of staff) will take part in specified staff development activities in their own classrooms. Each participating teacher will be regularly released from teaching in order to participate in these classroom-based aspects of the project.
- Teachers will use their participation in the project as a basis for accrediting their professional development work.
- Each school will participate in the evaluation of the project and share findings with other participants in the project.

From the demands this made upon participating schools, parallel demands on LEA partners and on project team members were identified. These were drawn together into a formal contract which identified the amount and level of support schools could expect, both from designated LEA advisers and from the project team.

Having established these expectations as far as possible, our next approach was to help each school design a strategy for achieving its developmental priorities and establishing appropriate conditions for improvement. As we have already noted, the details of this strategy had to be peculiar to particular schools, taking account of the nature of the priorities that had been agreed, the existing conditions and the resources that were available.

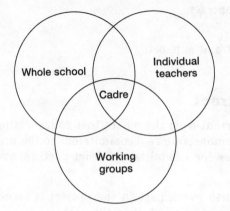

Figure 7.2 *Integrating the levels.*

The role of the cadre

Since the strategy must also be concerned with the school as a whole it must be designed in such a way as to impact upon all levels of the organization. Specifically our focus was on three levels (Figure 7.2) and the ways in which these interrelate. The *whole school* level is to do with overall management and the establishment of policies, particularly with respect to how resources and strategies for staff development can be mobilized to support school improvement efforts. Within the school there is a level where activity is carried forward by *working groups*. Here, the concern is with developing collaboratively the details of and support for improvement activities. Finally, at the *individual teacher* level the focus is on developing classroom practice.

We take the view that in very effective schools these three levels of activity are mutually supportive. Consequently a specific aim of the IQEA project has been to devise and establish positive conditions at each level and to coordinate support across these levels. It is in this connection that we have established a team of coordinators in each school whose task included the integration of activities across the various levels. We refer to these coordinators, in association with advisory colleagues, as the *cadre*. They are responsible for the day-to-day running of the project in their own school and for creating links between the ideas of the overall project and practical action.

Development and support

The cadre members take responsibility for coordinating the development of the project within the school, but there are a number of forms of support available. One is the training provided to cadre groups, which takes place away from the school. It has the advantage of building a network between cadre members from different schools, but it needs to be supplemented by support which reaches into the school.

LEA advisers linked with the project have been one way of providing such support. Many of the project schools have an identified LEA adviser/officer who has taken on this role. Project team members have also taken on this role: each school has a link with a particular team member and through that link access to the whole team. Support provided from these sources ranges from simply joining in the school's deliberations and discussions, via help in planning or guidance towards possible sources of help or ideas, to involvement in staff development activities alongside cadre members, which can be offered to the whole staff or to staff groups.

A further source of support is the project manual, a collection of information, activities and readings grouped around the conditions outlined in the following chapters. The resources in the handbook include many short, focused staff development activities which cadre members are encouraged to try themselves, and (where appropriate) to organize for colleagues in the school.

Evaluation

IQEA places considerable importance on the need for inquiry, reflection and evaluation. The collecting of school-based data of various kinds for purposes of informing planning and development is seen as a powerful element within each school's strategy. Consequently the schools are expected to collect data about progress towards the achievement of developmental priorities; about progress in establishing conditions for improvement; and, of course, about student and teacher outcomes. Agreement that these data are to be shared is one of the specifications of the project contract.

Within the project the journals kept by all the cadre members provide a common approach to recording relevant information. In general terms the journals provide a detailed account of events, decisions and processes that occur, as well as summaries of significant outcomes that are noted. Cadre members are also requested to write reflective comments, indicating their personal reactions to what occurs and mapping their involvement in the project over time. In this way individuals can monitor the progress of their school's project and, at the same time, record developments in their own thinking and practice.

Towards the end of each term cadre members prepare an evaluation report which provides a summary of developments in their school. In preparing these reports teams are asked to address the following questions:

1 How well do school development priorities reflect the principles presented in the IQEA materials?
2 What progress has been made towards the achievement of these priorities?
3 What progress has been made towards the establishment of the conditions outlined in the IQEA materials?
4 What organizational changes have occurred?
5 What significant student and/or teacher outcomes have been noted?
6 What tasks have been undertaken by cadre members?

It is intended that the reports and the process leading up to their preparation will be of value within the school. Indeed, it is assumed that they will be distributed to all members of staff. The reports are also used by the project team to gain an overall picture of the developments in each school's project. Issues raised in the reports are discussed during follow-up visits and cadre meetings.

Throughout the period of the project the project team make regular visits to each school to support cadre members in their work and, at the same time, to collect additional data. All these data are systematically processed on a continuous basis in order to build up a clearer picture of the activities going on in each school. These findings are also being fed back to the school in order to inform development processes. In this respect the project can correctly be characterized as a process of collaborative inquiry within which all partners are contributing to its evolution.

'STORIES FROM SCHOOLS'

In the following chapters we bring together a collection of accounts written by colleagues in schools. Many of these accounts are drawn from IQEA project schools; others have been included because they seem to us to demonstrate how priorities lead to school improvement strategies which operate on the conditions and culture of the school. For a number of reasons we have organized these accounts around the conditions:

- staff development;
- involvement;
- inquiry and reflection;
- leadership;
- coordination;
- collaborative planning.

First, as we have indicated, we feel that these conditions identify those key areas where management arrangements influence the school's capacity to engage in improvement activities. Second, we have noted that in many cases it is necessary to start by building one or more of these conditions before substantive improvement effort is possible. Third, though we have previously stated and underline here that it is the school's priorities which drive improvement, rather than, for example, 'doing staff development', we expect each school to have its own unique priorities, and are reluctant to suggest any 'ideal type' set of priorities as organizing categories. Nevertheless, we hope that in each case the link between priority and condition can be discerned by the reader. Finally, we recognize that any method of categorizing an activity as complex as school development must be, to a degree, arbitrary. We have therefore looked for a method of contextualizing these stories which will allow the reader to use them as access to a range of literatures which help to increase understanding of the intellectual resources available.

Chapter 8

Staff Development

Staff development is inextricably linked to school development. In the quest for school improvement powerful strategies are required which integrate these two areas in a way that is mutually supportive.

The professional development of teachers has traditionally been based on attendance at courses and workshops. Here the main concern is with increasing the knowledge and skills of individuals. However, over the past few years there has been increasing interest in school-focused staff development. Here the emphasis is on meeting the identified needs of the school as a whole, with the major goal of improving the quality of what occurs in classrooms. Thus the concern is with the development of the work of the staff as a team, as well as their individual thinking and practice.

Recently this attention to school-focused in-service has been endorsed by national policy in England and Wales. Schools are, therefore, expected to have a policy for staff development, with time and resources allocated to support its implementation. However, so far this has tended to encourage a search for 'quick-fix' responses, with a particular emphasis on using external consultants to provide one-off inputs. Indeed, many current schemes are conceptualized in a highly instrumental way; that is, identify needs then seek solutions within extremely strict financial limitations. The implications of this formula are not only increased incidence of the short-term and often ineffective response but also, in the longer term, the growth of an 'improvisation' response rather than a serious attempt to address teacher development.

This concern is coupled to another point: a naive interpretation of the supposed main purpose of arrangements for staff development. The way in which present arrangements tend to be interpreted leaves little opportunity for the genuine professional development of teachers given its narrow focus on identifiable needs at the school level which are then tackled in the most expedient way. These instant responses tend to be situation specific. Consequently they do not encourage a broader, more ambitious perspective on teacher development. Quality education is achieved to a large degree by a commitment to the professional learning of teachers that is on-going, developmental and not necessarily circumscribed by particular problems currently faced. Staff development, although it may respond to short-term needs, also transcends them in order to achieve longer-term purposes.

Powerful strategies that link staff development to school improvement need to fulfil two essential criteria: first, they need to relate to and enhance on-going practice in the school, and second, they should link to and strengthen other internal features of the school's organization. Unless the staff development programme leads towards overall school improvement then it tends to become a series of marginal activities.

In this chapter we consider the following issues:

- the creation of a school policy for staff development;
- the importance of the context of staff development activities.

A POLICY FOR STAFF DEVELOPMENT

Until recent times few schools had written policies for staff development, or a coordinator (or committee) with responsibility for its planning and evaluation. Previous policy has tended to focus on the professional development of individual teachers attending INSET courses by choice. The weaknesses of such an approach are as follows:

- Staff receive inadequate advice on their professional development.
- INSET is a matter of individual choice, so some staff get a lot and some get little or none.
- Professional development and INSET are often not related to the needs of the school.
- Most INSET takes place outside the school, leaving staff with a problem of how to integrate their learning into their usual working environment.
- The outcomes and gains of individual professional development are not necessarily shared within the school.

The growth in school-focused and school-based staff development, the existence of professional training days and the experience of appraisal schemes are beginning to lead to better policy and practice for staff development. A school policy for staff development should build upon these initiatives in the following ways:

- It should focus on the school's needs and the professional development required to meet these needs.
- Appraisal schemes should be used to provide links between individual needs and those of the school as a whole.
- Every teacher should be seen as having rights to professional development so there is a more equitable distribution of opportunities for INSET.
- Since professional development is directed to the support of teachers working on agreed topics, the knowledge and skills acquired through INSET should be put to immediate use in the interest of the school.
- Staff who undertake INSET should have a framework for disseminating their new knowledge and skill.
- There should be improvements in the design and use of professional training days.

- Information on external courses should be collated and checked for relevance to the school's needs.

- School-based INSET and external courses should be used to complement one another.

- Staff development must be included in the school's budget and the school timetable.

It is important not to lose sight of the fact that a staff development policy is about the quality of education made available to pupils — something which Hewton (1988, pp. 89-90) makes clear:

> What is staff development? A staff development programme is a planned process of development which enhances the quality of pupil learning by identifying, clarifying and meeting the individual needs of the staff within the context of the institution as a whole. The programme has three strands relating to the individual, interest groups and the whole school.
>
> Why school-focused? Because it moves professional development from being something 'in addition', to a part of the life of every teacher and every school. It recognizes the specialized needs of each member of staff and their professional potential in contributing to developmental activities. It demands more relevant design of INSET experience to meet needs and avoids reliance on the general 'course'. It provides a useful forum for curriculum continuity and innovation across traditional subject boundaries and it involves all staff in the development of the school as well as sharing responsibility for their development.
>
> The primary aim of staff development is to increase the quality of pupil learning by the development of staff potential. Subsidiary aims are:
>
> (i) To recognize and employ staff strengths in seeking the best teaching practices.
> (ii) To identify staff needs.
> (iii) To provide experience and guidance likely to contribute to career development.
> (iv) To make professional development a right and duty of all staff, and the responsibility of management and the LEA.
> (v) To create the most favourable climate for ensuring the continuance of staff development.

We could quote many examples of schools that have used staff development as a central strategy for supporting teachers as they have attempted to engage in improvement activities. All of them work from an assumption that attention to teacher learning is likely to have direct spin-offs in terms of pupil learning. All of them demonstrate the pay-off of investment of time and resources in teacher development.

An excellent example is that of Village Infants' School in Barking and Dagenham. There, over the past couple of years, a sophisticated strategy has been adopted to create conditions in the school that support the development of the staff. At the outset there was a concern with how to find time to observe children in the classroom for the purposes of new assessment requirements. With this in mind a staff development day was led by an external consultant. This event had an enormous impact on staff thinking. Specifically, the consultant led the staff through a series of problem-solving processes focusing on the arrangement of one classroom. Gradually the teachers rearranged furniture and resources in order to make the classroom more autonomous. Subsequently similar activities have been carried out in other rooms. It does seem that the impact of this approach was to do with the tangible nature of the task (rearranging equipment, etc.) and the context (the classroom).

Following from this initial day the staff explored classroom management issues. This led to the formulation of a house style involving the use of learning centres (that is, workstations) in which pupils carry out assignments. By the end of the first year there was clear evidence of increased pupil autonomy in the classroom.

During the second year, staff began to question the quality of learning going on in the workstations. Their concern was that pupils might simply be completing tasks without any significant learning taking place. With this in mind, they decided to work in small teams to observe in one another's classrooms. Observation focused a quality of engagement in the workstations. To facilitate these observations the headteacher covered classes to free teachers. She asked them to plan the observation and also allocated time for them to debrief what had occurred.

Overall, the evidence suggests that the strategy has had a significant impact. Specific changes in teaching style are evident in all classrooms; there is clear evidence of increased pupil autonomy in learning, even with very young pupils; and the quality of dialogue about teaching and learning among the staff is very striking to the outsider. Indeed it does seem that the strategy adopted has brought about a significant change in the culture of the school.

Vignette 8.1 is an account of these events in diary form by the head-teacher, Jan Featherstone, and the deputy head, Lyn Newman, of Village Infants'. It gives a real sense of the evolution of their work over the two-year period.

Vignette 8.1 Creating the autonomous classroom

Part one *It all started in 1991 with assessment. The problems of 'how' and 'when' had to be addressed. Time had to be made for the teacher to stand back, observe and reflect on the children's behaviour and learning. In addition, evidence to support the assessments had to be collected.*

We had no problem isolating points of weakness in the system that prevailed. A major time-waster for teachers was the excessive preparation of resources. We were doing things that children were perfectly capable of doing for themselves if we organized and resourced the classroom appropriately.

Now, there was a person who was willing and eager to demonstrate his principles of classroom management. His reputation for being dynamic went before him. We at Village Infants' were curious and an INSET day was organized. He was invited, he arrived and we were not disappointed.

In one day he launched an already very receptive staff into immediate action. Following a stimulating, amusing and occasionally unnervingly apt talk and slide presentation on bad practice in the primary classroom, he challenged us to make a start on and possibly even finish reorganizing one room, on the principles of good practice, of course.

We couldn't wait! Under his direction sleeves were rolled, screwdrivers were held ready and a 'don't take no for an answer' approach was employed.

Two to three hours later, tired, filthy but supremely satisfied, the entire staff stood in a classroom that had been stripped, sorted and rearranged on the basis of easy access to resources on a 'workstation' principle. Refinements would have to be made and some structural alterations were needed to enable the system to work more efficiently.

One class done, there were seven more to go! We now wanted to work on the remaining classes but, like building Rome, it couldn't be done in a day. However, we adopted the 'strike while the iron is hot' approach. Over a period of a few weeks and working in teams we moved from room to room. The team system meant that everyone had their turn and could benefit from advice, muscle power and one child-free day to reorganize their room.

It was dynamic and it did work!

Part two Money, quite a lot of it, was directed into the project. Alterations, improvements, refurnishing and carpeting need commitment, and are still going on.

Meanwhile, what was now happening in the classroom? Children were gradually being encouraged to help and think for themselves. Simple systems for handling equipment and resources were introduced throughout the school with slight variations according to the experiences of the children.

By 1992, it was time for an interim evaluation of the effectiveness of the reorganization. We had worked well as a large team but now we adopted a smaller, more intimate grouping to look at how the workstation system was operating in the classroom.

Peer observation, peer coaching or 'Tweedling', as we nicknamed it (as in Tweedledee and Tweedledum), was introduced. However, it was not without its teething problems. We did not know how to observe and we certainly did not know how to record our observation, so that we could draw conclusions.

We enlisted the help of an expert. Armed with a bit of theory, we focused on the success criteria we had identified. We persevered. Reservations about the value of our observations and the time commitment they demanded arose from time to time. It seemed to us that we were seeing what we expected to see. The value of feedback from the observations, however, was undisputed. Although we were not finding many answers, the questions that were raised stimulated lively debate and helped to clarify our thoughts and map out a way forward.

So into 1993 we go. We are learning all the time. The children are becoming more independent in the way they use the classroom and their time. Now we will focus our *observations on what the children are doing rather than how. What are they learning? How much are they learning? Are they learning what was intended they learn?*

Could this be leading to assessment?

THE IMPORTANCE OF CONTEXT

A crucial element of the Village Infants' strategy is the importance placed on locating staff development in classrooms. This seems an obvious point and yet it is one that is usually overlooked. So much of in-service education occurs away from the usual context in which teaching takes place and, indeed, is led by people who have not visited the specific contexts in which their participants have to operate. Eisner (1990, p. 102) suggests that this is 'akin to a basketball coach providing advice to a team he has never seen play'.

As we noted in Chapter 4, Bruce Joyce and Beverly Showers' (1988) work on staff development, in particular their peer-coaching strategy, has in recent years transformed thinking on staff development. Joyce and Showers (1980, p. 380) identified a number of key components which when used in combination have much greater power than when used alone. These are:

- presentation of theory;
- modelling or demonstration;
- practice in simulated settings;
- structured and open-ended feedback;
- coaching for application.

On the basis of this analysis, Joyce and Showers (1984, p. 85) summarized their 'best knowledge' on staff development like this:

- the use of the integrated theory-demonstration-practice-feedback training programme to ensure skill development;
- the use of considerable amounts of practice in simulated conditions to ensure fluid control of new skills;
- the employment of regular on-site coaching to facilitate vertical transfer — the development of new learning in the process of transfer;
- the preparation of teachers who can provide one another with the needed coaching.

More recently Joyce (1992) has distinguished, helpfully in our opinion, between the two key element of staff development: the workshop and the workplace. The *workshop*, which is equivalent to the best practice on the traditional INSET course, is where we gain understanding, see demonstrations of the teaching strategy we may wish to acquire, and have the opportunity to practise it in a non-threatening environment. If, however, we wish to transfer these skills that the workshop has introduced us to back into the *workplace* (that is, the classroom and school), then merely attending the workshop is insufficient. The research evidence is very clear that skill acquisition and the ability to transfer vertically to a range of situations requires support on the job. This implies changes to the workplace and the way in which we organize staff development in our schools. In particular this means the opportunity for immediate and sustained practice, collaboration and peer coaching, and studying development and implementation. We cannot achieve these changes in the workplace without, in most cases, drastic alterations in the ways in which we organize our schools. Yet we will not be able to transfer teaching skills from INSET sessions to a range of classrooms without them. Learning enriched schools pay careful attention to their workplace conditions.

In the light of these arguments within the IQEA project we have encouraged the establishment of partnerships of various forms that are intended to help individual teachers to develop their own classroom practice. There is considerable evidence that such partnerships can facilitate improvement in practice and, in so doing, encourage a general ethos of support within a school.

Three forms of partnership are worthy of consideration. These are outlined below.

Peer observation

Peer observation refers to the observation of one's teaching by another (usually a friendly colleague). It is ideal if teachers in peer groups can act as observers for each other, and this mutual exchange of roles quickly breaks down barriers and encourages collaboration. The observer can play any number of differing roles. He or she can observe a lesson in general, focus on specific aspects of the teaching and talk to pupils, all during one observation period. In addition the observer may note incidents that the teacher would ordinarily miss.

The major advantage of peer observation is that it lightens the teacher's problem of analysis and ensures, through the use of an observer, more unbiased and objective data gathering. Although it may sometimes be difficult to obtain the services of an observer, his or her ability to be flexible and to focus on a wide variety of teaching situations outweighs that disadvantage. It is now fairly well established that teachers learn best from other teachers, and take criticism most easily from this source.

Clinical supervision

Clinical supervision is a technique that has enjoyed much popularity in North America, where it was developed as a method of supervising student teachers, but it is also suited for use in classroom research. It is a more structured form of peer observation that focuses on a teacher's performance, utilizing a three-phase approach to the observation of teaching events: a planning conference; classroom observation; and a feedback conference. The planning conference provides the observer and teacher with an opportunity to reflect on the proposed lesson, and this leads to a mutual decision to collect observational data on an aspect of the teacher's teaching. During the classroom observation phase, the observer observes the teacher teaching and collects objective data on that aspect of teaching they agreed upon earlier. It is in the feedback conference that the observer and teacher share the information, decide on possible actions (if necessary), and often plan to collect further observational data. It is important to realize that to be effective all three phases of the process need to be gone through systematically.

There are a number of principles that are important to consider in clinical supervision (Hopkins, 1993):

1 The climate of interaction between teacher and observer needs to be non-threatening, helping and trusting.

2 The focus of the activity should be on improving teaching and the reinforcing of successful patterns, rather than on criticism of unsuccessful patterns, or changing the teacher's personality.

3 The process depends on the collection and use of objective observational data, not unsubstantiated value judgements.

4 Teachers are encouraged to make inferences about their teaching from the data, and to use the data to construct hypotheses that can be tested out in the future.

5 Each cycle of supervision is part of an on-going process that builds on the others.

6 Both observer and teacher are engaged in a mutual process of professional development that can lead to improvement in teaching and observational skills for both.

Coaching

Coaching is a teacher-to-teacher interaction usually carried out by a peer and aimed at improving teaching. Because of its personal nature, a climate of trust needs to be established. Partners select each other and work on problems voluntarily; they must feel that their confidentiality cannot be breached. The primary purpose of peer coaching is support, not evaluation; thus, peers are more appropriate partners than administrators in this professional growth scheme.

There are several entry points for peer coaching: a teacher might pose a problem to another teacher; a school might identify a curriculum change that requires new teaching skills; or a department might reorganize students. All of these events could precipitate meetings between teachers to decide on a response. These meetings generally serve as pre-conferences to identify concerns and map strategies for working on the problem together.

Generally, once a concern has been identified, the peer, acting as coach, arranges a time at which to conduct an observation, gathers descriptive data, and confers with the teacher. The coach's role is that of a facilitator or supporter; he or she works with the teacher to focus on the concern, plan improvement strategies, and follow through in the classroom. A variety of observation instruments can be used, depending on the nature of the problem and the desire of the teacher being observed. All data gathered become the property of the teacher observed.

In the two vignettes that follow, Pamela Hughes writes about her experience of setting up various types of partnership arrangement. This work has been carried out as part of a teacher education project, 'Developing Successful Learning', involving teachers in a range of schools. In Vignette 8.2 Pamela explains how this work evolved in Sharnbrook Upper School in Bedfordshire.

Vignette 8.2 Staff development: partnership teaching

When I first undertook the role of individual needs coordinator at Sharnbrook Upper School, I wanted to reorganize the learning support for those students with special educational needs. Prior to my appointment these students had been withdrawn from classes and as a school we now wanted to shift the emphasis to in-class support. To do this we needed to create conditions within the classroom for all students to have a positive and successful learning experience.

It soon became evident that there was an urgent need for some form of staff development, as many class teachers were uncomfortable at having another adult supporting in the lessons. Also the support teachers and teaching assistants felt de-skilled within the whole-class situation.

A staff meeting was used to heighten awareness. Video stills showing good practice within the classroom were shown, and then the staff, teachers and teaching assistants were divided into small cross-curricular groups in order to share ideas on how support could be used effectively to enhance the learning of students within the classroom. Four questions were given in order to focus discussion. The results of the discussions were compiled into a booklet and distributed to all members of staff.

Undoubtedly, the process of discussion reinforced by the booklet did raise awareness, as the staff were more confident and comfortable, but we were not convinced that the conditions for effective learning had been improved. The first sentence of the booklet, under the heading 'Defining classroom support for effective learning', was, 'Support is a partnership within which the boundaries are difficult to define.' We needed somehow to make this 'partnership' effective. The partnerships between class teachers and supporting staff had to be more than just a shared philosophy.

As a staff, we accepted that teachers learn from their own and one another's experiences by reflecting on practice in the context of our normal teaching. A shared experience would provide the best opportunity to talk ideas through with a colleague, but we would need some form of support in order to move into a developmental phase rather than a purely reflective one.

This led to the idea of 'partnership' as a means of fostering successful learning; creating opportunities for teachers and teaching assistants to work together and with their students to review and develop some aspect of their work. By encouraging working together in this way, we were also hoping to create a more collaborative culture within the school. Teachers working in partnership, emphasizing mutual interest in development, are likely to be more committed and accept a challenge better than those working in isolation.

In order to educate ourselves about the learning in our classrooms, we felt there was a need to develop supportive structures. These structures would need to incorporate strategies for mirroring, reflecting upon and analysing the learning as it took place.

It was difficult to know where to start, as we could not be given any more staff meeting time. All the support team were eager to form partnerships, so we decided to ask for volunteers to partner them. The response was overwhelming and finally partners were selected from just two areas of the curriculum, mathematics and humanities ('partnership seeds' had already been sown within science and English). We formed a team of thirteen, consisting of six class teachers, three support teachers, three teaching assistants and myself.

We had several informal lunches during which a group identity was built. This was very important, as there needed to be a firm base of mutual respect and trust before we could work in partnerships and observe in each other's classes as 'critical friends'.

A system of observation, reflections and 'target setting' was established between pairs of staff. Then, in order to share and develop practice further, wider partnerships were formed between the staff in two areas. By using our time creatively, there was only a necessity to use supply cover for lessons when it was a class being supported by a teaching assistant.

What have we learnt? We are now able to look at our teaching and the conditions within our classrooms to support the effective learning of all of our students through different eyes, the lessons observed being 'imprinted' on our minds. As we recalled 'success' and discussed 'failure', we generated questions which challenged our own learning and that of our students. We have also learnt how to create time to listen, challenge and support each other and to share ideas in 'real settings', opening up many avenues for further staff development.

Perhaps one of the most important lessons we learnt was that change does not happen overnight. 'Professional friendships' evolve between partners and further collaboration develops as partners wish to share their experiences with other. Once the structures are in place, this process of staff development is continuous.

Following this early work, Pamela worked with a team at the Cambridge Institute of Education to introduce the partnership approach to other schools. Vignette 8.3 is an account of what went on in one of the schools that were involved in this initiative.

Vignette 8.3 Developing successful learning: a partnership approach

The school is an upper school suffering from falling rolls. It was one of the deputies who first heard about the partnership approach. Interested to discover more, he came along, together with some of his colleagues, to the first unofficial meeting the project team organized to promote this method of staff development. He could see the practical benefit of teachers working together in the classroom and was able to secure the support of the senior team for development in the school. Two coordinators were appointed from the school and they attended a day conference about the partnership approach. Each felt that there was expertise within the school for the development of practice and that staff were becoming disillusioned and apathetic towards courses arranged externally. The strength of the partnership approach was the teachers 'doing it for themselves'. The following extract from the LEA's 'partnership framework' outlines the process of establishing a partnership:

(i) Purpose of the partnership
The first step is to think about what you hope to achieve through working in partnership. Your choice of partner may depend upon this. Some partnerships may, as part of a particular school initiative, have a tightly focused aim (e.g. to evaluate the implementation of some new curriculum materials). Others may prefer a more open-ended approach, valuing the opportunity to learn from others through working together, without a specific focus in mind. Both kinds of partnerships can stimulate worthwhile developments. What is important is that these purposes should have been discussed, and that both partners are clear about one another's intentions.

(ii) Ways of using a partner
There are a number of ways of using a partner to help you develop your work. In the early stages, a partner may be used to help you to identify aspects of your teaching which you wish to review. Once a partnership is established, a partner may be used to provide support in exploring new approaches.

(iii) Choosing a partner
Your choice of partner will be influenced by the purpose of the partnership. It is important to choose somebody with whom you can work comfortably.

(iv) Establishing ground rules
Partnerships need to establish guidelines and agree upon partners' responsibilities towards one another and towards others who may have an interest or involvement in the work.

The coordinators were anxious that this initiative was not seen as part of teacher appraisal, which was at that time being piloted within the school. Some of the processes were complementary but the partnership project was voluntary and based on peer support. It was foreseen that partnership approach might help to make teacher appraisal a more positive experience, as those involved would become accustomed to being observed and reflecting on their own practice. The coordinators had the trust of the staff, who knew that they would not report back to the headteacher. By taking the whole responsibility for its effective implementation, the coordinators felt they were enhancing their own professional development and personal accountability.

'Developing Successful Learning — A Partnership Approach', once adopted, became integrated into the school development plan and received the support of staff and governors. In the first phase, over half of the staff volunteered and formed partnerships, which have now successfully completed at least one cycle; all wish to continue the process next year and other staff are seeking to join the project. An extract from the school development plan follows:

Rationale
We believe that the primary aim of our school is to facilitate the successful learning of all our students. One of the main elements in achieving this aim is to have an enthusiastic, reflective and highly skilled teaching staff, able both to respond to a range of new curriculum demands and to meet the individual needs of our students. This in turn can best be achieved by developing classroom practice in the context in which it occurs and with the support of other colleagues.

Policy
Our main purpose in our involvement in this project will be to foster successful student learning by creating partnerships of teachers who are committed to helping one another to develop their classroom practice. These partnerships will usually involve two colleagues who, for the purpose of this work will regard one another as equals. Participants will be expected to set agendas, enter into classroom observation, reflect and evaluate the shared experience and develop personal action plans.

Expected outcomes
1 The identification and the promotion of successful learning.
2 The development of mutually supportive strategies.
3 The creation of a staff culture in which professional growth is firmly based in developing classroom practice.
4 Development of this staff culture as other staff become involved.
5 The ownership by the school of the partnership approach.

Time has not been a problem, as staff have volunteered to cover a lesson if necessary and the senior team have supported this well. One partnership highlighted the fact that they were actually able to sit down for over an hour to discuss teaching styles, different approaches and reflect on their lessons. Neither partner had been given the opportunity to observe a colleague's teaching before. They now feel much more open and relaxed when reflecting on and working out strategies for developing their practice together. They also feel able to move beyond the initial limited focus.

Staff in the school felt that it was already on the road to a collaborative culture, but the coordinators are convinced that, through the partnership approach, the culture of the school has become far more open, with teachers willing to share and develop their classroom practice.

The fact that there were two coordinators in the school was one feature of its success (especially as one was seconded during the second term). Any coordination role can lead to a sense of isolation, but the two were able to share the burden, bounce ideas off each other and give encouragement when things did not appear to be happening quickly enough or as planned.

The coordinators also appreciated the 'twilight meeting' halfway through the spring term, when the coordinators from all the schools involved were able to share developments within their own schools. Even those who felt that they had not progressed very far realized that, in fact, they had managed to sow the seeds of a more collaborative and developmental culture within their schools.

They welcomed, too, the continued support of the development team; a telephone call just added the encouragement that was needed to prevent them from feeling isolated. The project newsletter was also helpful.

Both coordinators commented that this approach requires a long-term effort; it cannot 'happen overnight' and be successful. It must be embedded within the school's culture, and consequently add to the staff's understanding of what staff development is and how much they can provide for one another.

As a result of the 'Developing Successful Learning' project Pamela Hughes and her colleagues have developed the guidelines on p. 123. This is a useful resource, particularly in contexts where colleagues are not used to the idea of working in one another's classrooms for the purpose of professional development.

MESSAGES

It seems reasonable to assume that improving the conditions for supporting the learning of teachers in a school will have an impact on the conditions they provide for their pupils. To this end it is important that a school has a well-thought-out policy for teacher development. This must go well beyond the traditional patterns by which teachers attend external courses, or, more recently, the use of one-shot school-based events. It is vital that strategies for staff development should be *linked to school improvement*. These should therefore be concerned with the development of the staff as a team, as well as with the evolution of its thinking and the practice of individuals.

Schools with successful staff development arrangements tend to have long-term policies that link individual needs to school improvement efforts. They also see one-off events as part of a wider strategy. Critical to their success is an emphasis on providing *support in the classroom* using various types of partnership arrangements. In other words, successful staff development depends upon quality *workshops* that encourage understanding and provide demonstrations of good practice, coupled with modifications to the *workplace* in order to provide support on the job as teachers attempt to explore aspects of their practice.

In establishing staff development in schools it is helpful to create the following conditions:

- a written school policy for staff development;
- procedures for ensuring that the staff development policy responds to staff needs:
- discussion of staff's professional needs;
- support to staff involved in development activities.

Chapter 9

Involvement

In the research literature on effective schools there is strong evidence that success is associated with a sense of identify and involvement that extends beyond the teaching staff. This involves the pupils, parents and, indeed, other members of the local community. It does seem that some schools are able to create positive relationships with their wider community that help to create a supportive climate for learning.

Referring to a series of studies carried out in Wales, David Reynolds (1991) refers to the existence of what he calls an 'incorporative approach'. He notes that this seems to have two major elements: incorporation of pupils into the organization of the school, and incorporation of their parents through supportive roles. We believe that this approach can and should be widened to include members of the local community. In the UK it is also particularly important to adopt a similar attitude to school governors.

In this chapter we will consider two main aspects of this topic. These are:

- pupil involvement in schools and classrooms;
- approaches for encouraging parental involvement.

PUPIL INVOLVEMENT

Pupil involvement seems to be a particularly important factor in school improvement. The research suggests that this can occur at an organizational level, by involving pupils in decision making and encouraging them to take responsibility for day-to-day routines; and at the classroom level, when pupils can be encouraged to take responsibility for their own learning and, though involvement, to learn organizational, planning, discussion, decision-making and leadership skills (Stoll, 1991). We will consider both of these levels in turn.

When pupils are less involved it is likely that their attitudes to school will be much more negative. Then, when innovations are introduced, they may well become barriers to change. Their resistance may not be open and tangible but nevertheless their intuitive reactions may create the negative atmosphere that discourages staff from pursuing their goals.

As we have noted, the reactions of pupils to attempts to bring about change can be particularly significant. In the IQEA project we have observed how a number of schools have used the power of pupil involvement to support their development activities. A particularly good example of this approach occurred at Sanders Draper Secondary School in the London Borough of Havering.

During the academic year 1990-1, four cross-curricular groups were established in the school: each group was chaired by a senior member of staff and investigated various issues. One group took as its focus 'open learning', and developed two aims: the organization of a flexible learning week and the development of a learning resources centre (LRC). The existing school library was book based, located at the back of the school and used mainly by the English department; it was felt that this was a poor use of resources.

A working party of four staff was formed to manage and direct the LRC project. It was decided to move its site to a more central location being vacated by the sixth form. During the summer of 1991, they began to extend the range of resources in the LRC in consultation with departments. However, they recognized that, if they were to succeed in raising the quality of education offered at Sanders Draper, they had to do more than simply create a physical area. Therefore in September 1991 they began a programme of staff development aimed at enabling and encouraging staff to widen their range of teaching approaches.

In Vignette 9.1 Gill Daly, who coordinated this initiative, explains what happened.

Vignette 9.1 Pupil involvement in school improvement

We called a meeting of all the staff teaching Year 9 as we had decided to monitor the effects of our initiative on that year group. We asked for volunteers to join in with an investigation into characteristics of good practice. Staff formed partnerships to conduct some paired observations, which helped them to reflect upon how children worked in their LRC-based lessons. 'Twilight sessions' were arranged to give staff the skills in observation techniques which were required and to share ideas and experiences.

By the summer of 1992 we felt that we were ready to launch our work school-wide. We organized a whole-staff INSET day for the autumn term to investigate teaching and learning style. During the day, staff were exposed to a series of experiences such as working out their own preferred learning style and learning that a wide range of preferences existed among the staff. Pupils were used as witnesses during the morning session, helping staff to reflect on what it was really like to learn at Sanders Draper School. Towards the end of the day, departments were asked to respond to what they had learned by drawing up action plans to meet the needs of all the pupils.

Since the INSET day we have continued our staff development work by setting up what we have called our 'flexible learning support group'. At the first meeting, staff identified their own training needs if they were to become more skilled at a wider range of teaching techniques. By using the skills of the teachers in the group we have set up a programme of workshop sessions to try to meet those needs. For example, recently, two teachers from the art department ran a very lively session on organizing whole-class practical work.

Throughout the project we have tried to involve students. Initially, we were concerned to give them information about our work: they were told in assemblies that they were to be part of an experiment! However, their contributions developed far beyond that originally intended, and they have taken on a variety of roles as:

- Monitors *of the classroom impact of the project. Year 9 pupils were asked to complete an initial questionnaire and a follow-up questionnaire in June 1992. The aim of this exercise was to detect any shift in pupils' perceptions of how they learned. Almost all noticed a change in the ways in which they had worked. Mel Ainscow and David Hopkins from Cambridge Institute (UCIE) and Professor David Hargreaves interviewed our students and were able to draw some positive conclusions about the effects of our work in the classroom.*

- Motivators. *Staff were encouraged by the response of pupils. Transcripts of the pupils' conversations with UCIE were made available to staff and governors: positive pupils' comments made far more effect than we could have. The aims of our work were explained to the pupils at an early stage and they were keen, therefore, to know how we were getting on.*

- Resources *for staff development. Pupils at work in the LRC were videotaped and this was used to sharpen our classroom observation skills. In November 1992, students were used as 'witnesses' as part of a whole-staff training day. Teachers talked with pupils to enable staff to learn about how pupils learn in our school.*

- Practical helpers. *Students were invited to apply for the posts of resource assistants to help with the day-to-day running of the learning resources centre. The helpers have regular meetings with a member of the project team to discuss day-to-day running of the LRC issues. A pupil chairs this meeting.*

During the next term we are evaluating the impact of our work, using mapping exercises, classroom observations and interviewing. We will use this information to inform the next stage of our planning.

We have learnt a great deal about the nature of change in our school. This is best illustrated by our experiences in the summer of 1992, when we were asked by management to reflect on our experiences so far and come up with suggestions, perhaps in the form of a flow-chart, about the route a person trying to implement whole-school initiative might take. We drew several time-lines chronicling our project, which would have been of very limited use to a person starting out, although they were useful as a record. Then we began to think about what had helped and hindered us along the way, and produced a rather more specific spider diagram, showing the characteristics of our project which had helped to make it 'successful' as well as those things which had had a less positive effect. In essence, we learned that change or growth will not fit on a flow-chart, but that it is an organic process that happens at different rates at different times, and that it is the conditions which exist in the school which determine its success or failure.

The ideas presented in this chapter assume that schools are places where children and adults are skilful in working together, sharing their ideas and supporting one another. They are based on the assumption that there are two major resources for learning, the teacher and the children. They also assume that teachers have skills in organizing their classes in ways that encourage

cooperation. It is, of course, in the classroom that pupil attitudes have the greatest impact. It is here that interactions can provide barriers that prevent learning or, indeed, the most powerful stimulus that can inspire the learning of all members of a class.

Karen Jones, an English teacher at Oakbank School (13-18) in Keighley, saw the potential of pupil involvement for creating better learning conditions in her classroom. In Vignette 9.2 she tells the story of what occurred.

Vignette 9.2 Learning to learn at Oakbank

The project arose from three main concerns:

1 *I perceived a decrease in motivation in a Year 11 English class. Their pastoral tutor had noticed this too. Their poor attendance and time management skills were cause for considerable concern. It was a difficult class to teach because the sporadic attendance made the setting and collection of work haphazard and difficult to follow up. The regular attenders were being affected: who could blame their tardiness at handing in work when the truants were getting away with the bare minimum? Clearly my classroom had to be organized differently. I could no longer 'class teach'. Some sort of supported self-study seemed to be the answer. But that led me on to another problem . . .*

2 *The flexible learning projects I had done before left me feeling that much more work had to go into defining the teacher role in these situations. Too much work had gone into preparing materials and individualized workpacks. To be honest, I had let myself off the hook by handing out the pack and expecting the students to get on with it. This gave me some nice, easy lessons in which to pretend that the students were 'working at their own pace', but the results were disappointing to say the least. I had failed to appreciate the importance of my new role in this different style of teaching. I needed to try a fresh approach.*

3 *Part of our IQEA school improvement work has been concerned to examine our school as a learning institution and to explore ways to encourage whole-school involvement in this notion. We needed some sort of mechanism whereby we could begin to build a picture of the types of learning going on. If we really were serious about developing our craft by learning from one another, then staff and students needed to be made aware of the range and variety of teaching methods and learning styles already available within the institution.*

It was finally decided that one way to tackle all of these concerns would be for my Year 11 class to research, compile and produce a booklet called 'Learning to Learn at Oakbank'. The audience for the booklet would be the parents and students of the new Year 9 intake. It was hoped that the Year 11 class would enjoy a chance to do something 'real' that might have an effect on their motivation. By analysing learning and teaching styles, the pupils might come to some beneficial conclusions about their own progress and how best to use the little time left before their examinations. The project would also give me the chance to develop my teaching technique. I enlisted the help of an observer to sit in on some sessions and provide feedback. Finally, the very process of making the learning picture would at least raise some questions about learning and teaching. With a bit of luck, the finished product, if good enough, would make a positive contribution to school life for students, parents and staff.

It did not take long for my classroom to look and feel quite different. Students each had responsibility for two or three sections of the booklet, working with different combinations of people for each section. They had to be scrupulously fair and well organized when it came to time management, otherwise they ran the risk of letting their classmates down. Some devised questionnaires which went out to heads of department; they were dismayed when they discovered that it was difficult getting returns back and that teachers also had problems in meeting deadlines! Fortunately, most heads of department did return valuable information on teaching styles to be found in their curriculum areas. They also gave an insight into what a newcomer to the school could reasonably expect to happen in these subject lessons and what skills would be developed.

Another pair selected three teachers to interview in depth about their preferred teaching methods. These two, a boy and a girl, became totally engrossed in this work and were to be seen painstakingly transcribing the tapes and drawing some interesting conclusions from their evidence. One group wrote to some parents and organized afternoon tea in the classroom. The parents accepted the invitation and seemed to enjoy the opportunity to have their say about Oakbank and to explain the importance of their role in helping their children to learn. They were, incidentally, extremely enthusiastic about the idea of a learning handbook and said they would have found it very useful when their children had started out at the school.

Others interviewed past students to find out if they had any advice that they could pass on to future generations of learners at Oakbank. One pair interviewed the headteacher about his vision of the school as a learning institution. Some wrote help sheets on homework, and managing and coping with revision.

We are still a long way from completing the finished product. At present the booklet exists only in raw, draft form. However, even if we don't get to publication date (which we will!) it has been worth it. First and foremost, the students enjoyed themselves. What threatened to be a difficult final term turned out to be purposeful. The attendance problem did not go away but at least the regular attenders were being stimulated and challenged and there was a sense of continuity.

I have had the opportunity to begin to explore my role not only as coordinator but also as time-keeper and setter of expectations. Each session began and ended with circle work in which the students were expected to tell the others what they had been doing and what they planned to do next. This group accountability provided a positive pressure point: the group dynamics dealt with any motivation problems, and this was far more effective than any nagging on my part.

As far as the whole-school initiative goes, the success of the 'Learning to Learn' project cannot be tested yet. Before we publish the booklet, we need to go back to departments to make sure that they have been properly represented and that everyone is happy with the content. I suspect that the booklet will be trialled for a year with a few classes, their parents and their teachers and that we will go into full publication the following year. So as with all learning the process will be continuous.

Clearly Karen's willingness to take some risks in her own classroom opened up possibilities for learning for both her pupils and her colleagues.

The ways in which teachers go about their tasks do have a significant impact upon classroom interaction. Unfortunately, few teachers have the opportunity to observe other colleagues at work and so may not consider alternative ways of organizing their lessons. It can also be instructive to put ourselves in the place of our pupils, in order to see what is is like being a consumer (Hargreaves, 1982, p. 3):

> At the end of the day I tried to summarise their response to their schooling. There had been no hostile rebellion from them, though they had been rebuked many times for 'talking' and for not paying attention. School lessons for them appeared to be like seven very dull television programmes which could not be switched off. They did not want to watch and made little effort to do so; occasionally the volume rose to a very high level, so they listened; occasionally the programme became sufficiently interesting to command their attention, but it was never more than a momentary diversion from the general monotony. Part of the problem appeared to be that they were not, in fact, seven new independent programmes. All of them were serials, which demanded some knowledge of earlier episodes. Indeed, most of the teachers generously provided a recapitulation of earlier episodes at the beginning of every lesson. But the girls had lost track of the story long ago. Two of the programmes were, in fact, repeats; since their first broadcast had aroused no interest in the girls, it is not surprising that the repeat evoked no new response. So these two girls responded as most of us do when faced with broadcasts of low quality that we cannot switch off: they talked through the broadcast whenever they could. The easiest form of resistance was to treat the lessons as background noise which from time to time interrupted their utterly absorbing sisterly gossip. And of course they made the most of the commercial breaks, as it were: they were the first to leave each lesson and the last to arrive at the next one.

It is accounts such as this that draw our attention to the need for teachers to have feedback upon their practice. In particular they need to have opportunities to know about the pupil perspective on the way they carry out their tasks as teachers. This is why involvement of pupils is such an important issue.

What is clearly important is for teachers to plan their lessons and organize their classrooms in ways that encourage involvement in the tasks and activities that are set. Whilst a variety of approaches should be encouraged in order to respond to pupil differences, a case can be made for some degree of emphasis on structured group work. In effect group work is a way of presenting tasks in a form that encourages participation.

Despite the rhetoric of education in Britain, with its emphasis on group problem solving within the curriculum, it is not uncommon to see pupils working alone for large parts of the school day. Often they are seated in groups, but it is still quite rare to see them carrying out their tasks collaboratively. It is difficult to know why this is so, although one possible explanation is that many teachers have not received training in ways of organizing group work in the classroom.

In recent years there has been increased interest in various forms of group work in schools. In particular, the work of David and Roger Johnson (Johnson *et al.*, 1986; Johnson and Johnson, 1989) and Robert Slavin (1983) has been influential. They suggest that classroom tasks can be set in one of three ways:

1 In terms of a win-lose struggle to see which pupils are best (that is, *competitive* learning).

2 In a way that requires pupils to work alone (that is, *individualized* learning).

3 Where pupils work in pairs or groups (that is, *cooperative* learning).

Let us look at the main features of these approaches to task setting in a little more detail.

Competitive learning

Here pupils:

- work against each other to achieve a goal that only one or a few can attain;
- are graded by their ability to work faster and more accurately than their peers;
- seek outcomes that are personally beneficial but also are detrimental to others in the group;
- either study hard in order to do better than their classmates or take it easy because they do not believe they have a chance of succeeding.

Individualized learning

Here pupils:

- seek achievements and complete tasks that are unrelated to those of others;
- are graded against a required set of standards;
- seek outcomes that are personally beneficial and ignore as irrelevant the achievements of their classmates.

Cooperative learning

Here pupils:

- work together to accomplish shared goals and tasks;
- perceive that they can achieve their goals only if other group members achieve theirs;
- seek outcomes that are beneficial to all in a group.

While working alone on individual tasks is an important and legitimate approach, used excessively it is a limiting form of learning. This has been recognized in many schools, where attempts are being made to encourage pupils to become more skilful in learning cooperatively. This is not an easy task since it requires sophistication of curriculum planning and implementation for which many teachers feel ill-prepared.

Where pupils are to be encouraged to adopt cooperative ways of working, these have to be planned and introduced in a systematic way, as with any other new learning experience. It is important to recognize that cooperative learning assumes an approach that goes well beyond a simple commitment to encourage children to work together. It requires, for example, careful attention to:

- the setting of tasks in ways that necessitate collaboration;
- helping children to recognize that their success is dependent to some degree upon the success of the other members of their group;
- group size and membership that is appropriate given the skills and experience of the children, and the nature of the tasks that are set;
- the development of the pupils' skills in aspects of group working, including communication, sharing and decision making.

Effectively it involves the introduction of an additional series of demands, requiring pupils to work towards objectives associated with the content of the curriculum at the same time as achieving new objectives to do with their skills in collaboration.

When this works well, the benefits are enormous. Cooperative learning that is successful can have a positive effect on academic outcomes, self-esteem, social relationships and personal development. Furthermore, it has the potential to free teacher time as a result of making pupils less dependent on the teacher for help and support.

Cooperative learning can take a variety of forms. For example:

- pairs of pupils may read the same book together, helping one another with difficult words and discussing the content of their reading;
- pupils may work in pairs preparing a joint statement about a topic, which they will be responsible for giving to a larger group;
- a group may be involved in a task that can only be completed if separate materials that are held by individual members are pooled;

133

- group members may brainstorm ideas, which are recorded by one member who acts as scribe;
- individual members of a group may be assigned particular roles; for example, chair, recorder, summarizer, reporter;
- a group may be told that they will be scored or graded as a result of the aggregate performance of individual members.

We should add that, when we have seen teachers being successful in increasing their use of cooperative learning approaches, this often seems to have been in the context of a whole-school development. In other words, cooperative learning in the classroom is facilitated by cooperative planning in the staffroom.

In Vignette 9.3 Julie Payne of Frances Bardsley Secondary School in the London Borough of Havering describes how the school carried out an initiative to improve the quality of classroom interactions. The focus was on the idea of flexible learning.

Vignette 9.3 Flexible learning

Since 1988 we have been developing a policy to ensure that the curriculum is accessible to all students and that they become more autonomous in their learning. The vehicle for this has been flexible learning.

Flexible learning is a fresh approach to the problems of teaching and learning in that there is an identifiable structure, or framework, which can enable teachers to effect long-term change. In addition, flexible learning styles are an important means of responding to the National Curriculum requirement for a broad, balanced and differentiated curriculum. The emphasis is on the learning process and learning how to learn.

The thrust at Frances Bardsley School has been to:

- give the pupils learning experiences appropriate to their ability, as the curriculum needs to be made accessible to all, starting from where the child is — in particular, extending and challenging more academically successful pupils;
- encourage the pupils to become independent learners, through growth of personal skills and various cross-curricular skills;
- encourage the staff to explore their methodology and its outcomes, and to become reflective about their practice;
- evaluate and plan learning by talking to pupils and through the use of Records of Achievement;
- seek feedback from pupils on how they prefer to learn.

The introduction of flexible learning has been managed by innovation on an incremental basis. INSET has been provided on:

- interviewing skills in supported self-study;
- classroom observation and partnerships;
- differentiation;

- *gifted children;*
- *multimedia resources.*

Resulting from this, change started to occur through one or more small-scale developments in some curricular areas. Gradually some of these discrete areas of the curriculum acted as a catalyst for changes elsewhere. The most significant change occurred when the senior management team became committed to the innovation at the onset of our involvement in the IQEA project.

We have attempted to evaluate the work in a number of ways. It has been found particularly helpful to take account of the reactions of our pupils. These ideas can be summarized as follows:

Positive findings:
- *Pupils enjoyed working at their own pace and found it more fun than working as a whole class.*
- *Pupils enjoyed the freedom of choosing their own activities.*
- *Pupils found it more relaxing as there was less pressure from the teacher.*
- *Some pupils thought it helped them to reach their own highest possible standard.*
- *High-ability pupils enjoyed the challenge of having to find out for themselves.*
- *The majority of pupils enjoyed being able to choose their own homework and the time spent on it increased in some cases.*

Negative findings:
- *Many pupils were frustrated because the materials they wanted were not always available.*
- *Pupils were sometimes confused and insecure at not being told specifically what to do.*
- *Some pupils found supported self-study boring, which demotivated them.*
- *More able pupils felt that they were not covering the syllabus as effectively.*
- *Many pupils found that supported self-study did not help with their understanding of the subject.*

Overall I feel the whole-school approach to bringing about an innovative change has altered the culture of the school. By encouraging and supporting teachers to become more reflective about their teaching and the learning process of the pupils, the school has moved forward towards a common vision of improving the experience of the pupils and the learning outcome. Teachers working together have learnt to explore their classroom practice for the benefits of the pupils and their own professional development. This new approach among the staff must be encouraged to continue if the school is to grow further. It is evident that consideration must be given to allowing time for teachers to work together, and adequate resourcing — within both departments and the resources centres.

To date, the learning experience of a substantial proportion of the pupils has been enhanced and our initiative has enabled pupils to have learning experiences appropriate to their ability. They have become more autonomous in their learning, too, and there has been a growth in their personal and cross-curricular skills.

Pupils have also learnt to evaluate their own learning as well as the methodology used. They have been involved in the process of planning their own work and their assessment. Further development will be necessary to link in with Records of Achievement.

PARENTAL INVOLVEMENT

The incorporative approach can be extended beyond the school gate to involve parents and, indeed, members of the local community including, of course, governors. Here the attitudes of staff are a major factor.

Ainscow and Muncey (1989) suggest that teachers may see parents as:

- *a hindrance*. For example, the teacher may consider that the parent, by following an irregular marital life or by being lukewarm about the child's education, may actually be hindering the child's progress and contributing to difficulties.

- *a resource*. The teacher may consider that a parent is a potential source of help; for example, to help with reading practice at home.

- *partners*. Teachers may feel that they can drop the professional-client relationship and work on an equal level with parents.

- *consumers*. Some parents see the school as supplying a service about which they are entitled to complain if it is not providing what it claims to offer. If parents adopt this viewpoint it automatically throws them into the role of consumer.

Similarly, parental views of schools and teachers vary. Often parents' views of teachers are based on their own experience in school. This may have been negative, and the parents may see the school as an institution that fails people. Consequently, it is important that the whole issue of communications between school and parents is handled effectively. When teachers and parents meet there is a lot of potential for conflict, though much of it can be avoided by careful planning and skilful interviewing techniques.

One research project asked some parents of pupils to describe the kind of information professionals should be giving families (Ainscow and Muncey, 1989). The parents wanted, for the most part, honest, concise and useful information. They wanted to be given some practical advice directed towards immediate problems and some indication of the likely long-term outcomes for their child. But the parents also talked about the manner in which information should be transmitted. For example, one parent said:

> It would have saved a lot of pain and perhaps meant more rapid progress if we had been treated as adults. We would have liked it if the terms they were throwing out at us had been explained. Professional honest and candour would have increased our level of confidence in their competence. (Ainscow and Muncey, 1989, p. 116)

Respect was another term frequently used by parents. For example:

Why can't teachers realise that no matter how well informed they are about the child, the parent still knows more about their own child than anyone else in the world? Why can't teachers accept that this information might be very important? (p. 117)

Another group of parents were asked to give advice to professionals on how best to deal with parents. They suggested the following four points:

1 Be frank and open. Excuses or vague explanations are often interpreted by parents as an over-protective attitude or simple evasion of the truth on the part of the professional.
2 Listen. Teachers must recognize that all parents have knowledge of their child that they cannot possibly have. This knowledge may well be valuable in helping the child overcome some difficulty.
3 Do not be afraid to say 'I don't know'. Parents often appreciate the honesty of the response, and this may well help to foster a sense of partnership between home and school.
4 Encourage. Parents feel that they need encouragement and reassurance from teachers rather than attempts to lay blame.

With these ideas in mind, it makes sense for a school to review arrangements for parental involvement. Below is a set of questions from Ainscow and Muncey (1989) that have been found useful for this purpose:

1 Do you know the school policy for contacting/meeting parents?
2 Are the parent involvement procedures arrived at by consensus?
3 Is there a record-keeping system of parent contacts?
4 Is there a method for evaluating parent contacts?
5 Is time made available for staff to discuss with parents?
6 Is information routinely provided for parents?
7 Do parents have opportunities to meet and discuss together?
8 Is there a physical parent base in the school?
9 Is there a clear written statement of parent involvement available to staff and parents?
10 Are parents seen as individuals and given individual attention?
11 Do interactions between staff and parents indicate mutual respect and equality, as opposed to professional distancing created by the idea of the 'expert'?
12 Is information provided to parents which helps them evaluate:

 • school attainments generally;
 • own child attainments?

13 Does the school project a welcoming, valuing image for child and parent?

14 Is there flexibility in ways to involve parents?

15 Is parent involvement largely problem oriented?

16 Are school records on families open to parent inspection?

It is interesting that some schools are particularly successful in creating a strong sense of partnership with parents, while others find this almost impossible. In Vignette 9.4 Mike Cassidy, the headteacher of St Louis Middle School, describes the ways in which he has developed a policy in this area.

Vignette 9.4 Encouraging parental involvement

St Louis is a Catholic voluntary-aided middle school with 430 pupils on roll. It draws pupils from a very wide catchment area in a 25-mile radius from Bury St Edmunds. The majority of pupils transfer from five main feeder schools which are situated in towns across west Suffolk.

This large catchment area naturally brings challenges to the school in terms of pupils having to travel considerable distances, as well as creating additional difficulties for parents who previously enjoyed the opportunity to 'pop into' school whenever there was a need or to help out when required. Consequently parents could feel very detached from the school.

Despite this, the school has long enjoyed considerable support from parents. Their involvement ranges from fund-raising and organizing social events through the PTA, helping with supervision on residential trips and day visits, paired reading with children, running the school bookshop, selling uniforms and helping with many other activities and school events. The school's motto 'Ut sint unum' — 'that they may be one' — provides the traditional foundation for staff, parents and children to work together.

However, it is interesting to note that although the school has sought to involve parents in a supportive role, there has never been an invitation for them to participate in the decision-making process or in formulating school policy. Traditionally this has always been the preserve of the governors and staff.

However, during the spring term of 1992 this traditional model began to change, owing to an initiative proposed by the head and staff. The school wanted to stand back from itself in an attempt to appraise its strengths and weaknesses. The objective was to involve parents in the entire process. A framework for appraisal was agreed between staff and governors. Parents were then invited to join the 'appraisal team'. The rationale and proposed framework were introduced to parents by the chairman of the governors and the head. Parents were asked to comment and make further suggestions if necessary. The role of the parents was strongly emphasized, as their perceptions and opinions were to provide the raw data.

Response from parents was very positive and many volunteered, offering both views and support. Eventually, following a series of discussions, a range of issues was identified and a short list of targets was agreed. Five working groups consisting of parents, governors and staff were formed and given an area of school life each to evaluate:

1 *Presenting the school to parents.*

2 *Continuity and liaison with feeder schools.*

3 *Links with the local community.*

4 *School–home transport arrangements.*

5 *School buildings/site development for the future.*

Each group was invited to elect a chairperson who would present the group's findings to a termly meeting of all group representatives. The chairman of the governors was asked to coordinate communications between all working groups.

All five groups have been actively engaged with their respective appraisals. Each group has identified further targets for evaluation, and proposals have been presented to the head and governing body. The key activities are as follows:

Group 1: Presenting the school to parents

Focus:
- *the school uniform;*
- *open days or evenings;*
- *communication between the school and parents — school newspaper or magazine, school brochure and termly newsletters;*
- *new parents' initial perceptions of the school.*

Outcome:
- *There have been changes to the school uniform.*
- *There is a new school brochure.*
- *Open evenings have been modified.*
- *A parent directory of support available from parents has been set up.*

Group 2: Continuity and liaison with feeder schools

Focus:
- *exchange of staff to be timetabled within the middle and feeder schools;*
- *opportunities for feeder-school and middle-school pupils to work in each other's schools.*

Outcome:
- *Middle-school staff in PE and music are now working in all five feeder schools.*
- *Activity days are now planned into the diary for school cross-phase events, such as a kite-making exhibition.*

Group 3: Links with the local community

Focus:
- *sponsorship from local business;*
- *teacher placement in local industry;*
- *displays of children's work in the local town.*

Outcome:

- The school's new brochure has been published and sponsored by a local printer.

- Seven members of staff have enjoyed the opportunity to work in local industry, which has offered personal and professional development.

- Displays of children's work are being planned for public exhibition;

- A local restaurant has been decorated and designed by Year 8 pupils (technology project).

Group 4: School–home transport arrangements

Focus:

- improving the quality and efficiency of the current service;

- negotiating with the LEA on funding and administrative support;

- setting up parent transport committees to organize transport from areas where there is no current service.

Outcome:

- The LEA is now much more involved in terms of arranging contracts/tenders on behalf of parent committees.

- There is a newly formed parent committee on transport.

- A transport link has been established for Haverhill children. Twenty-seven children are now able to attend the school, so the school roll has increased.

- The school is using delegated funding to subsidize transport.

Group 5: School buildings/site development

Focus:

- identifying areas in the greatest need of improvement.

Outcome:

- The school has agreed building and landscape projects for the next five years.

There is now ample evidence to support the advantages of parental involvement within certain aspects of decision making and the formulating of new developments or new school policy. Feedback from parents so far is encouraging, as they value the opportunity to contribute, although many still believe the final decisions should be taken by the head and governors. As head I feel more secure and confident about introducing change, since everyone now has an opportunity to give his or her views and become involved in the consultation process.

Furthermore, the school has introduced more changes than it previously intended. This has been achieved because of the additional time and support which have been freely given by its parents.

It does seem, therefore, that even where parents live long distances from a school it is possible to encourage meaningful involvement. The evidence suggests that the most vital factor relates to attitudes among head and staff.

MESSAGES

Effective schools seem to adopt what might be called an *incorporative approach*. In this way they are able to mobilize pupils, parents and other members of the community in support of school activities.

Pupil involvement is particularly important. When pupils feel alienated it discourages learning. It can also mean that pupils act as barriers to attempts at innovation. Some schools have found that pupils can be a positive force in supporting improvement initiatives. Pupil involvement can operate at both an organizational and classroom level. An emphasis on *cooperative learning* in the classroom is a way of facilitating pupil involvement. Such approaches can also improve academic standards, self-esteem, social relationships and personal development. It has been found beneficial to introduce reforms in teaching on a whole-school basis.

An incorporative approach can also be used to encourage *parental and community involvement*. Teacher attitudes seem to be a key to the success of such ventures.

In encouraging involvement in schools it is helpful to create the following conditions:

- an agreed policy to involve pupils and parents;
- procedures that encourage pupils and parents to participate in decision making;
- parent and pupil understanding of whom to approach in order to comment on policies;
- open discussion between pupils, parents and staff.

Chapter 10

Inquiry and Reflection

As we have pointed out, national reforms in the education system of England and Wales have produced unprecedented pressures for change at the level of the school. Changes in curriculum content, processes and assessment have been enshrined in legislation, requiring adoption at a pace which many schools feel is beyond their capacity. In addition to creating a potentially de-skilling context in which individual teachers must work, the logistics of implementing these changes has proved a severe test for even the most confident of management teams — so much so that it may seem strange to be arguing that schools should actively adopt a focus upon school improvement activities at a time when many teachers are finding that all their time and energies are consumed in trying to assimilate into their schools the range of unavoidable changes currently required.

However, there are a number of reasons why schools should strive to impose their own agenda on the overall pattern of change. First, it is important to know what is actually 'new'. Though the specifics may vary from school to school and it seems unlikely that any school was already working wholly as required by recent legislation, nevertheless the majority of schools already have significant experience which is relevant to current demands. It is important to recognize that working out from identified strengths tends to be easier and more rewarding for those involved than being constantly challenged to make good 'deficits'. Locating relevant experience, and developing from it, is therefore a sensible way forward.

Beyond the arguments which arise from the view that, even in the current climate of quite extraordinary external pressure on schools, it is both vital to the individual character of schools and consistent with the drive for school improvement to maintain a firm control of policies and priorities at school level, there are more general cases to be made for school-level inquiry and reflection processes. Willms (1992) summarizes some of the more important reasons for engaging in school-level monitoring. His point that the 'working knowledge' of decision makers is frequently seen as inadequate is one which we have come across increasingly in our work with schools. Indeed we have found ourselves both individually and collectively 'retained' by schools to provide precisely the kind of 'specific knowledge' to which Willms refers. But what are we arguing here very much supports Willms's notion that routine data collection within the school is likely to be a more useful and enduring basis for decision making than is commissioned external investigation (Willms, 1992, p. 2):

School boards, administrators, and teachers rely heavily on their working knowledge to make decisions ... The 'working knowledge' of decision-makers includes the large body of facts, principles, and perceptions that determine their particular view of the world. It is influenced by their values, attitudes, and beliefs, and by the steady stream of information gathered from friends, colleagues, clients, and the public. But decision-makers often view their working knowledge as inadequate for confronting certain issues: it is too subjective or shallow, or biased because it does not represent the opinions of a wide constituency. Thus they regularly seek 'specific knowledge'. They appoint committees, hire consultants, conduct evaluations, commission research, and attend courses to obtain information focused on specific problems or activities. Although specific knowledge is often more objective and relevant, obtaining it requires time and resources. Also, specific knowledge is sometimes at odds with working knowledge, and does not always fulfil decision-makers' need ...

Monitoring information can fill some of the gaps between working and specific knowledge. If data are collected routinely from a variety of sources, then many regular information needs can be met more quickly. Monitoring data on some topics can be more objective than those obtained through in formal observations and conversations. Monitoring data tend to cover a wider variety of topics than those obtained through evaluations, consultancies, or commissioned research. In some cases monitoring information is insufficient for addressing particular problems, but it can provide a basis for the kind of specific knowledge required.

Nevertheless, while fully supporting the link between the production of school-level performance data and school improvement activities, we need to acknowledge that simply collecting data, however systematically and routinely, will not of itself improve schools. There needs to be a commitment to scrutinize such data, to make sense of it, and to plan and act differently as a result, if we are really going to make the exercise worthwhile. In practice, this means that school improvement activities are frequently small-scale and focused. This is not to say that whole-school development is not possible, but to accept that the time and complexity involved in carrying through whole-school review militate against data collection and analysis on this scale. What seems more likely, and more appropriate to the current educational climate, is the acceptance that school improvement will come about in a rather uneven way through a range of different initiatives, with different inquiry processes supplying the data (Hargreaves and Hopkins, 1991, p. 33):

> It is advisable to carry out a series of small-scale focused or specific audits in key areas and in implementing the action plans that may result from these enquiries. A planned series of specific audits creates a *rolling programme* which provides a picture of the school built up over successive years.

Thus, while the pattern of improvement may be uneven, it can nevertheless be resourced and supported and will influence the whole school over time.

Central to this book is the proposition that certain conditions, if they can be created within the school, will provide an environment in which school improvement will flourish. The systematic collection and use of school-based data is one such condition, and there is growing evidence for its importance (Wilson and Corcoran, 1988, p. 20):

> The Californian Study (Overcoming the Odds: Making High Schools Work) found that more effective schools were clearer about their indicators of success, and used data to assess their progress more frequently, and conducted diagnostic assessment of students more regularly.

This commitment to inquiry was also listed as a feature of unusually effective schools by Levine and Lezotte (1990). Most recently, Levine (1992, p. 34) has pointed out that school improvement is a process which needs to be 'data-driven in the sense that appropriate information should be collected and utilized to guide participants in preparing and carrying out plans for improvement'.

But what does this look like in practice? Vignette 10.1 offers one example. Robin Dixon, of Tong School, Bradford, outlines how a school improvement initiative has been carried forward in the school, highlighting the important role played by data collection and interpretation as the initiative developed. The initiative involved a school-level project focusing on ways in which pupils' personal development could be fostered through the development of classroom materials and activities. The project has been carried out over a school year, during which time it has been coordinated by a small group of staff. However, as the vignette makes clear, the project drew heavily on data available before the year started, and will leave an important legacy of data available to inform school planning in the subsequent year. It also drew in most members of staff at some point through the year, as data sources, data gatherers, data interpreters and planners, using the school-based data generated. Finally, the staff are functioning as implementers — carrying the results of their collective inquiry and reflection back into the classroom in the form of new approaches and materials.

Vignette 10.1 Using data to inform planning processes

Embarking upon a whole-school project concerned with personal development required a focus with which all members of staff, or at least a good majority of them, could readily identify. The project team looked at and analysed the data that were already in the school at that time with a view to identifying what focus might be achieved.

The solution was not that far away. A working party had just completed a report on the curriculum. This highlighted the issue, through their own deliberations and, more importantly, through the results of a questionnaire filled in by 85 per cent of the staff on an individual basis. Prior to this the LEA had conducted a review of special needs provision which later prompted a more detailed and searching review in school. The latter had included a questionnaire filled in by departments. The final piece of the data jigsaw was a feedback document from a whole-school training day on special needs. On their own these documents were important enough, but put together they produced a heady cocktail that was too good to resist. The project team recognized that a focus was emerging from these documents, namely one of access to the curriculum for all pupils.

The project team presented the focus to staff at an evening meeting. The data collection activity which followed this stage was fast and furious but allowed staff to develop their own individual ideas. A questionnaire to all staff brought up issues about staff involvement in school development activities. This was followed immediately by an open-ended invitation to staff, via a response sheet, that proposed a series of general areas of study that staff might be interested in. Both of these were to be filled in anonymously, giving the staff an opportunity to think around the problem and report their activities. The format was very simple and designed to make responding straightforward.

These data were analysed by the project team, who produced a series of generic groupings of staff, allowing people to opt into a group that would comprise those with similar objectives. These groups met and a series of twenty-three sub-groups formed over a period of two weeks, during which each individual project group filed a simple pro forma outlining the objectives of their projects.

Thus far the project team had tried to ensure that all responses from staff had been in the form of questionnaires, short-sentence responses, small dialogue boxes and memos not exceeding fifty words, so as not to make unreasonable demands on their time.

A training day on action planning led by an external lecturer in education was organized at this point. It was felt to be a very worthwhile session, resulting in individual project action plans that were detailed in terms of planned activities, expected outcomes and resources required. The project was up and running.

An interim report giving an overview of progress to date was written by the project team, outlining the whole-school approach and some common issues and problems. Within three weeks of this report the project team wrote individual reports based on the data that were held for each project. Even so, discussion was required with many members of staff to make sure that the data were giving a true picture of what was happening.

The volume of data held by the project team was at this stage getting rather burdensome. So to make sense of the range of data held and reduce it if possible, an analysis of each project was made, identifying common elements. This analysis and the individual reports required that all data had to be re-read and synthesized by the project team. This process helped them in developing future plans for INSET and the evaluation phase of the project.

The final stage of the year's work was brought about by the idea of a celebration of the hard work put into the project by the staff. Each individual group has agreed to write an evaluation based on a common framework and in addition produce a display for the 'big day' when all will assemble, with invited dignitaries, friends and colleagues. This will be the very final piece of data and will inform us of the work that has gone on in the classroom as a result of the project. I am, as of now, charging up the batteries on my minicorder to record some of the verbal data that will be in evidence during the party. This will be added to the notes, fleeting conversations (unrecorded), essays, reports, resumés, demands, pleas, diatribes, lists, charts and minutes that have accumulated over the year. However, the most important pieces of data are the classroom outcomes, as they are the raison d'être of the *project. The principal driving force of all the projects has been to develop new materials and test them in the classroom.*

The function of the data development throughout this project has been to support the staff in their research, to inform each other of our progress, to simplify the process of informing interested parties, to aid the project team in managing the wide range of activities, and, above all, to log the project in a simple and undemanding way.

The final piece or pieces of data will be 'documents' that will inform the way ahead. Hopefully, the experience of collecting and analysing data we have gained will help the new project team that will be 'on line' next year.

This account shows how school improvement can be facilitated through focused data gathering. It also shows how important are other conditions, such as leadership and staff development, and how much more powerful the conditions become when they combine. It underlines, too, the role *each* member of staff can play in this process. Indeed, much of the impact of this initiative on the school stems from the opportunity for all staff to become involved, and much of the impetus for experimentation by staff arises from their own involvement as data sources and data analysers. Perhaps most important, the experience staff gain through this one, highly focused, classroom-centred initiative adds to their understanding of the importance of inquiry and reflection by teachers, thus increasing both their capacities and confidence to engage in similar school-based developments in the future.

The experience from Tong School also shows that 'data' can comprise several different types of material: 'objective' information provided by an LEA or other external review (Table 10.1); 'formal' internal review (perhaps less objective, but described as 'more searching'); staff surveys; 'brainstorming' sessions; notes; and fleeting (unrecorded) conversations. It is important to recognize that initiating formal or semi-formal procedures for inquiring into a particular aspect of school life does not create a 'new truth' — it does not invalidate those data which already exist in documents and records, and also in the minds and experiences of staff and pupils. Rather it should seek to complement and draw together such information into a richer and more detailed picture in which comments, discussions, observations and perceptions are used to enhance the kind of data which an audit or a measurement-centred approach can supply. Currently this activity has been prompted in a number of schools as a result of involvement in quality management initiatives. Such initiatives are most common in the post-compulsory sector — incorporated status for further education establishments has brought with it the need for some form of business plan. A feature of these plans seems to be a commitment to the introduction of a quality management programme throughout the establishment. British Standard (BS) 5750 is the most widespread approach to quality management at present, though schools and colleges are also beginning to experiment with total quality management (TQM) programmes.

The use of such programmes originated in the engineering industry as a method of ensuring that organizational processes and transactions conformed to a previously specified quality or standard. It has spread to a large number of manufacturing and service organizations as a certifiable quality indicator.

Table 10.1 *Using outsiders as a source of data*

Advantage	Limitations	Sources of advice/examples
Impartiality: outsiders will not be associated with particular areas of school performance	*Lack of 'local' knowledge*: outsiders may not be aware of the school's history, traditions, etc.	Gray (1988)
Different perspective: outsiders will not necessarily share the assumptions and rationlizations which are present in the school's thinking	*Personal agendas*: some of those who act as external consultants bring with them their own views and interests to promote	Stillman and Grant (1989)
Informed view: some outsiders, because of their own work, will have experiences and ideas which can be valuable to the school	*Credibility and trust*: school staff will need to accept the competence of the outsiders used, and to feel secure about the process	HMI/Scottish Education Department (1988a, 1988b)
Little demand on school resources: normal work patterns will be largely unaffected	*Cost constraints*: some external consultants will need to be bought in	Cabinet Office (1981)
	Time-scales: existing reviews by outsiders (e.g. inspection) may not match the school's review schedule	Winkley (1985) Becher *et al.* (1981) Millman (1981) Pearce (1986)

Adapted from West and Ainscow (1991).

Organizations which adopt BS 5750 are subjected to regular review or audit by an accrediting body, and in order to retain the British Standards Kitemark must be able to demonstrate that quality management procedures are in place. Strong support for this approach from the Training Enterprise Councils has stimulated interest among educational organizations, and the British Standards Institution has responded to this interest by publishing guidance, for educational organizations interested in gaining accreditation, which covers four aspects of the quality cycle: management responsibilities; the use of personnel and resources; the creation of quality systems; and relations with 'customers'.

King Harold Grant Maintained School, Waltham Abbey, is one of the first secondary schools to be awarded BS 5750 registration. In Vignette 10.2 Frances Howarth and Malcolm Wright describe how the school's commitment to the identification of quality systems took them, via an initial focus on teacher appraisal, into the scrutiny of one aspect of the school's performance: the development of pupils' basic numeracy skills.

Vignette 10.2 King Harold Grant Maintained School, Waltham Abbey

The school was looking for a team approach to teacher appraisal that focused on outcomes for pupils. We wanted to generate a quality improvement process that:

147

- *focused on how teams operate together;*
- *unleashed the potential that all staff have to apply their experience to solve problems facing their team;*
- *generated self-managing teams who have an understanding of their individual and collective responsibility for delivery quality in their area.*

We asked for volunteers to form a steering group. Fourteen members of staff came forward. They had visited a range of organizations and industries noted for their team approaches to quality improvement. Drawing all the data together, a model was generated with our school context in mind. Four teams piloted the model, of which the maths department was one. The model required the whole school — parents, staff, support staff and governors — to reaffirm in the form of mission and vision statements what the school was about. The team selected one of the vision statements and identified one or two main targets that would be the focus of their work over a specified and agreed period of time:

The quality of education and commitment to academic achievement encourages students and staff to achieve their highest potential.

The team target was to raise the standard of basic numeracy across the curriculum for Years 7 and 8. Two key result areas were:

1 *To improve numeracy test scores by 10 per cent.*
2 *To enable pupils to feel more confident and secure using numeracy skills across the curriculum.*

Once the time-line and agreed target focus were set, a snap-shot survey was completed. All staff were asked to comment on Year 7 and 8 pupils' numeracy competency as revealed within their specific curriculum area. These data were analysed, revealing an interesting range within the year groups, ranging from 'lacking in confidence' to 'reasonably confident'. A base-line test was administered to all Year 7 and 8 pupils to establish a measurable starting point that would be used in the evaluation.

The team came together and discussed what evidence they would expect to see to ensure that the basic level of confidence and competency had increased. Performance indicators were set once areas of weakness within existing provision and among individual pupils had been identified. Good practice was shared in terms of strategies staff had used in the past, which could now be formalized and used across the whole team. Individual staff set individual targets related to the team targets. They also agreed on what would be used as evidence of individual achievement, which they would bring to a final review meeting when the team would assess the extent to which the team target had been met. The date for this meeting was set.

A range of strategies was devised. Staff generated over a hundred specific worksheets to target pupils, groups of pupils and classes who, from the test, had been diagnosed as having a weakness in certain areas. Specific lessons were drawn up on aspects of numeracy skills that would be used across the curriculum. From cross-curricular skills mapping, curriculum areas had already been identified where cross-skill competency would be needed. These specific lessons drew all the class (but in smaller groups) out of the School Mathematics Project individualized scheme that the school generally operates.

All pupils were tested at the specified time to discern the extent to which the team had

Table 10.2 *Results of the King Harold School quality improvement process*

Class	Class average		% improvement
	January	March	
7FWY	52.2	65.0	24.5
7ASF	54.1	64.0	18.3
7ASF	48.3	64.0	32.5
7LGK	56.7	62.0	9.3
7LPS	48.5	62.0	27.8
8LYT	56.3	69.0	22.6
8LPM	59.0	70.0	18.6
8FDH	52.3	71.8	37.3
8FJH	54.6	64.0	17.2
8AJS	62.7	74.0	18.0
8AFG	58.3	71.0	21.8

met its target. The results are shown in Table 10.2. Only one class failed to achieve a 10 per cent increase, and they had started with a good performance score. There was an 18 per cent increase overall. One class went up 37 over per cent.

The review meeting took place at which individual staff members publicly reviewed their targets and the extent to which they had been realized. The team co-ordinator generated an agreed statement that highlighted achievements to date and the need to maintain the level of provision over the coming months. One lesson every two weeks to address cross-curricular numeracy skills has now been established for Year 8, and one per week for Year 7.

The process was successful for the following reasons:

- *Motivation lay with the team, in the invitation to come on line.*

- *Leadership empowered the team. The coordinator for this project was not the usual team leader.*

- *The vision building was generated by all the staff who work on the site. Team targets, in aligning effort with the vision statements, made staff feel they were all moving in the same direction. It gave cohesion to the work of their team.*

- *Time was spent on it. The process can be applied to any focus — it is a way of approaching task developments facing the team — but finding time is vital.*

- *From the outset, staff had a very clear idea of what was expected in respect of the given area. Understanding has been gained as to what the developments/outcomes look like in practice, and this enabled good practice to be shared and reinforced.*

- *The focus is outcome for students, so that the quality improvement focuses on the classroom and curriculum delivery. Teachers are meeting and discussing aspects of their classroom practice in the light of real data.*

- *Staff reflect on their own practice and select their own targets in relation to the team target set. The motivation comes from the staff members themselves.*

This account demonstrates how powerful a force for improvement school-based inquiry can be, underlining the sense of empowerment teachers feel when

Table 10.3 *Using classroom observation as a source of data*

Advantages	Limitations	Sources of advice/examples
Provides information on teacher behaviour: allows access to data about teaching styles and approaches	*Restricted focus:* appropriate for reviewing only certain aspects of school life	Croll (1986)
Provides information on pupil response: allows access to data about pupil attitudes and behaviours within the classroom	*Data recording and analysis:* data can be difficult to classify and summarize	Delamont (1983)
Stimulates reflection: those being observed will tend to think hard about their own classroom practice	*Judgemental:* it can be difficult to maintain a neutral stance rather than making judgements about what is being observed	Flanders (1970)
Gives feedback to teachers: it can be used to provide developmental feedback to teachers as well as to review pupil experiences	*Time-consuming:* classroom observation takes time to prepare and conduct	Hopkins (1993b)
Benefits observers: observing colleagues in action can be a powerful factor in personal development	*Threatening:* some teachers find the presence of another adult in the classroom disturbing	Hook (1981)
	Distortion: the presence of an observer can change the normal pattern of classroom interaction	Anderson and Burns (1989) Acheson and Gall (1980) Galton (1978)

Adapted from West and Ainscow (1991).

actively involved and able to influence. It also illustrates the importance of a school-wide strategy for review and development. The 'answers' the teachers came up with were their own, grounded in their own inquiry and interpretation processes, but the impetus to engage in inquiry stemmed from a school-level commitment to quality review. Even under the present pressures for change, King Harold School has found time to impose its own agenda on development activity within the school — in fact thus far some seventy-five specifications have been evolved. Clearly the amount of effort which goes into producing such quality standards would not be possible if it was seen as an additional burden: it has been possible because quality management is seen as a vehicle for securing the school's agreed policies. The outcome is teachers who work not harder, but more effectively. The collection, analysis and appropriate use of school-based data is a key to the more effective use of staff time and energies.

Of course, instructive as the examples from Tong School and King Harold School are, they are only examples. There are many aspects of school's functioning which can benefit from systematic review. Correspondingly, there are many different approaches to inquiry which can be used. Table 10.3 lists some of the advantages and limitations of an increasingly important and frequently used method of data gathering in schools, classroom observation.

What matters is that review methods are selected which match the needs of the inquiry. The final part of this chapter offers some advice on data collecting which we hope will help schools to identify, collect and make sense of information that can promote school improvement and develop teacher skills.

CHOOSING INQUIRY METHODS

How, then, can the school make best use of inquiry and reflection? There is a wide range of possible inquiry methods and the aim must be to choose one which is appropriate to the purposes at hand. This choice is likely to be influenced by the following factors:

1 *The nature of the topic that is under review.* Some topics will be relatively straightforward, thus lending themselves to be examined by methods that involve simply the gathering of factual information. So, for example, a review of how frequently a resource area is used at particular times in the week may be undertaken by recording use on some form of tally sheet. However, many aspects of school life require much more complex and sensitive methods if they are to be reviewed. Often matters of policy will be perceived in different ways by different members of the school community. Consequently, understanding these policies requires us to find ways of taking account of these multiple perspectives.

2 *Contextual features of the school.* Schools vary from one another in many ways. Apart from obvious differences in size, shape and location, there is an individuality in each school arising from its traditions and the collective experiences of its staff and pupils. In choosing an appropriate method for a particular review, therefore, it is necessary to take account of this individuality. A method that will be ideal for one school organization may cause very negative reactions in another.

3 *The level of previous knowledge and experience available.* When a school is seeking to review an area of policy about which it already has considerable experience, it is likely that the emphasis will be on collecting and making sense of knowledge that is already present. Procedures for drawing together information can be based on structures and category systems drawn from this experience and knowledge. If, on the other hand, the matters to be reviewed are relatively new to the school, a more open-ended perspective may be appropriate. This means that those involved in the review may have to collect general information without having a clear focus to their investigations.

4 *The management style adopted in the school.* If it is to be conducted in way that will facilitate further action, it is important that the inquiry is carried out in ways that will be comfortable for

those involved. Consequently it is important to adopt approaches that are consistent with the school's usual ways of doing things. An inquiry that necessitates high levels of participation in a school that is normally characterized by a directive management style, for example, is likely to run into difficulty.

Keeping these four factors in mind, methods for inquiry should be chosen that:

- relate to the questions that need to be answered;
- are feasible in the time that is available;
- will be acceptable to those who are likely to be involved;
- are not too disruptive to the day-to-day life of the school.

It also makes sense to review the methods themselves, in order to be aware of their strengths and weaknesses. Common sense would suggest that whatever approach is used will have its limitations. To be aware of such limitations is a starting point for assessing the value of the information that is collected.

MESSAGES

In this chapter we have argued that the processes of inquiring and reflecting on practice create conditions which foster school improvement initiatives. In particular we suggest that:

- systematic collection and interpretation of school-based data are at the core of school improvement;
- in the current climate of educational change there is a particular need for schools to have effective strategies for reviewing the progress of policies and initiatives;
- all teachers have a role to play in data-collection and analysis activities.

Chapter 11

Leadership

Those writing about effective schools make frequent reference to the importance of leadership. As long ago as 1977 HMI opined, of each of the 'ten good schools' featured in the first publication of the influential 'Matters for Discussion' series (DES, 1977), that:

> What they all have in common is effective leadership and a 'climate' that is conducive to growth ... Emphasis is laid on consultation, teamwork and participation, but without exception, the most important single factor in the success of these schools is the quality of leadership of the head.
>
> (p. 36)

This observation (interesting in that it separates out the use of teams and a participative approach to decision making, thus presenting leadership as a series of personal qualities rather than a process in which many can share) has been echoed and amplified in many publications addressing school effectiveness since. Persell *et al.* (1982), in a review of research into what constitutes effective leadership in schools, note that this emphasis on the *person* is frequently mentioned — it seems that 'strong personalities', 'dynamic' and 'energetic' are descriptions often associated with successful school leaders. However, their review also begins to map out wider aspects of the head's role — for example, in relation to climate-building and consultation procedures — which have come increasingly to be associated explicitly with effective leadership.

This broadening of interest in and understanding of the head's leadership role parallels the pattern of development of leadership theory generally. Readers familiar with writing about leadership as a general management issue, rather than a school-related one, will recognize this pattern, and the growing links between industrial and educational models (Murphy, 1991, p. 13):

> Advocates for school restructuring have found support for fundamentally different methods of operation from modern management theory and from activities in the corporate sector ... Faced with a series of problems not unlike those confronting schools — diminished product quality, low employee morale, unhappy consumers — businesses looked inward to see how the most successful of their group were operating ... By and large, it was discovered that the most effective corporations had transformed their businesses by decentralizing operations — by pushing decisions down to the level of the organization in closest contact with the customer, by reorienting

their management philosophy from control to empowerment, by establishing scrupulous reputations for attention to quality, and by changing their views of workers — from property of the company to partners in the corporate undertaking ... In short, they had restructured themselves from more hierarchically organized units to more fluid and organic systems. These lessons are now being held up to schools, especially by corporate managers ... as blueprints for educational reform. There is considerable pressure on educators to adopt these blueprints and transform school operations consistent with the organizational revolution occurring in the private sector.

Murphy (1991) summarizes this development as follows:

- initial interest in the personal qualities and characteristics of 'successful' leaders which results in *personality* or *trait* theories of leadership;

- increasing focus on what it is that leaders actually do — are there some behaviours and approaches which are consistently associated with successful leadership? Such inquiries support the development of *behavioural* theories of leadership;

- growing awareness that task-related and people-centred behaviours may be interpreted quite differently by different groups and in different contexts, prompting explanation of how the particular context might best be accounted for within a general theory, and resulting in a variety of *situational* approaches to leadership;

- most recently, emphasis on the links between leadership style and the culture of the organization — a movement away from the notion of leadership as a series of transactions within a given cultural context and towards a view of leadership as *transformational*, having the potential to alter the cultural context in which people work.

Of course, this shift in thinking about leaders and leadership is neither an even nor a linear process. Nor should we assume that progression from one way of conceptualizing leadership to the next necessarily means rejecting the validity of the previous approach; it is wiser to view such development as the addition of new layers of understanding rather than alternatives. This means, for example, that HMI were probably right in identifying the leadership qualities of headteachers as an important variable; but we need to recognize that it is only one variable, and that even those who start with a set of appropriate personal qualities are likely to become more effective still if they have a range of appropriate behaviours to select from, have some knowledge of and sensitivity to situational variables, and are able to conceptualize links between leadership and culture. As Owens (1987, p. 156) points out:

Recent research in school — such as reported in Ernest Boyer's *American High School*, Theodore Sizer's *Horace's Compromise*, and John Goodlad's *A Place Called School* as well as more popular portrayals of good schools, such as Sarah Lawrence Lightfoot's *The*

Good High School — have strongly underscored the importance of managing schools so that teachers in them feel that they belong to effective work groups, feel good about the work they do, and feel that they achieve something on the job that is worthwhile. From such research, it is becoming increasingly clear that the leaders of excellent schools take care not only to preserve the traditions that may happen to have been inherited from the past, but they set about the building of new higher-order traditions. In this regard, findings from research in schools seem to parallel findings being reported from studies in the corporate world such as in John Naisbett's *Megatrends*, Thomas Peters' and Robert Waterman's *In Search of Excellence*, and Terrence Deal's and Allan Kennedy's *Corporate Cultures*.

Leadership through the development of an organization's culture means building behavioral norms that exemplify the best that a school stands for. It means building an institution in which people believe strongly, with which they identify personally, and to which they gladly render their loyalty. All of this gives meaning to the work that they do, gives it significance, and this — as we know — is highly motivating.

One outcome from this increasing emphasis on the links between school effectiveness and leadership as a process variable is the growing recognition that a school which looks to the headteacher as the single source of direction and inspiration is severely constrained. It is dependent on a single individual's supply of intellectual, emotional and physical energy — it is restricted by a single imagination. But often school structures reinforce this somewhat limited view, confusing what is essentially a hierarchy of roles with the real distribution of knowledge and skills. We believe that research into effective schools provides clear evidence that challenging this traditional order and promoting a more dynamic and decentralized approach to leadership have often been associated with school improvement. Anne Jones (1987, p. 10) summarizes the implications of this recent reassessment of the head's leadership role:

> giving other people genuine authority does not mean giving up one's own authority; empowering others does not mean enfeebling oneself; encouraging others to give creative leadership does not mean abdicating from having ideas of one's own; giving others real responsibility does not mean leaving them to sink or swim, but rather to support them in developing the best possible way of going forward.

The exercise of such leadership by a headteacher involves a significant shift away from structure as control — rather, structure becomes the vehicle for empowering staff, a network which informs and supports staff as they seek to bring to life the values and goals of the school community in its day-to-day activities.

Beare *et al.* (1989) map these recent developments in thinking about leadership, putting forward a set of generalizations about the leadership role which they evolve from studies in educational and non-educational contexts. They go

155

on to offer examples of what each generalization might look like in a school context (Beare *et al.*, 1989, p. 108):

Generalisation	*Illustration*
1. Emphasis should be given to transformational rather than transactional leadership	Principal takes action to change community attitudes towards school
2. Outstanding leaders have a vision for their organisation	Principal envisages school as a learning centre for whole community
3. Vision must be communicated in a way which secures commitment among members of the organisation	Principal seeks commitment of teachers in devoting time and energy to change community attitudes towards school
4. Communication of vision requires communication of meaning	'Community' is metaphor for school; Principal rewards related teacher activities
5. Issues of value — 'what ought to be' — are central to leadership	Principal has strong commitment to equity in terms of access to schooling
6. The leader has an important role in developing culture of organisation	Principal involves members of community in all ceremonies at the school
7. Studies of outstanding schools provide strong support for school-based management and collaborative decision-making	School policy is determined by group representing parents, teachers, students and community at large
8. There are many kinds of leadership forces — technical, human, educational, symbolic and cultural — and these should be widely dispersed throughout the school	Planning for the various programmes in school carried out by teams of teachers, each having its own leader
9. Attention should be given to institutionalising vision if leadership of the transforming kind is to be successful	The vision of the school as a learning centre for the community is reflected in goals, policies, plans, budgets and activities
10. Both 'masculine' and 'feminine' stereotype qualities are important in leadership, regardless of the gender of the leader	Principal is sensitive and caring about personal needs ('feminine' stereotype); Principal fosters competitive, team approach in raising school's academic standing ('masculine' stereotype)

The development of a clear vision of where the school is going is central to the transformational approach — that is, shared vision rather than supervision, which provides for the coordination of individual efforts. The building of a school culture in which individuals at all levels enjoy a degree of autonomy in relation to their own work, and the possibility of bringing their own knowledge, skills and creativity to bear in resolving problems and pursuing opportunities, is the challenge facing school leaders. Of course, decentralization of decision making within the framework of agreed and clearly communicated school goals and priorities will not of itself improve schools — we need to be assured that staff do indeed possess the relevant knowledge and skills. Our own experience is that capability is widely distributed within schools, though this is not always understood by senior staff. One consequence of this has been the tendency to designate individuals to fulfil leadership roles in relation to particular issues by dint of position rather than suitability. Since research findings from a range of work environments indicate that task-relevant expertise is a major determinant of leader effectiveness, we need to be willing to locate such expertise, or, from time to time, to develop it, if we hope to create a school in which leadership enjoys the confidence of the staff.

Malcolm Ward, headteacher of King Harold Grant Maintained School, Waltham Abbey, has made a deliberate effort to change both the way leadership operates and the way it is perceived within the school. In Vignette 11.1 he describes how his approach to leadership has developed over the past seven years, building towards the introduction of a quality management programme which the school expects to see accredited under BS 5750 during this year.

Vignette 11.1 One headteacher's reflections on leadership

The essential feature of good leadership is having the capability of employing the appropriate style in any given situation. This has meant for me a change in role over a period of time. Starting out as a new head I placed myself at the authoritative/manipulative end of the management spectrum with very little enable/open style coming through. The head at this point was the fount of all knowledge, setting the agenda for whole-school policy, directing the work of task groups closely, managing the outcomes so that a whole-school policy could be established — the school's development plan.

During the next five years team work and team responsibility were established. Progress was made towards the targets set in the development plan. Some measure of value sharing was established.

A second school development plan was established, this time with far less direction from the head and much more involvement of staff, governors and parent groups. This plan gave us the opportunity to set a variety of groups to work on short-term goals. More staff were willing to acknowledge that there was a genuine opportunity to influence the development of the school and therefore more willing to commit time and effort to task groups. This process of involvement continued, so that, by the time we undertook an effectiveness review three years ago, I was confident enough to involve all staff, governors, inspectors, and parent and pupil representatives. It was now clear to all that a school ethos had developed that was both confident and open in its nature.

The effectiveness review was carefully managed, but the outcomes were genuinely spontaneous and not contrived, as they would have been some years earlier. The developmental work that had led the school to this point guaranteed a constructive dialogue during the effectiveness review. A culture of participation had been firmly established and the notion of change being a process rather than an end was beginning to take root amongst staff.

During this seven-year period, senior managers and other representatives on the staff had taken a larger and larger part in setting the pace of change, with the head gradually letting go of the total control that he felt was necessary in the early years.

The dynamic effort of thus letting go led to the energizing of senior managers and others as they grasped opportunities to lead development in their own fields that contributed to the overall school targets. The latest development work that the school has been involved in required many more staff outside the senior management team to lead task groups. It is now possible to have task groups led by junior staff. The work on total quality and BS 5750 has been the most exciting and productive so far and the most significant in its potential for change. This work has touched all staff, with parts of it being led by a variety of people at different times and at different levels.

Senior managers have coordinated this work on a day-to-day basis, keeping the head fully in the picture on a weekly basis with developments. The input by the head is now only at a strategic and not at a hands-on level. It is only possible to make effective progress with work of this scope and significance if large numbers of staff are willing to take part in task groups. Staff are only willing to do so if they feel that they have a deal of autonomy within a general but clearly defined framework and that their efforts will lead to meaningful change.

This account underlines the importance of vision building and communication, both as a basis for empowerment and as a stimulus to participation. It also suggests that collaboration develops as an *outcome* from groups of teachers working together to secure common goals — the intention was not to develop collaborative patterns *per se*, but to create circumstances in which teachers could see the benefits to be gained from collaborating. Further, it suggests the process of collaboration altered the culture of the school, transforming it into a much more dynamic and self-questionning organization, in which staff were nevertheless more confident in engaging with the new uncertainties than they had been in the relative security of central direction.

But how did those staff who were newly empowered feel about this transformation? Mary Healy, a senior teacher in the school who has been a member of the senior management team during this period, reflects in Vignette 11.2 on what has happened to her own role and the roles of others as the leadership style of the headteacher has altered.

Vignette 11.2 Developing leadership in the school

Our whole-school approach to development necessitates the identification of needs, encourages a sense of ownership and enables us to develop appropriate strategies to accommodate development needs. This has not been achieved overnight; in fact, it has taken a number of years to move from an authoritative style of management to a much more flexible and autonomous approach. The guiding principles have been involvement, ownership and the belief that all contributions are valued and acted upon.

This process began some years ago with a review of the school's philosophy. As a senior management team we felt it was necessary to update and reaffirm our values and aims for the school. During this process we involved teaching and non-teaching staff, pupils, parents, governors and members of the local business community who had developed links with school. This activity enabled us to establish a team approach to our development work and introduced us to the concept of team responsibility.

The resulting school aims and values were documented and provided a focus and starting point for school development planning. We progressed over the next two years through a curriculum review and a school effectiveness review. We continued to develop our team-work approach, establishing research and development groups with long-term goals and steering groups/task groups with short-term goals. All members of staff had the opportunity to join these groups. Membership has always been on a voluntary basis, but as they become the established way of working they were viewed not only as a means of school development but also as a vehicle for the personal and professional development of staff. This in turn increased staff commitment in terms of their time and effort input; as did the fact that their recommendations were seen to be acted upon.

By the end of the effectiveness review we believed that the team approach with full staff participation was taking root and seen to be an effective approach. The management of these groups was also changing. Initially their tasks and organization were directed and the team leader was usually a senior member of staff. We were beginning to let the reins go, encouraging a wider group of staff to lead the teams, with back-up support and consultation from members of the senior management team. This enabled members of that team to work closely with a wide range of staff. Concurrently, our view of school goals was changing from one of 'will we ever get there?' to 'where shall we go next?'. A sense of capability and achievement was spreading through the school.

Most recent development work has centred on total quality. It has two main strands: the introduction of a quality improvement process, including team reflection and review; and gaining school accreditation in BS 5750, which sets out how an organization can establish, document and maintain an effective quality system. The focus has been on those processes that affect and impact upon the delivery of the curriculum and the outcomes for pupils. Through this process we are constantly reinforcing the culture whereby self-managing teams increasingly have an understanding of their individual and collective responsibility for delivery quality in their area. There is a greater sense of shared direction, and increased understanding of the role individuals and teams play in the organization of this. It has enabled us as an institution to tie together and manage our agenda in terms of:

- *development planning;*
- *aligning the work of all the various teams with that of the school;*
- *making explicit what we are about and what we are striving for (and as such it is a useful monitoring tool);*
- *broadening staff perceptions of what constitutes 'staff development', to embrace the opening up of one's own practice in a supportive environment and the sharing of ideas and successful approaches used.*

159

Staff are discussing and negotiating desired outcomes, which raises their understanding and increases commitment to improving individual and collective performance.

We believe that our approach to development work has had a major impact in terms of promoting the idea of leadership throughout the school, giving greater autonomy to teams and investing real responsibility in their work, and promoting a shared understanding of what we are striving for.

In getting this far a number of issues have emerged:

- *Full staff commitment and understanding must be earned, not assumed.*

- *Enabling change has to be a school priority; meeting time, INSET, training days and supply cover all need to be seen as part of the wider processes of school development.*

- *Good communication is essential — communication which informs all members of staff about proposals and decisions which affect them, and supplies information relevant to their own decision-making needs.*

- *Leadership is no longer centralized. It extends to and is shared by the staff group, encouraging self-direction and an increased (but shared) sense of accountability. All this is supported by encouraging debate and openness amongst staff.*

For us, effective leadership has involved embedding a culture within, rather than imposing a structure upon, our school.

We believe that the introduction of self-managing empowered teams is leading to raised esteem, morale and performance in individuals and teams.

Caldwell and Spinks (1992) have written in some detail about what Mary describes as 'embedding a culture'. They suggest that the creation of a culture capable of promoting and sustaining excellence has a number of implications for school leaders/headteachers:

- It is necessary to be able to describe and analyse the culture of the school.

- It is necessary to ensure consistency between the values and beliefs the school proclaims and the manifestation of the school's culture.

- We need to recognize that changing school culture takes time.

- It is helpful to be able to make links between what is happening in the school — seeing the larger picture.

- The capacity to cope with continual change needs to be built into the culture.

- Leadership must function at technical, human and educational levels as well as the cultural level.

- As there are few individuals able to fulfil all these requirements, empowering others is necessary for the development of the organization. It is also desirable for the development and motivation of individuals.

The King Harold example begins to show us what can happen in a school when empowerment is extended.

A commitment to participation in the leadership process seems to grow from the headteacher's commitment to securing participation — once staff believe the invitation is authentic then the quality of individual involvement increases. However, the building of openness and trust hinges on the quality of the communication which is established alongside and around the decentralization of decisions. This communication needs to flow upwards and sideways as well as down, and to be seen as an important part of the influence process — where information replaces authority as the basis for decision making, additional information inevitably changes the equation and sometimes the decision. Nurturing such an influence pattern is difficult in the larger school, where groups and individuals do not always meet one another regularly; it may be even harder in the smaller school, where staff see each other daily and patterns of headteacher patronage are well established.

Carol Robinson, headteacher of William Ford Church of England Junior School, Dagenham, describes in Vignette 11.3 how she set about transforming staff expectations of leader behaviour in such a context.

Vignette 11.3 Establishing a just new leadership style

I came to the school in January 1990, at the same time as the deputy headteacher. I had not met the deputy headteacher until 2 January — his appointment was made by the previous headteacher. My previous experience was that of being a teaching head in a four-class junior school. I was therefore used to a relaxed atmosphere where everyone contributed to the development of the school, albeit informally.

When I met with the staff on that first INSET day I made all sorts of incorrect assumptions. I knew that previously staff had addressed the headteacher by her full title and there were real expectations of a formal and hierarchical structure being maintained. My chief aim was to gain the trust and respect of the staff as well as of the children. I knew that I had to take time to view and appraise 'where the school was', as well as how best to support the staff. My previous experience had taught me the folly of leaping in to change everything just to prove to myself that I could do the job. I made (and continue to make) several mistakes (like stating that I wasn't out to change things, when many of the staff were crying out for change).

I also had to realize the pressure put on the staff — they were to have two new people in the most 'powerful' positions in the school. They didn't know what to expect, and must have dreaded the spring term.

My over-riding aim was to take time and gain respect. Even getting staff to call me by my first name took time — I remember when the last person actually addressed me as 'Carol', it was quite a day for me!

But to leadership: I believe that everyone in a team has something to offer. Sometimes we need to listen to experience, sometimes to the person with expertise, sometimes to the person with vision and sometimes to the person who feels they are going under because they don't know what they are supposed to do. The leadership pattern established in the school was of the 'pyramid' type — head, then deputy head, then senior management and so on. What we discovered was that there were a few 'powerful' members of staff (not

161

necessarily members of the senior management team), with the majority seeing themselves as powerless. There were two sections to the school, the upper school and lower school, and the planning, except for one year group, was done very much by the individual for their own class. We soon recognized that we had to adopt a different approach to staff meetings to make it possible for everyone to participate — in fact, the first thing to establish was regular weekly staff meetings! We attempted to circulate information before the meeting so that we knew what we were going to discuss. I deliberately chaired the meetings so that no one felt under undue pressure.

It seemed that the people with posts of responsibility had been given little opportunity to develop their own expertise or to learn the management skills needed for the post. They also had not been given the opportunity to decide on resources in their own areas.

We soon identified the fact that although we were increasing the 'power' of the majority, we had taken away some of the power of a minority. I believe that this must have caused distrust and uncertainty for those teachers. However, all of these influences were happening below the surface. There was still not enough trust for open discussion to take place.

At the beginning of the autumn term 1990 we began to see the way ahead as encouraging planning to take place within year groups. We also had recruited probationers whose only experience was working in the way we suggested. I had at that stage written a provisional school development plan, which was submitted to the staff for comments. People were beginning to increase in confidence. The deputy headteacher took full responsibility for a Year 3/4 class — a significant departure for the only man on the staff, as well as someone in that position, to be with Year 3 or 4.

We had involved the LEA advisory teams, initially science and then maths, in the training of staff. There were after-school INSET sessions as well as in-school working alongside the class teacher and children. The main aim was to enable the class teacher to develop the expertise which would remain when the advisory team left.

We soon discovered that people were happy to be trained and thereby felt more able to share their expertise. We were able to view the introduction of the National Curriculum in a more balanced and less frantic way.

In the spring of 1991 the whole staff set out their priorities for the school development plan, and working groups began to take off. We were able to respond to a request to set aside school time for planning for the next term. Initially it was one session (a.m. or p.m.) at the beginning of the term; then we moved to one session at the end of the previous term; and we have now agreed that we allocate one day at the end of each term when the whole year-group team are released for planning for the following term.

At first we worked as a whole staff at core subjects — English, maths and science — but then people began to feel that this was taking too long. Working groups or subject coordinators, with advice and help from the authority, now prepare policies and schemes of work, which are presented to the whole staff for discussion and adoption as working documents. So much has been achieved in a relatively short time by very dedicated members of staff who work flat out all of the time to get the best for the children. The whole ethos is one of commitment and enthusiasm, although most of us are exhausted! It's an exhaustion that comes from achievement.

Once the staff became empowered, it became necessary to respond to their demands, knowing that any demands that were made were for the benefit of the children. It is the recognition that no one person has all of the answers, even if theoretically that person has the power, that has changed the way decisions are made.

The belief that a team committed to working together with the same aim has more to offer than an individual wielding power is a very basic one. It is also a very uncomfortable one at times, because the team can propose something that the head does not totally agree with, and yet the style of management means that we try it. Throughout the whole of this is a total unwritten dependence on the support and professionalism of the deputy head-teacher. So much is discussed and honest opinions are exchanged — we are not afraid to challenge one another and yet all of the time there is this interdependence, an essential ingredient of the development from hierarchy to team.

Carol's description underlines the importance of relationship building — the mutual trust which is needed for genuine empowerment to occur hinges on the quality of the relationship between head and staff — and also shows how trust builds once relationships are right. Communication is clearly important here too: new opportunities were created for staff to meet and talk about what is happening — occasions when the formal communications hierarchy gave way to whole school meetings where horizontal, vertical and, most importantly, upward communication were possible. But better-quality communication does not mean universal agreement — indeed, it has been 'very uncomfortable ... at times'. What is important is that although certain issues or discussions create discomfort, the staff feel able to raise them. This leads to a much healthier environment for handling conflict (that is, by acknowledging and exploring it) than is usually the case in leader-dependent cultures, where differences in view tend to be minimized or hidden, rather than viewed as opportunities for growth.

This account also demonstrates the motivational potential of shared leadership — the staff feel more enthusiasm and commitment to their jobs because they are actively involved in decisions about them, creating a strong sense of personal identification with organizational jobs.

Owens, as we have seen (pp. 154-5), suggests that beyond the functional aspects of leadership we have focused on here there are important symbolic dimensions, and also that leader behaviour is a central determinant of the kind of cultural structures which promote excellence in schools. Angus (1989) also acknowledges the links between leadership and culture, although he reminds us too that many of those who made this link look from a rather simplified or unproblematic definition of culture. One aspect of this is the tendency to assume that educational leaders will exhibit values which reflect the cultural expectations of the school's community (Angus, 1989, p. 70):

> By asserting and defending particular values, it is argued, leaders so strongly articulate and endorse their vision that it becomes also the vision of followers, and so bonds leader and followers together in a shared covenant ... which incorporates what then comes to be the non-negotiable core values and beliefs of the organization ... This core, according to the argument, amounts to an organizational culture in which effective leaders can utilize particular rituals and values 'to mobilize and focus the energy and commitment of employees on organizational goals' ...

The notion of an organizational culture that can be in a sense manufactured and manipulated, and the influence upon it of leaders, ... has been influential in attempts to define educative leadership ... According to Duignan and Macpherson for instance:

> ... educative leadership is part of the process of modifying or maintaining an organizational culture.... Educative leadership helps to articulate, define and strengthen those endearing values, beliefs and cultural characteristics that give an organization its unique identify in the minds of participants ... educative leaders use the tools of culture to build an ethos, to create shared assumptions about responsibilities and relationships, and to gain the commitment of groups to the achievement of tangible and intangible goals and objectives. (1987, pp. 51, 55)

As [has been pointed] out in criticism of the growing emphasis in administration literature on the importance of culture in the management of organizations, successful management has become as much a matter of getting the culture right as it is of getting the technology right. As [has also been pointed] out, the particular notion of culture being applied is regarded in this literature as curiously unproblematic. There is virtually no sense, for instance, of an anthropological concern with culture as a shifting and contested concept which is continually being constructed and reconstructed and which must be subjectively understood. Instead, there is only a managerial concern with the manipulation of and intervention in culture to shape it in ways that enhance the efficiency of the organization.

In both King Harold School and William Ford School we see how school leaders have begun to transform their ways of working so that the culture is, to a degree, shaped by the values and expectations of the teachers themselves.

Clearly, these transformations represent the first steps towards a more empowered and autonomous staff group, rather than its realization, but the willingness these school leaders have shown to begin to share the leadership process with colleagues points the way ahead.

MESSAGES

We began this chapter with the suggestion that vision building, relevant expertise, relationships and the quality of communication and participation are all factors in effective leadership. We have tried to illustrate within the chapter how such factors can be brought to bear within schools to create a new agenda for school leaders — that of transforming the school culture into one where leadership is spread widely among the staff group and all members of staff are capable of contributing.

To devise management arrangements that empower is a challenging task. Yet this challenge is already being attended to in many schools, since the pressures for change are creating a strain on the existing arrangements, and are leading governors, heads and staff to review traditional ways of managing and leading the school. Governors in particular are looking for new ways of working with the head and staff, which build upon the good relationships already established. Teachers are also realizing that the management of classrooms cannot be isolated from the management arrangements for the school as a whole. As budgets are delegated to schools, systems for managing finance and resources have to be created to complement or replace existing arrangements. The National Curriculum is leading to a new approach to the whole curriculum, to the deployment of teachers and to the organization of teaching, learning and assessment.

Schools that are more successful in coming to terms with change will clearly need more leadership. There will be visions to be identified, agendas to be built, new ways of working to be designed, and climates of problem solving and learning to be nurtured — among the many other major tasks. But there will be a need for better management as well. The school will inevitably become a more complex organization. More day-to-day interventions will be needed to make sure that the relevant teams have the resources to function effectively. Although the roles of teachers may expand and develop considerably, the head's role will be no less central. All heads need to become better versed in the skills of leading and managing change.

In a recent article on leadership Tom Sergiovanni (1987, p. 27) addressed the question, 'What motivates and inspires teachers anyway?' He argued that the rule of motivation basic to most of today's leadership practice is 'what gets rewarded gets done'. Though the rule works in practice, teachers end up working for rewards rather than for the job itself. A busy kind of leadership is required to sustain the rule. Leaders must constantly monitor the exchange of rewards for work, and guess which rewards make most sense for different people. As a result, teachers become increasingly dependent upon the rewards themselves and upon their leaders to motivate them. 'What gets rewarded gets done' discourages people from becoming self-managing and self-motivated.

We need, therefore, to develop within our schools a set of leadership practices which complement management behaviour, and bring life to the concepts of participation and collaboration, which are more often voiced than experienced. We believe that there are a number of aspects of leadership which will provide a basis for transforming the school, including:

- establishing a clear vision for the school;
- valuing task-relevant expertise;
- building positive relationships between leaders and followers;
- a commitment to widespread participation in decision making;
- two-way vertical and horizontal communication patterns;
- the acceptance that leadership is a function to which many staff contribute rather than a set of responsibilities vested in an individual.

Chapter 12

Coordination

Schools are not just buildings, curricula and procedures such as timetables. Much more importantly, schools comprise relationships and interactions among often quite large groups of people. How these interpersonal interactions are carried out largely determines how successful a school is in achieving its purposes.

In the literature on educational management (e.g. Weick, 1985), schools are sometimes referred to as 'loosely coupled systems'. The looseness of the coupling occurs because schools consist of units, processes, actions and individuals that tend to operate in isolation from one another. Loose coupling is also encouraged by the goal ambiguity that characterizes schooling. Despite the rhetoric of curriculum aims and objectives, schools consist of groups of people who may have very different values and, indeed, beliefs about the purposes of schooling. Weick uses the metaphor of football to illustrate the point. He describes a school as a soccer game in which players enter and leave the pitch at will, and attempt to kick the ball towards several goals that are scattered haphazardly around an oval, sloping field.

How, then, can such an organization be coordinated in order for those involved to work in a more efficient way? It does seem that relationships are the key to establishing greater coordination.

It has been suggested, as we have seen on pp. 132-4, that school relationships may be structured in one of three ways: individualistically, competitively or cooperatively (Johnson and Johnson, 1989). In schools with an individualistic form of organization teachers tend to work alone to achieve goals unrelated to the goals of their colleagues. Consequently there is little sense of common purpose, no sharing of expertise and limited support for individuals. Furthermore, such schools often move towards a more competitive form of organization.

In a competitive system teachers strive to do better than their colleagues, recognizing that their fates are negatively linked. Here the career of one teacher is likely to be enhanced by the failure of others within the school. In this win-lose struggle to succeed it is almost inevitable that individuals will celebrate difficulties experienced by their colleagues, since they are likely to increase their own chances of success.

Clearly, therefore, the organizational approach which is most likely to create a positive working atmosphere is one that emphasizes cooperation. The aim must be to encourage a more tightly coupled system within which the efforts of individuals are coordinated in order to maximize their impact. In such a school, individuals are more likely to strive for mutual benefit, recognizing that they all share a common purpose and, indeed, a common fate. Furthermore, individuals know that their performance can be influenced positively by the performance of others. This being the case, they feel proud when a colleague succeeds and is recognized for professional competence.

A school that is based upon a cooperative structure is likely to make good use of the expertise of all its personnel, provide sources of stimulation and enrichment that will foster their professional development and encourage positive attitudes to the introduction of new ways of working. In short, it is well on the way to becoming a learning-enriched school.

Having said all of that, we feel a word of warning is necessary. Establishing a cooperative way of working is not a simple matter, partly because it is necessary to do it in ways that do not reduce the discretion of individual teachers. Teaching is a complex and often unpredictable business that requires a degree of improvisation. Teachers must have sufficient autonomy to make instant decisions that take account of the individuality of their pupils and the uniqueness of every encounter that occurs. What is needed, therefore, is a well-coordinated, cooperative style of working that gives individual teachers the confidence to improvise in a search for the most appropriate responses to the situations they meet. In other words, we are seeking to create a more tightly coupled system without losing loose-coupling benefits (West and Ainscow, 1991).

In this chapter we look at the following ways in which schools can encourage greater coordination:

- staff working groups and task groups;
- communication networks;
- key individuals as coordinators.

STAFF WORKING GROUPS AND TASK GROUPS

Working groups

Ultimately the success of a school depends upon the success teachers have in working with their classes. There is little doubt that teachers teach better when they experience support from their peers. In many schools, however, little emphasis is placed on developing the coordination mechanisms that will encourage such support. As a result teachers may feel threatened, isolated and alienated.

Establishing various kinds of staff working groups is a way of providing teachers with the opportunity to share ideas and to support each other's efforts to improve the quality of education provided for all pupils. Working groups can, therefore, provide the basis for coordination and support throughout a school. More specifically they can:

- provide help, assistance, support and encouragement as colleagues seek to improve their practice;
- serve as an informal support group for sharing, letting off steam, and discussing problems;

- serve as a forum in which more experienced colleagues can help others as they plan developments;
- create a setting in which camaraderie and shared success occur and are celebrated.

Working groups of this type succeed when they are carefully structured to ensure not only active participation by members but also, where possible, concrete products (for example, lesson plans or teaching materials) that can be used later. The structure of meetings should point members towards increasing each other's expertise, in order that they do not degenerate into gripe sessions, destructive criticism of each other, or amateur therapy. Members need to believe that they sink or swim together, ensure that considerable face-to-face discussion and assistance takes place, hold each other accountable for implementing personal action plans between meetings, and periodically initiate discussion of how effective the group is in carrying out its mission (Johnson and Johnson, 1982). Task-oriented discussion, planning and problem solving, as well as mutual support, should dominate the meetings.

Recently Andy Hargreaves (1992) has pointed to some difficulties that may occur when a school attempts to improve coordination by means of increased collaboration. As we have seen, he notes the existence of four types of school culture: fragmented individualism, balkanization, contrived collegiality and true collaboration. Too often schools are characterized by two of these types: fragmented individualism, whereby teachers work in isolation, or, in larger schools, balkanization, in which sub-groups of staff may be in competition when major decisions or actions are necessary. However, Hargreaves also points to the potential dangers of contrived collegiality, involving a proliferation of unwanted contacts among teachers that consume scarce time with little to show for it. Rather what we should seek is true collaborative cultures that are deep, personal and enduring. These are not strings of one-shot deals; a culture of collaboration is central to the day-to-day work of teachers.

Task groups

Some staff working groups may be set up for more formal, policy purposes. Of course, some policy decisions can be made by governors or the management team alone. Other decisions may be made in a staff meeting after a few minutes of discussion. However, there are decisions that require much longer consideration before a recommendation can be formulated. In particular, school-wide issues call for careful review and planning involving the whole staff.

In such situations, a useful strategy is to appoint a task group representing the whole school that is given responsibility for considering the issues and planning the actions that the staff might take. For such a group to be successful it needs to be given clear goals, a time-scale and the resources required for it to function. Membership of such a group may be on a voluntary basis, but sometimes teachers are asked and expected to serve.

Some useful practical guidelines for setting up task groups (or forces) are provided by Johnson and Johnson (1989). Our experience is that many schools are using various types of staff group but that too often these become rather aimless talking shops, consuming time and, sometimes, reducing morale. What is proposed here is meant to be purposeful and cost-effective.

From our work with schools in the 'Improving the Quality of Education for All' (IQEA) project we have seen many examples of schools that encourage a high level of coordination through the use of staff working groups. These examples always result from careful planning along the lines we have described. In Vignette 12.1, Monica Adlem, deputy headteacher at Britannia County Primary School in Ipswich, describes how this is planned in her organization.

Vignette 12.1 The use of task groups

We are a large primary school with twenty-four staff. The use of staff groups has developed as an effective way of enabling staff to focus on planning and be engaged in the development of specific curriculum areas, while maintaining their involvement in the development of the whole curriculum and whole-school issues.

There are three parallel mixed-ability classes in each year group. Each year team of teachers is released for one half-day towards the end of the summer term so that they can make an overall plan of work for the coming year. Our school curriculum framework outlines the content for their plans. The year team decide how to group the subject content and in which order to teach it. This enables each team to work in the most effective way, making use of their expertise. They can also ask other subject coordinators for advice.

At the end of each term they are also released to make detailed plans for the coming term. One hour per week is included in the time budget for year team meetings. This enables them to refine and adjust their plans as well as to discuss any problems. The strength of the year team is in mutual support and inspiration. The time spent on planning is valued as enabling the more efficient use of time and resources during the term. It is also seen as helping to raise the standard of work produced in the classroom.

Monday is our regular staff meeting time. There is a sequence of staff meetings, middle management meetings (year coordinators and senior staff), staff INSET and curriculum groups. All staff are members of curriculum groups. Each year coordinator is also a subject coordinator. Our present curriculum groups are PSE, humanities, and aesthetic and creative. These groups change according to our priorities for development. The mathematics, science and language coordinators continue to develop their subject areas and these curriculum groups will be reconvened when necessary.

In the current climate of change, staff are working to implement and monitor National Curriculum requirements. The use of groups means that a few staff can concentrate on developing one subject area and construct policy statements and school guidelines to ensure continuity and progression. All policies and documents produced by any group must be discussed by the whole staff and amended if necessary before being passed to the governors for approval.

We were concerned that large time gaps were occurring between a group's producing draft policies or guidelines and these being discussed in a staff meeting. Also, with a large staff, we could not be sure that all staff felt able to contribute to the discussion, because of pressure of time and items on the agenda. We therefore started giving draft copies of the policies to the year coordinators for discussion within their year team. Each team can scribble their comments on the draft version, either during a team meeting or individually at a convenient time. This has proved to be a most effective way of getting useful responses from all members of staff. The revised draft is again given to year teams for comments. The senior staff approve the final version before submitting it to the governors. This process emphasizes the management role of year coordinators and ensures that all staff are fully involved in the decision-making process.

All staff are also involved in producing the school development plan. The curriculum groups and subject coordinators produce their own plans for the coming year. Whole-school issues can be raised by any member of staff. All staff discuss all aspects of the plan, something that we regard as essential if all staff are going to be committed to implementing it. After the whole-staff discussion, the plans are discussed by the senior management team and the middle management team so that the advantages and disadvantages of each element can be discussed and prioritized.

Our school development plan is organized on a financial-year basis, as many of the aspects will be dependent on money. Each coordinator is then allocated a budget to support his or her subject area.

The use of staff groups enables our staff to work more efficiently and effectively, to maximize the expertise available within the school and to develop their own professional skills. The effective use of teacher time is further enhanced by the support of non-teaching staff. A secretary does all the reprographic work; any duplicating handed in before school is ready by lunchtime. Teachers do not handle dinner money, they only count the numbers for school dinners, packed lunch or going home. A librarian is responsible for the children's library and the staff library. Any books or other resources purchased are catalogued by the librarian, who will also help staff with the preparation of material — labelling, covering, etc.

Our staffroom is also a resource base. All new resources are displayed there before going on to the shelves, so that staff are aware of what is available. Frequently, informal INSET takes place through discussion of problems and strategies. Staff are quite happy to ask for help from whoever has the relevant expertise, regardless of the 'allowance hierarchy'.

This format is not static but developing. Each year refinements or changes are made, either in response to staff requests or in anticipation of future needs. Our aim is to improve the quality of the education for our children. In order to achieve this we need all of our staff working together to provide a stimulating and cohesive curriculum with a happy and structured environment.

Monica's account is an excellent example of how effective working groups can be when they are well thought through. Particular features that should be noted are:

- **the way in which groups are constructed to ensure that all staff are involved;**
- **the allocation of time to support staff as they take on additional responsibilities;**
- **the accountability of individuals who are designated to take on coordination tasks;**
- **the attention paid to ensuring good communication between the various groups.**

COMMUNICATION NETWORKS

The issue of communication is a vital component of overall school coordination. In order for a school to organize itself to accomplish its goals, maintain itself in good working order and, at the same time, adapt to changing circumstances, sound procedures for communication are essential. Meetings must be scheduled, reports from task groups distributed; departmental meetings organized, and summaries of various activities written and sent round to all staff. All of these responses are structured communication opportunities. The communication network thus created determines the amount and type of information a member of staff will receive from colleagues.

In the IQEA project we have emphasized the importance of creating an effective communication network within schools. In particular we have stressed the importance of all staff being aware of progress related to project activities and decisions that require them to take particular actions.

Fullan (1991) stresses the importance of effective communication within a school during improvement initiatives. He notes that no amount of good thinking by itself will address the ubiquitous problem of faulty communication. Since change is a highly personal experience, and since schools consist of numerous individuals and groups undergoing different (to them) experiences, no single communication is going to reassure or clarify the meaning of change for people. A cardinal fact of social change is that people will always misinterpret and misunderstand some aspect of the purpose or practice of something that is new to them.

To be successful in coordinating developments in school, therefore, it is necessary to work at communication. A study of the theory of change indicates the importance of frequent, personal interactions as a key to success. Indeed, Fullan argues that two-way communication about specific innovations that are being attempted is a requirement of success. To the extent that the information flow is accurate, the problems get identified. This means that each person's perceptions and concerns get aired.

KEY INDIVIDUALS AS COORDINATORS

As staff become more involved in development activities, they become increasingly aware that they can take a broader view of their work. Overview becomes possible and longer-term plans are legitimate. In itself this becomes a feature of staff development and management training for all colleagues. At this stage it is crucial for the senior management team to take the risks inherent in devolving responsibility in order to foster this staff development process. It is also important that certain individuals take on specific coordination tasks.

Within the IQEA project we have recommended that schools should appoint at least two coordinators, at least one of them being a member of the senior management team. These coordinators, referred to as the cadre (see Chapter 7), take responsibility for the day-to-day activities of the project in the school. Watching the ways in which different coordinators have operated has confirmed our belief in the importance of the tasks they perform if school improvement initiatives are to be sustained. Vignette 12.2, by Les Fearns, the deputy headteacher of Marshalls Park Secondary School in Havering, illustrates this.

Vignette 12.2 The tasks of the coordinator

The school became involved in the IQEA project in June 1991. It was decided to involve three members of staff as the coordinating group, one of whom was to be a deputy head in order to give authority and management expertise to the school's involvement. I was keen to get involved personally as I felt that the processes envisaged by the project could be of benefit to the management of the school in general, not just with respect to making learning more effective. In particular, the emphasis on staff involvement in both planning and implementation of change was especially attractive.

In general, my role was:

- *to act as a link person between senior management and the project and to facilitate similar linking between the project and the staff in general;*
- *to provide for direct access to the management structure of the school for the project (for example, for resourcing and meeting times);*
- *to lead a cadre of three and to provide, with the other two members, initial frameworks for both the management of the project and the issues to be focused upon;*
- *to help facilitate amendments to the school management and development structure which would enable the outcomes of the school's involvement in the project to be more effective, and which would also be of benefit in making the planning process in the school more effective, open and accessible to all staff in general.*

With regard to the first three points above, a decision was made very early on with the two other initial staff representatives at the first IQEA session to set up a specific structure for managing our involvement in the project. It was at this stage that the need for a larger staff group, known as the expanded cadre, was felt. Such a group would allow for wider staff representation, and would also help deal with some problems of perception which had arisen early with the staff: concern that participation would mean extra work at a time when initiatives were mounting, that the project was a back-door way to introduce appraisal, and that the involvement of the school had taken place with insufficient staff consultation.

In the early phases, the expanded cadre was quite tightly directed. Working with the two cadre members, precise schedules were drawn up for each term, and targets were set prior to each meeting of the expanded cadre. To play down the role of senior management in the expanded cadre, the meetings were chaired by the staff member of the cadre, although items for the agenda were discussed fully prior to each session by the cadre. As part of this initial schedule, interviewing was suggested by myself and adopted by the expanded cadre for the first area of involvement. This allowed for a precise initial initiative to be used which was already on the school agenda and enabled a process of staff INSET, focused on small groups, to be implemented. Later, developing effective learning strategies was adopted by all the staff after a prioritization session.

To help make this more effective, through my working with the headteacher and senior management, training days were set aside for staff to work on IQEA-related issues, a residential weekend was resourced for the expanded cadre to help develop a group identity, and regular meeting time was allocated on the school calendar for meetings, both of the expanded cadre and for staff in general working on project-related issues.

However, it was clear to me from the start that the main value of involvement in the project lay in what it had to offer to the management structures of the school in general, and in particular with regard to perceptions among some of the staff concerning a lack of involvement and openness in connection with decision making and planning. Consequently, in discussions with the headteacher, it was decided to discuss with the school policy group ways of reforming its composition to reflect staff more fully and to enhance its role within planning. This resulted in the formation of the school development group, which now meets on alternate Wednesdays and focuses its attention on issues of planning. Working through this group, I also drew attention to the need for greater formal all-school involvement in the school development plan and its role in setting targets and structures for future effective planning and implementation of policy. A training day is now set aside each year for development planning to be discussed by all staff, and the drafting and planning from and with reference to the development plan are now established within the school management structure.

With regard to the project directly, the interviewing process was well received by staff as a consequence of the process used, which was based upon IQEA ideas. Its introduction has been more effective as a consequence. The expanded cadre has become much more confident, especially following the residential weekend, and there is good, positive discussion at its meetings. This was seen most clearly during the session in which the individuals spoke of their involvement before receiving the Certificate of Further Professional Study award.

From anecdotal evidence, the changes to the policy group and development planning have led to staff in general feeling more involved and able to participate in planning and decision making than in the past.

However, a number of aspects need to be considered at this stage:

- With regard to the second phase of the project (effective learning strategies), momentum has been harder to maintain. Partly as a consequence of general staff concern that National Curriculum assessment is now the priority which should be tackled above all else, staff have not seen the need to work so urgently on effective strategies. The original schedule which I drew up with the cadre was extended. With hindsight, the tighter timing should have been retained to keep staff working at a brisk pace. Matters concerning this were brought to a head in quite a vocal expanded cadre meeting, and amendments were made to the programme and initial plan as a consequence.

- Much time has been devoted to ensuring that staff were informed of what was taking place to ensure as much openness as possible. However, in the first year of the project, I should perhaps have taken more care to allay the concerns of fellow deputies about the work of the project and to keep them fully apprised of what was taking place, especially with regard to the changes to the management and planning structure.

- At the end of the first year, a number of issues combined to provide a significant episode for the project and school. The structural changes were now *taking effect within the management structure and the position of the school development group was now beginning to be established. However, this was resulting in changes to other groups which traditionally were predominantly involved in planning and decision making, such as the senior management team of deputies and senior teachers. Eventually a working relationship between the two was established, with both having defined roles, and this is proving both productive and effective for both. This, though, came after considerable discussion, and it was at this stage that the problem outlined in the previous point also came to a head. The outcome, however, has been positive, with greater communication and a good, structural, supportive relationship having developed between senior staff and the school development group. This has been crucial for the future progress of the school.*

- *As pressure on staff has mounted with regard to National Curriculum changes, there has been an increase in staff demands for time to be allocated to the administration of education. I feel that our established involvement in the project should now be used to protect time for staff to be able to plan ahead and to work on effective learning methods. Without our present involvement and staff expectations of it, such time would be harder to conserve from staff and for staff.*

From my involvement, I have learnt:

- *The need to work with a supportive team who get on with each other personally as well as professionally. The cadre was made up of staff who knew each other socially and who had already worked together on school visits. This made the management of the project much easier and allowed each cadre member to be that much more supportive of the others.*

- *That staff scepticism can be overcome, but only through involvement and trying to present as much professional integrity as possible. This means taking time to communicate and interact with staff, informally as well as formally.*

- *The need for long-term planning, especially where different groups of staff are concerned. There must be some concept of where you are going eventually.*

- *The need to communicate fully with everyone involved. One cannot rely on assumptions or perceptions being shared implicitly. Time needs to be spent cultivating staff at all levels.*

- *The importance to the project of having the support of senior staff, in both a personal and structural sense, to help ensure the effectiveness of what is being implemented, and for what is being done to be seen as a whole-school programme.*

As we see from Les Fearns's account, a coordinator needs to have clear views, but also to be able to listen to, and accommodate, the views of others. This flexibility will enable the coordinator to judge when to move things on, when to be willing to change the agenda and when to provide time and space for staff to explore ways forward. This implies that he or she will have a strong sense of personal security. The coordinator's function ought not to be that of control, but rather to provide guidance to staff as they seek to participate in constructive developmental activity. This guidance will be based upon:

- the coordinator's perspective on the overall aims and plans which exist in the school;
- the coordinator's knowledge of areas of developmental activity and expertise already in existence in the school;
- the coordinator's awareness of, and contact with, individuals and agencies that can provide external support and expertise.

A sensitive use of influence can often move people in directions which they would not themselves have chosen, but in directions which can be of greater benefit both to the school and to them. Above all, the coordinator needs to be involved in the activities of the group in order for empathy to exist, so that he or she can show encouragement and generate self-confidence within each member of the group.

At its most effective, the coordinator's work of facilitating, enabling and encouraging others may not be readily apparent in the outcome of the activity. This may be a source of some threat to a coordinator who feels the need to be seen to be effective.

As we have noted, with the appointment of a coordinator there is likely to be a significant change in the degree of delegation of power from senior management to the staff. This is particularly the case when a group of people are drawn around the coordinator to act in an advisory and planning capacity. A range of issues relating to INSET and to curriculum planning and development is likely to form the remit of such a group. The group may identify issues to address which have traditionally been the responsibility of members of senior management teams.

The effective functioning of the coordinator in this situation would appear to be crucially dependent upon the quality of delegation from the head, who needs to create a climate in which staff as a whole are able to respect and relate to the coordinator. It appears that this can best be achieved when:

- there is positive support for, and effective definition of the limits of, the responsibility of both the coordinator and any groups which may be established;
- all relevant matters are communicated to or channelled through the coordinator;
- the coordinator is able to feel supported by the whole of the senior management team;
- the coordinator's role is clearly understood by all of the staff;
- the staff are able to relate to him or her on a personal level.

The coordinator's effectiveness is likely also to depend upon the quality of the INSET and support that he or she has been offered. Consequently the provision of INSET support for the coordinators is a key element.

Many schools establish a staff development committee in support of school improvement initiatives. These committees are usually chaired by a coordinator. Their function includes identification of needs, together with planning and delivery of programmes to meet those needs. The coordinator is ideally placed, in sensitively harnessing the energy, knowledge and expertise of members, to link the outcomes of the committee's discussion and planning to the overall objectives of the school.

The existence of a staff development committee chaired by a coordinator provides a formal structure for the effective implementation of informal processes. In many schools the establishment of such a committee has been in addition to the existing consultative provision and, depending upon the status accorded to the committee, has significantly changed the role and function of other groups. For example, the head of one school now regards the staff development committee, which contains representatives from across the staff, as the group upon whose recommendations he bases many of his major decisions. The effect of this has been that individuals such as heads of departments have needed to accept some redefinition of role. The existence of a formal staff development committee can therefore be both a strength and a weakness.

There are, however, specific ways in which a staff development committee, as a formally recognized group, can support informal activity. Individuals or small groups of staff working together find it difficult to share information with others and to involve others in their work. These difficulties can be overcome by the provision of some formal support. The sharing and channelling of information through a coordinator can enable others to join in or benefit from the work of colleagues. In the same way, a coordinator can offer invitations or give guidance to staff, enabling them to undertake specific tasks on behalf of others. Such an invitation validates that member of staff in providing inputs to INSET programmes for groups of colleagues. A specific example of this in one IQEA school relates to a small group of teachers who, as a result of attending a course, became involved in a programme of paired observation. Formal requests to undertake a particular activity such as this can move it up the list of priorities for the individual involved, making action more likely. Sharing experiences via a coordinator and a staff development committee has enabled the group to expand and has provided a means by which their findings could be shared.

Whatever the status of the staff development committee, the coordinator will need to be the link between it and the formal consultative structures in the school. As coordinators, and staff development committees where they exist, become involved both in identification of needs and in planning and delivery of programmes, there is a need to identify in detail the source and nature of the power that is actually devolved to them. Whether proposals can be developed into programmes which can be implemented is a question which immediately focuses attention on resource availability — time, money, materials, expertise, energy — and the degree of control which the coordinator can exercise over these.

MESSAGES

Successful schools encourage coordination by creating a *collaborative environment* which encourages involvement, professional development, mutual support and assistance in problem solving. Such an approach should not, however, limit teachers' discretion to teach in ways that seem appropriate to the individual.

One important way in which such a collaborative way of working can be created is through the use of various forms of *staff group*. These need to be well organized in order to be effective. Poorly conceived group approaches consume precious time and can lead to reductions in morale. School-wide task groups set up to address particular policy issues or organizational problems can be a particularly effective response. However, such task groups must be carefully planned to ensure appropriate representation, accountability, sense of purpose and good use of time.

Successful coordination also requires an effective *communication network*. In addition to formal procedures it is important to emphasize frequent, personal interactions.

Given the complexity of life in schools, all of these coordination strategies need themselves to be coordinated. In this respect it is helpful to designate particular individuals who take on the role of *coordinators*. They should see their task as involving the coordination of both formal and informal processes.

In coordinating school improvement activities it is helpful to create the following conditions:

- policies that keep staff informed about development priorities;
- coordination of links and overlaps between activities;
- awareness of one another's responsibilities;
- informal contacts which contribute to work.

Chapter 13

Collaborative Planning

The quality of school-level planning has been identified as a major factor in a number of studies of school effectiveness. Such studies also regard the nature and quality of school goals as important. Purkey and Smith (1983), for example, list both collaborative planning and clear goals as key process dimensions. Caldwell and Spinks (1988) advocate goal-setting and planning as two of the phases of the collaborative school management model which emerged from the Effective Research Allocation in Schools Project (ERASP), linking these two activities within one cycle of the management process. Similar linkage can be found in the writings of Louis and Miles (1990) and Snyder and Anderson (1986).

Despite this emphasis on the centrality of planning, others have pointed out that schools frequently find it difficult to engage in high-quality planning activity — perhaps taking their lead from the headteachers in the NFER observational study who (Hall *et al.*, 1986, p. 205): 'in general, spent more time on "teaching activities" than on "leading professional" matters of curriculum and other educational policy; more time on "operations" and "human management" than on "educational policy".'

In their recent book about total quality management, Murgatroyd and Morgan (1993) suggest a number of traditional problems which have inhibited the development of effective planning procedures. These problems can be broadly grouped into those which relate to the school's understanding of the planning process, those which arise from the difficulty schools have in identifying suitable and feasible goals, and those stemming from a failure to link planning into action. In the first grouping fall those schools which approach planning on a piecemeal or *ad hoc* basis, and which restrict their planning to single time periods or 'short-termism'. The nature of educational goals often creates difficulties for planning, because they can be difficult to measure, or so broadly defined as to be meaningless. Sometimes, measurable goals are not measured, and where goals are seen as long term, it is often only too easy to distance these from the day-to-day life of the school. Links from planning into action fail because plans are often drawn up without reference to the actual resources available. Sometimes excellent planning is frustrated by a failure to communicate planning goals to those who will be working towards them — staff can only work on those plans they know about. It is not difficult to find examples of all of these problems — though the UK government's recent school development planning initiative certainly went some way towards alerting schools to their shortcomings in this area, and, in many instances, prompting an increased emphasis and expertise in relation to planning processes

(Hargreaves *et al.*, 1989). Most importantly, this initiative explicitly linked the process of establishing goals or vision building into planning, underlining the need to relate plans to the core mission of the school. Louis and Miles (1990) suggest that successful schools are more likely to work towards general goals and around general themes than with polished mission statements, implying that it is a broad understanding of where the school is going that matters, rather than one clear image. They describe such themes as 'interim change goals that helped to organize and direct energy' (p. 207) and note that such themes tend to be arrived at as much by induction as by analysis, and to change over time.

They also report that in their own studies of schools there was little evidence that the kinds of planning models most frequently put forward in management literature were being used — though they did find examples of 'good planning'. This, they argue, underlines the fact that the reality of planning may be rather different from the theory, and they identify a number of variables which they feel should influence the method of planning a school adopts:

- the degree of consensus which exists between and within the various communities which make up the school about the school's 'problems' and possible 'solutions';
- the amount of energy for change the school has available (a resource much depleted in the UK by centrally directed reforms);
- the degree of stability or turbulence which is associated with the school's context;
- the levels of autonomy and flexibility which the school enjoys.

Though the specific planning system adopted would need to reflect these factors, Louis and Miles conclude that evolutionary planning offers the best way forward. This is a process based on three premises:

1 Act — then plan.
2 Pay less attention to missions and goals and more to inspirational themes.
3 Reflect on the relationship between action and improvement.

This third premise is a crucial point: action needs to be focused on improvement — unless planning leads to improvements, why plan? Working from rather different assumptions, the recently issued framework for school inspection (OFSTED, 1992 p. 16) echoes this point, though it clearly sees the link between planning and improvement emerging from a somewhat more rational approach to school-level plan making:

> Management is to be judged in terms of the extent to which the governors, head and staff, particularly those holding incentive allowances, determine and implement the school's objectives, set individual and group goals, promote quality and plan improvement, take responsibility for performance in the areas they manage, enable people to give of their best, and manage resources effectively and

efficiently. Planning is to be judged by the extent to which the school has a means of evaluating its provision, identifying strengths and weaknesses, and maintaining a development plan to address priorities. Plans are assessed in terms of whether the priorities for action are appropriate; whether the implications of the development programme have been assessed (including an assessment of the costs, steps to be taken, staff to be involved and training needed); and whether criteria have been developed to evaluate success.

The aim of planning is, then, to secure improvements in the quality of teaching and learning by identifying appropriate educational and organizational goals, and improving the way the necessary activities (and changes) are managed to achieve these goals. This interdependence of mission building and planning is illustrated in Vignette 13.1. Jean Graham of Broomfield Special School, Leeds, describes how the school was created from a reorganization of special education in the authority. Though the headteacher and deputy headteacher were appointed some nine months before the school was due to reopen, planning for the new school was complicated by limited information about staffing — the process of assimilating existing staff into newly created schools being one which was likely to drag on well into the summer term. Nevertheless, they were clear about the sort of structure and relationships they wanted to see in the school, a preliminary vision which was shared with all staff when the school did open. Following from this, staff became actively involved in planning for the development of the school, and, inevitably, as a result of their engagement in the planning process the vision is refined, leading in turn to new priorities and a further round of planning activity.

Vignette 13.1 Planning — involving staff

On 31 August 1991 twenty-two special schools within our local authority closed and then the following day twelve reopened as new schools. This major reorganization was prepared for over an eighteen-month period, and during this time the process of assimilating staff into the jobs in the new schools was protracted, placing us all under considerable strain and stress with regard to what our futures might hold.

From January 1991, as headteacher and deputy headteacher designates, we were faced with the challenge of planning the development of our new school which would open in September. Both of us were already familiar with the school site and its physical resources since we had worked there beforehand for some time. We knew that the school would have an additional intake of a small number of new pupils transferring from closing schools. At this point, we knew what the staffing establishment would be, but we had no idea, or control over, who might fill these posts. Given this situation we discussed how we could best plan a school structure which would allow us initially to welcome everyone aboard on as equal a footing as possible, and would also encourage the development of staff involvement, commitment and collaboration from the outset.

After much discussion, and the consideration of many ideas, we decided our best course of action would be to develop a totally new form of organization, clearly different from that of the existing schools from which staff had come. We hoped this would ensure the removal of any previous power bases and also ease the assimilation of any new staff. So, having rejected the familiar top-down hierarchical model, we worked towards the development of a more collegial management structure that would group staff in horizontal bands across the whole school. We ended up with the following framework:

- Four 'syndicates' were created, responsible for policy development, planning and implementation, within designated areas but across the whole school.
- The syndicates were:
  - staffing — responsible for all matters relating to adults in the school;
  - students — responsible for all matters relating to pupil behaviour and wellbeing;
  - resources — responsible for finances and the school's physical resources;
  - curriculum — responsible for ensuring that pupils' educational needs are met.
- All staff, including those with support and medical roles, are attached to a syndicate.
- Syndicates are led and coordinated by the members of the management team.

Our next task was to plan and write post descriptions to implement this framework, and to consider the specific briefs of each syndicate in more detail. At this point, the headteacher and I felt that any further planning and decision making should be at a whole-staff level. We envisaged that the aims, ethos and methodology of the school would evolve as the staff worked together and developed a collective philosophy to meet the needs of the pupils.

By the end of the summer term the staff assimilation exercise was almost complete and we were surprised to find that our staffing would remain largely unchanged for September. We held our first meeting to enable the headteacher to explain the vision for the organization of our new school, and how we anticipated this would be achieved. We reached a joint decision to use some training days at the beginning of September to facilitate joint planning with all staff.

When we opened in September one of the first tasks was to elect staff to the syndicates. These would immediately have to tackle significant planning areas, such as the number and composition of pastoral groups, the allocation of teaching time, and determining how best to organize the timetable. In terms of staff development, team building featured highly and activities were arranged to develop this aspect. The autumn term saw everyone trying hard to come to terms with the new organization and the implementation of the new structures.

After the first term, though pleased with the progress, we recognized that the system was by no means perfect. Accordingly, in February a questionnaire regarding the general running of the school was given to each member of staff. The intention of this was to gain some initial feedback and gather early reactions to the system, and also to pinpoint any specific difficulties that needed attention. The perceived strengths and weaknesses of the school's structure emerged from the resulting data and, not surprisingly, contained a request for greater clarity, with specific roles and responsibilities defined, particularly with regard to the communication network. As a direct consequence, a number of changes were made; for example, we decided to amend our staff meeting cycle, and also reorganized the presentation and circulation of information.

We are now well into the second year of operating our structure and as time passes we have continued to evaluate and adjust our systems to best meet our needs. A collegial organization ideally involves consensus decision making, and that is the challenge we are *tackling now. It is not always easy, but we think that the commitment to collaborative planning is now firmly rooted in the school, and this will help us to face present and future challenges.*

This account of evolutionary planning activities shows how the school's goals and priorities are emerging from the planning carried out by staff, and also how the planning activities are themselves influenced by emerging goals and priorities. As the plans became translated into actions for implementation, monitoring becomes increasingly important, providing feedback which will in turn influence the whole cycle of progression from priorities to plans to action. Though this example is unusual in that it relates to the creation of what was effectively a new school, the school development planning model can usefully be applied to the emerging cycle of analysis planning and action. Hargreaves and Hopkins (1991) suggest that schools can begin to approach planning more systematically by working through a number of steps or questions:

- Where is the school now?
- What changes do we need to make?
- How will we manage these changes over time?
- How will we know whether our management of these changes has been successful?

Broomfield School has begun to establish 'where it is' and consequently necessary changes are presenting as priorities. Some of these — the need for greater clarity about roles and communication systems, for example — are already being tackled as part of a planned process of development. Initial feedback is becoming available which offers the staff group the opportunity to assess how successful their actions to tackle these areas have been. Other priorities — for example, the need to develop decision-making procedures — are emerging as major points of focus for the next planning cycle.

We can see in this one case, then, that though it is helpful sometimes to delineate discrete stages in the planning process — vision building, setting priorities, planning objectives to secure these priorities, etc. — such delineation has more to do with increasing our understanding of the ingredients of an effective planning cycle than producing a description of what planning really looks like in schools. On the ground, the various stages constantly interact, seem often to spill over into one another, and come together into an apparently seamless cycle of thinking, action and reflection. This does not mean that identifying the separate component parts of the planning cycle is not a valuable exercise — it both helps us to conceptualize what we are engaged in when we plan and provides us with a model which can be used to examine whether the component parts have been give attention in a particular case. But we need to be aware that it is most unlikely that the kind of separation implied in many planning models can be — or even should be — achieved. Rather, we need to be able to understand that there is a continuous process of planning and replanning going on in the school. We may well, at particular points in the school year, wish to take stock, to set down what we hope to achieve in the following year; but this must not be seen as the first point when planning goes on and, once the plans have been drawn up, the end of the exercise for another year. Such points merely bring the school's planning activity into focus, providing one 'still' from a continuous movement: they are frames drawn out of the film, not composed photographs which summarize or portray.

The Broomfield School account gives some sense of this dynamism, which is central to effective planning/action cycles. Indeed it is sometimes hard to know whether one is planning or evaluating, so closely are these functions linked. A different aspect of this same issue is raised in Vignette 13.2. Where schools take an overly 'rational' approach to planning — regarding it as something which takes place towards the end of the summer term, thereby creating a straitjacket upon, rather than a vehicle for, the next year's development — opportunities are constantly missed. Unfortunately, opportunities arise not when we would prefer to address them, but, like problems, at difficult times, when resources, including senior management time and attention, are fully occupied in dealing with the day-to-day and the predictable. Such opportunities may be small, such as the chance to alter the balance of knowledge and skills within the school every time a member of staff is replaced. Unless this is seen as an opportunity for growth there can be a tendency to replace existing resources instead of developing new ones. In effect, the departure of a member of staff is being treated as a problem to be solved rather than as an opportunity to be exploited. But occasionally, such opportunities can be very great indeed. In Vignette 13.2, John Brandon, headteacher of the Mark Rutherford Upper School, Bedford, describes such an opportunity, and outlines how the school was able to mobilize resources to create a plan which would both secure the opportunity and provide a framework for development once secured.

Vignette 13.2 Planning for the Technology Schools Initiative (TSI)

Like many schools we feel restricted by lack of funds. Small shortfalls in the annual revenue budget affect our ability to deliver the service we would wish, and to develop at the rate we would wish. The account that follows arises because of the virtual non-existence of large capital injections capable of supporting the kind of curriculum we would wish to see in the twenty-first century. The reader needs to bear in mind that much of the UK's school building stock, because it dates back to the pressures for expansion stemming from the creation (1944 Education Act) of a national system of education, and further growth in the 1960s and 1970s in response to the raising of the school leaving age, and the reorganization of the system following 'comprehensivization', will by then be more than forty years old. In design terms, much will be older still. On top of this, many secondary schools are coming to terms with a welcome, but very rapid, increase in post-16 staying-on rates. Mark Rutherford School in Bedford matches the above descriptions exactly, and our parent LEA, short of cash, has as its priorities the even older schools in the south of the county — and who can blame it?

The annual revenue we could do little about; but fairy godparents do exist when it comes to capital injections! The school was coming to the end of its TVEI contract, but was presented, along with all other secondaries in the country, with the opportunity to bid for extra-large funding within the TSI. In December 1991 we had no inkling of what was to come; at the beginning of January 1992 we were invited to bid; in March we were told that we had an award of £250,000 which must be spent by March 1993! The process was competitive, and in Bedfordshire there were two rounds; we supposed the odds against success as: fifty to one — so what happened in the sixteen days we had to put forward our proposals?

In spite of the desperately short time-scale we did manage to produce an action plan. It was coherent, it was consistent with the steady flow of development in the school, and it had three distinct phases. First, rather like Mrs Beeton in her recipe for jugged hare, we had to catch our hare! Phase 1 was to set out actively to gain the award. Second, if the bid was successful, the paper exercise of the bid document had to be capable of being turned into solid facts of bricks and mortar, of networks, hardware and software. Finally, there had to be a clear route into the school's normal annual development planning cycle as phase 2 unfolded. Any capital injection would be valueless if it did not support, sustain or further develop our curriculum of the future as well as the present. In the way of things, it too would need sustaining in the future, by way of maintenance, replacement and technician support.

The requirements of phases 2 and 3, of implementation and institutionalization, put immense pressure on the initial documentation for the bid. The document itself had to look good, and to be easily read and assimilated. We told ourselves that the reader would want to be interested in our document among a pile of fifty, and to remember it after reading it! An ex-student of the school produced a futuristic full-colour photograph of the buildings to match our chosen title, 'MR 2000'. Readers could get all the information they needed from just the first nine pages; the remaining pages were simply supporting evidence.

The bid had to be credible in curriculum, financial and community need terms. The senior management team (SMT) produced a 2,000-word briefing document, including all we knew about TSI, and circulated it to all curriculum providers, all local employing organizations in our existing networks, and all relevant departments in county hall, as well as to potential suppliers of equipment and services. Endorsement was obtained from the local MP. With this document went the questions:

- If you had access to large resources how would you wish to develop/change your department/area's curriculum and methodologies? Answers in forty-eight hours.

- How might your company feel able to support MR 2000? Direct sponsorship, teacher placements, contribution of ideas, even personnel . . .? Expect contact from the school's SMT within the week. Oh . . . may we use your logo?

- What are the likely building costs for a CAD/CAM area, for automotive engineering, for an arts performance/audiovisual studio suite? Again, answers within a week.

It all came together. Within the school, and externally, people were genuinely excited by the project. Departmental heads did know what they wanted to do; they had never dared to dream they might have a chance like this. The employers were superb: we did not get much finance, but there was a lot of advice, and the letters of support and the logos went into the bid document. County architects, and others, came up with solid estimates of cost. The bid document was written by one person to ensure consistency of style, was commented upon by two key governors, was tabled at the school's main policy committee, and was submitted twenty minutes before the closing deadline.

Even if we were not successful we knew we had achieved something worthwhile.

Targets for the future had been identified, although they would take longer to achieve if the funding was not forthcoming. Local community networks had been strengthened. Everyone got a huge lift, though, when we were in the list of award recipients.

Phase 2 was interesting, and at times difficult. The pace of events, so different from the annual planning cycle, or even TVEI, had left sixty-five teachers and fifteen technical and administrative staff at eighty different knowledge levels. Staff meetings were held, bulletins issued, an IT coordinator and support group designated (all after the event, of course). These were helpful but limited; they were, after all, bolt-ons to the schedules of already busy people. The early part of the implementation phase did give rise to misunderstandings, and even jealousies, which are only now becoming resolved as the annual planning cycle takes over, with curriculum providers now thinking happily of next year, starting from a much enhanced resource and equipment base. Decisions of detail were made by the headteacher and the IT and buildings team leaders in quite autocratic ways, very different from the school's normal, consensus building approach. We aimed to spend the money sensibly; in the long cycle of planning, permissions and tendering attaching to any new building, this is not always easy.

What we have got out of it is:

- *a fine new technology block;*
- *one of the best school libraries in the country, fully computerized, with full IT provision for pupil use, and with its databases, CD-ROM facilities, satellite information, and careers and other software programmes networked to every department in the school;*
- *local departmental networks, supporting the curriculum in all areas;*
- *better-defined curriculum targets;*
- *franchised links with our local further education (FE) college for the school-based provision of General National Vocational Qualification (GNVQ) work at levels II and III;*
- *sponsorship from local companies ranging across IT training for staff and pupils, teacher placements, industry personnel placements in the school, a joint industry–governors advisory group, promises of industry standard robotic and CAD/CAM equipment on short-term loan;*
- *even a new car from Vauxhall Motors!*

We also have better insights into the school's organizational structures, as we carried out a questionnaire/interview study among staff about the impact of TSI upon the institution, and better knowledge about the wishes of parents with regard to TSI, through the return of a questionnaire circulated to new-intake families. We asked them, among other things, why they chose this school: equipment levels did not come top, but it was close! Unlike Her Majesty's government, they do not want us to collect the title 'technology school'. We have a better understanding of the role of performance indicators, having built these into our bid document as part of the promised evaluation procedures.

What remains to be done? We have to integrate fully the resources we now have into our curriculum — departmental responses are patchy. Staff training lagged behind phases of TSI, in spite of the use of two non-contact half-days. Technician support has to be much more fully developed. Many challenges remain, but we feel we have made a good start and have learned a lot about planning along the way.

John Brandon's account demonstrates a willingness to take on extraordinary tasks, matched by an ability to find the necessary resources to tackle the opportunity. But he also makes another very important point about planning, reminding us that even if the bid had failed, the school had still achieved something worthwhile. What is it, then, that John had identified as an outcome of the planning process itself, irrespective of whether the project planned for would be realized or not?

We believe that his penultimate paragraph identifies what this 'something worthwhile' is. Involvement in the process of planning has itself been beneficial for the participants. The intellectual engagement with a set of issues and set of colleagues vitalizes the staff of the school. Where teachers actively debate goals, priorities, activities and the use of resources, and relate their thinking in these areas to the core purpose of the school, making links between the way the school is developed and the opportunities for development provided for pupils, then planning becomes a major staff development exercise. By comparison, the plans produced from these deliberations may be short-lived, but the creation of a staff group who can plan for the long-term improvement of the school is likely to be an enduring asset.

The development of this conceptually skilled group of staff who feel comfortable engaging in debate about the school's future may also produce other benefits. Rosabeth Moss Kanter (1990) has pointed out that successful and innovatory companies are places where staff focus 'more of their resources and attention on what they do not yet know ... than on controlling what they already know'. Binns (1992) describes the learning organization as a place where, because staff are guided by a shared mental model (vision) which is both objective (in the sense that it has been debated) and provisional (in the sense that it reflects assumptions rather than truth), planning can be recast as learning. Developing this notion, perhaps we could describe the 'planning school' as a 'learning school'. In both Broomfield School and Mark Rutherford School, explicit links between planning and learning have been made. There are also clear implications of planning for communication. In Mark Rutherford School the sheer speed at which a response was required meant that the staff were left at 'eighty different knowledge levels'. The first point to note is that the involvement of all staff meant that individuals were likely to be more aware of differences in knowledge than is sometimes the case. The second is that the school took immediate action to communicate with all members of staff. Similarly, in Broomfield School, initial feedback suggested that communication was stretched. It is important to remember that planning both relies on information and changes the status or importance of some pieces of information. When planning for change we need to communicate 'as never before', to borrow Plant's phrase (Plant, 1987, p. 33).

MESSAGES

We have argued in this chapter that collaborative planning can create conditions which stimulate and sustain school improvement activities. The effectiveness we achieve in anticipating decisions needed to resolve problems and exploit opportunities is likely to be increased if more staff are able to contribute their knowledge and experience to this process. Staff find it easier and are more likely to contribute when they are well informed. Hargreaves and Hopkins (1991, p. 26) have sought to capture the essential features of this open and informed approach to development planning:

> Learning to ask the right questions of itself is more empowering of a school than being given other people's second-hand answers:
>
> When everyone
>
> - is open about the planning and management of change,
> - gives development planning the time and status it needs,
> - draws upon the experience, talents and suggestions of others,
> - is willing to learn by making some mistakes,
>
> there arises a climate of partnership focused on enhancing the quality of teaching and learning in the school. This is the heart of development planning.

We believe that the process of school improvement will be further enhanced where:

- vision building and planning are directly linked to one another, ensuring that development is rooted in the values and expectations of the school's community;
- staff recognize that involvement in the process of planning is more important and valuable than the plans themselves;
- replanning is seen as both inevitable and desirable and there is a clear understanding that planning is not something done once a year, which then becomes a straitjacket for thinking and development;
- communication within and about planning is seen as a major priority and something that needs to be worked on daily.

PART 4

REFLECTION

Chapter 14

Seeing School Improvement Whole

We have, as the reader will have noticed, drawn extensively on the metaphor of a journey to describe our approach to school improvement. We noted in Chapter 7 that as we have travelled with these schools, we have continued to engage with the available 'knowledge base', to reflect on our interactions, the progress made and the problems encountered. We have suggested that what is distinctive about our work is that, unlike many of those working on school improvement projects, we attempt to support, intervene in and research the journey of school improvement as we are making it. We have also acknowledged the tensions which can arise from this dual role. This is most probably why developers stick to development and researchers research! The situation in the UK is further complicated by the radical reform agenda that schools are currently working through.

In this final chapter we want to begin to make sense of the complexity we have created for ourselves by working in this way, and to focus on what we have learned about the process of school development. There are three questions that we are attempting to grapple with here, which we will restate and to which we hope to respond. We believe that if we can find answers to them we will be in a position to unravel some of the complexities of educational change and begin to see school improvement whole. The three questions are:

1 What is the role of school improvement in an era of change?

2 In what ways does the process of school improvement lead to cultural change?

3 What have we learned about intervention, and how can we build on this?

It is our responses to these questions that provide the substance of this last chapter. The nature of our work makes this as interim account, rather than the final word. Nor do we apologize for that. Reflective stories from the field are, in our opinion, as useful to fellow travellers as a polished account of an expedition accomplished. Accordingly we have prepared this interim and reflective account of the 'Improving the Quality of Education for All' project in order to share our work with other colleagues, and as a contribution to the on-going debate on school development, rather than as a definitive statement. This chapter is therefore a reflection on school improvement, a review of what we have learned, and an account of what we will rely on as we continue the journey.

WHAT IS THE ROLE OF SCHOOL IMPROVEMENT IN AN ERA OF CHANGE?

We have argued at length in this book that the only way that schools can survive and enhance quality in an era of change is through school improvement. School improvement as a strategy for change focuses not only on the implementation of centralized policies or chosen innovations, but also on creating the conditions within schools that can sustain the teaching-learning process. Unless they can do this, the impact of reform initiatives will only be tangential to the daily life of the school. At times of great change, of innovation overload, schools need to be able not only to prioritize between competing policy or innovation objectives, and adapt these changes to the needs and aspirations of the school, but also to create the internal conditions for so doing. In order to illustrate this point we briefly describe the experiences of some of the schools we are working with that are attempting to implement changes that not only relate to centralized policies, but are also in line with their own aspirations.

A primary school had carried out considerable development activity with respect to classroom practice. Its initiative involved the creation of *learning centres* in which groups of children can work on self-directed learning tasks. During a staff meeting many of the teachers discussed their anxiety about the quality of engagement of pupils while they carried out tasks in the learning centres. In order to support staff in their pursuit of this work, the headteacher arranged time for them to observe children at work in colleagues' classrooms. Time was also allocated for pairs of teachers to discuss their observations in order to draw out implications and to plan modifications to the children's learning tasks.

This story is a particularly good example of how headteachers can support colleagues by allocating the most valuable resource that teachers need — time. By organizing the school day in such a way as to allow colleagues to spend time together, she is endorsing their activities and, in so doing, demonstrating her commitment to their professional learning.

Throughout this book we have stressed the importance of encouraging collaboration in schools. We see the isolation of teachers as a major barrier to improvement. At times it seems as though schools are deliberately organized to inhibit meaningful collaboration. It is an indictment of our educational system that many teachers do not have the opportunity to observe their colleagues at work in the classroom.

The priority for one of the secondary schools we have been working with was curriculum access. The term that is currently fashionable with respect to this issue is *differentiation* — in other words, the ways in which teachers take account of the individual differences of their pupils in the classroom. To address this issue, task groups were established that involved a majority of the staff. Although each group was working in a different curriculum area, they used a similar action planning format for their work. Each group appointed a coordinator, known as the 'conduit'. The choice of this name was to emphasize the role of these people in passing information around the system. All of this activity was coordinated by a cadre of three teachers, one of whom was the deputy head. This led to a school-wide debate about the meaning of the term 'differentiation'. After an initial period during which this seemed a relatively straightforward matter, the discussions gradually began to identify the complexity of the issues involved in teaching for diversity. Issues about differentiation by task and differentiation by outcome led to heated debate. Indeed some staff became increasingly uncomfortable about the use of the word 'differentiation', arguing that it might imply forms of teaching that could promote discrimination.

The importance of this story is to show how carefully organized task groups following a common process can be used to heighten awareness about a vital issue, even in a large secondary school. Such a strategy does, however, have to be supported and managed if it is to bear fruit. Another dimension to this account is the way in which such a debate necessitates a search for meaning. As we have already suggested, the evolution of new policies and practices within a school requires staff to establish a sense of personal meaning with respect to the areas to be developed. In this context curriculum change is not seen simply as the rational implementation of a pre-specified set of ideas. Rather it is a much more complex process whereby those involved seek to reconstruct their existing understandings and ways of working.

Two members of staff of a medium-sized secondary school were invited to lead an initiative looking at *pace of learning*. This priority was identified as a result of an inspection of the school. Since neither teacher was a senior member of staff, they chose initially to work with small groups of staff rather than go for whole-staff involvement from the outset. Working with colleagues in pairs, they carried out classroom observation in order to collect data about existing practice, and to develop curriculum materials and teaching strategies designed to enhance the pace of learning. Gradually they involved more teachers in their activities, and as a result the development work began to have an impact across the school. Time was allocated so that staff could work in one another's classroom in supporting development activities. Towards the end of the year, some of the staff who were involved in this classroom research presented some of their experiences during a staff development day for the whole staff.

This is a good example of the 'think big, start small' approach to change. At various stages during the first year of this project, however, the two school coordinators experienced periods of doubt as to whether their work would have any impact upon the school as a whole. Their main concern was that without the involvement of some senior staff their activities would become marginalized. Consequently they adopted various formal and informal strategies to encourage the participation of various senior colleagues. Their decision to involve senior colleagues was, we believe, a significant change in the conditions in the school. Indeed it represented a clear signal that the initiative was seen as important.

As the coordinators and senior staff reflected on the changes in teaching styles that had occurred as a result of this work, they recognized a number of key strategies. In our terms, the school had been successful in recognizing the need to review and adapt certain conditions to support staff in their development tasks. The provision of time to work on the development group was a significant factor. In addition, the skills of the two coordinators in maintaining momentum and disseminating the work were important. Their decision to find ways of involving students was also recognized as a major strength in their activities.

This linking of a small-scale initiative into an overall strategy for school improvement is, we believe, a vital factor. Elsewhere we have observed similar task groups that, despite doing excellent development work, have failed to have a wider impact. Ideally, of course, the widening of impact should not be left to chance. Indeed this is why we recommend that attention is given to establishing leadership roles for support development activities from the beginning.

In each of these examples the school was seeking effective strategies to increase its capacity to handle change. Being prepared to invest resources and, in particular, time to support activities is an important lesson. Despite our recognition of this principle, we find that some schools are incapable of accepting it as a necessary condition for improvement. We have experience of a number of schools that, despite good intentions, seem unable to cope with disruption to existing arrangements in order to mobilize resources and time for supporting development. We think, for example, of one school that for two years continued to establish task groups, issue policy statements and hold meetings. What it was unable to do, however, was to make the significant changes in timetabling arrangements so that individual staff could be encouraged and helped in pursuing the classroom implications of their discussion.

It may be helpful to locate this discussion of strategies and conditions within our framework for school improvement, discussed in Chapters 6 and 7. In Chapter 7 we explained that the strategy links the priorities to the conditions. Our own work has focused on how this link can be strengthened. Here we would like to consider what the school does to link priorities to conditions in the pursuit of school improvement.

In the examples related above, the strategy chosen by the school not only makes the links, but also has an impact on culture and on student outcomes. In the schools we are working with we have seen many strategies and combinations of strategies used to bring about improvement. The following list is not exhaustive; it is simply a composite of those strategies used by the schools we are currently working with. Obviously no school uses them all, but equally no school relies on just one. We have loosely grouped the strategies under the conditions to which they apply.

Staff development:
- staff development processes are used to support individual teacher and school development;
- teachers are involved in each other's teaching;
- where appropriate, external consultants are used to support teacher development.

Involvement:
- students are encouraged to take responsibility for their own learning;
- use is made of cooperative learning approaches to facilitate student learning;
- students, parents and governors are involved in the creation of school policy.

Inquiry and reflection:
- there is a search for increased clarity and shared meanings;
- reflection and review activities are used to monitor progress and enhance the professional judgement of teachers.

Leadership:
- staff throughout the school are encouraged to adopt leadership roles;
- temporary systems or working groups are created;
- individuals take on key roles in initiating change and supporting development work.

Coordination:
- efforts are made to maintain momentum;
- links are made between formal and informal structures;
- images of success are created.

Collaborative planning:
- planning processes are used to legitimize and coordinate action;
- resources for school improvement are specifically allocated.

Although it is helpful both conceptually and strategically to think of these approaches to school improvement as distinct, in reality they coalesce. Similarly, the priority or curriculum focus and the strategy combine in the minds of teachers to present a uniform reality. As we saw in our examples, on a day-to-day basis school improvement is an amalgam of broad strategies such as self-review, action planning and staff development, which link together the classroom and the school, as well as the more dynamic aspects of the change process.

From our work on the IQEA project, we have identified some themes that underpin the work of the most successful schools. Taken together they result in the creation of opportunities for teachers to feel more powerful and confident about their work. It is interesting if unsurprising that they relate quite closely to the principles we described in Chapter 7 as being central to successful school improvement.

Teacher learning In successful schools, teachers meet together regularly to discuss aspects of their work, share ideas, plan and help one another in problem solving. They also spend time in one another's classrooms, observing one another's practice and providing feedback on new approaches. In addition, teams of teachers might be formed to plan, implement, and evaluate experimental classroom approaches.

Living with ambiguity The evolution of new policies in the school involves the consideration of alternative points of view and the clarification of the policy in use. In this way policies come to be defined over time through social processes. During periods of intensive development, therefore, members of staff have to live with the uncertainties created by ambiguity. Successful schools seem to recognize the importance of providing support to colleagues during such periods.

Leadership Teachers in these successful schools are aware that different teachers take on leadership roles. Indeed, many colleagues seem prepared to take the lead at one stage or another. Leadership roles frequently arise through staff working groups, which are appointed with specific goals, a time-line and considerable authority. In most of these schools, virtually every staff member takes part in a working group sooner or later.

Student involvement An important factor in supporting policy creation can be the reactions of students in the school. When they are unaware of the reasons for change, they may unintentionally act as a barrier to progress. Some of our successful IQEA schools have found ways of overcoming this problem by involving students in the change. For example, the school that is introducing resource-based learning has enrolled some students as resource centre assistants.

Tying resources to development activities As we have seen in a number of vignettes in Part 3, it is helpful if time is allocated to individuals and groups that undertake development tasks. Our experience is that even small amounts of time are seen as being enormously precious and can encourage high levels of commitment. The availability of specific development funds is seen to be equally valuable in engendering enthusiasm and facilitating innovative work.

Vision Perhaps the most significant role for the headteacher, or other senior colleagues, is to nurture an overall vision for the school. In one large secondary school, for example, the headteacher occasionally holds meetings of the whole staff during which he muses about his views on important educational ideas. Staff members report that this helps them see their own work within a broader picture of the school's mission. Similarly, in a small primary school, teachers refer to the headteacher's habit of 'thinking aloud' about policy matters as she mixes informally with the staff. Again, this seems to help individuals as they think about overall school policy.

Celebrating success Equally important, staff members celebrate their success. For example, they may positively reinforce one another's work through informal discussion in the staffroom; by collecting and displaying press cuttings about the school in the entrance hall; and, in some instances, by accrediting their classroom practice through academic awards. In these ways, they are maintaining enthusiasm and generating ownership of and clarity about the school's aims and vision.

Further, these schools are marrying the internally generated goals and priorities with forces and opportunities which present themselves in the environment; finding what we have called consonance in priority setting. Mark Rutherford School, for example, managed to link together the school's desire to continue the work funded under TVEI — which provided a strong internal motive — with the invitation to bid for a TSI award. This combination of internal and external circumstances produced extraordinary and sustained effort from the staff of the school; effort rewarded by the success of the bid. In Britannia Primary School, their priority — the need to find ways of involving and making best use of what is a large staff for a primary school — has been carried forward in tandem with the pressure to implement and monitor the National Curriculum. In King Harold School, the maths department's priority of increasing competence in basic numeracy among Years 7 and 8 pupils interacted with the school-wide pursuit of quality improvement, deriving from a drive to gain external accreditation from the British Standards Institution. In these and many other instances where staff commitment has been very high, the outcomes secured were unusually impressive. We have noted the consonance between internal priority and external opportunity. Indeed, we believe that a predisposition towards school improvement equips a school to take maximum advantage of external circumstances. However strong the forces for reform, a commitment to internal development may offer the best way of dealing with such pressure.

This discussion and the various examples given in this section go some way to responding to the question, 'What is the role of school improvement in an era of change?' Unless schools are able to take a more proactive stance towards external policy initiatives and translate them into needs at the school level, they will continue to suffer from innovation overload and gradually lose control of their own educational agenda. It is the integration of themes such as these into the norms and expectations of staff and the wider school community that keeps the process going. To put another way, it is the culture of the school that sustains the improvement process and ensures enhanced outcomes for students. It is to a discussion of how this process evolves that we turn in the following section.

IN WHAT WAYS DOES THE PROCESS OF SCHOOL IMPROVEMENT LEAD TO CULTURAL CHANGE?

The key argument in this book is that school improvement strategies can lead to cultural change in schools through modifications to their internal conditions. It is the cultural change that supports the teaching-learning process which leads to enhanced outcomes for students.

In Chapters 6 and 7 we outlined a theoretical model, a framework for school improvement, that informs our work with schools. In these terms, school improvement is the process through which schools adapt external changes to internal purpose. When successful, this leads to enhanced outcomes for teachers and students, and ultimately affects the culture of the school, as well as its internal organizational structures. As we have continued to work with schools, we are finding some common patterns in the way in which this process unfolds.

Most of our schools are now familiar with the school development planning process that encourages them to express their developmental aspirations in the form of *priorities*. The school's development plan consists of a series of priorities which should be supported by action plans. These are the working documents for teachers. In them the priority is sub-divided into targets and tasks, responsibilities are allocated, a time-frame is established, and evaluation or progress checks are identified.

Through this approach to planning, priorities are then reformulated within a *strategy*. This typically involves teachers in some form of collaborative, classroom-based action. The exact nature of the strategy, or combination of strategies, is peculiar to each school. Strategies need to take account of the priorities that have been agreed, existing conditions and the resources that are available. So, for example, the priority in one of our secondary schools was developing resource-based learning; one of the strategies its staff used in order to implement this priority was classroom observation.

Schools are now used to planning in this way and to establishing working groups for developmental tasks. But it is as they move into action that problems tend to arise. Beginning to work on something new, to change, inevitably creates some difficulties, both for individuals and for the institution. Teachers are faced with acquiring new teaching skills or mastering new curriculum material; the school is often faced with new ways of working that are incompatible with existing organizational structures. In the the example of resource-based learning, teachers had to work out what it meant to them, to their teaching styles and to the curriculum content. They then had to adapt their classroom practice to match this understanding. The school, for its part, had to provide time on the timetable for classroom observation, and to give increased responsibility to relatively junior members of staff.

This phase of destabilization or internal turbulence is as predictable as it is uncomfortable. Yet many research studies have found that without such a period, successful, long-lasting change is unlikely to occur. It is at this point that most change fails to progress beyond early implementation. In these cases, when the change hits the 'wall' of individual learning or institutional resistance, internal turbulence begins to occur and developmental work begins to stall. Often the working group continues for a while, but eventually it fragments, or another priority is found for it to focus on. The change circles back on itself and nothing much is achieved — so we start something new. This is the cycle of educational failure, the predictable pathology of educational change.

Many of the schools that we have been working with have survived this period of destabilization by either consciously or intuitively adapting or accommodating the *internal conditions* in the school to meet the demands of the agreed change or priority. In order to overcome the 'wall' problem, we encourage schools to diagnose their internal conditions in relation to their chosen change *before* they begin developmental work. They can then start to build these modifications to the school's internal conditions into the strategies they are going to adopt. So in our running example, time was found for the classroom observation, staff training days were devoted to discussing the definitions that various curriculum groups had of resource-based learning, and the wall was successfully breached.

When this happens, we begin to see changes occurring in the *culture* of the school. In our example, as a result of the staff training day and the class-room observation, teachers began to talk more about teaching, collaborative work outside of the project became more common, and management structures were adapted to support this and future changes. When taken together, these changes in attitudes and structure created a more supportive environment within the school for managing change. The school's change capacity was increased and the groundwork was laid for future change efforts. Instead of rebounding against the wall, a virtuous circle of change began to be established. Schools that have been through similar change cycles either experience less internal turbulence, or are able to tolerate greater levels of turbulence, because they have progressively enhanced their capacity for change as a result of this developmental process.

When we talk about this process we often summarize it using the following notation: P stands for the priority the school sets itself, S the chosen strategy, the wavy lines the period of destabilization, Co the school's internal conditions that are modified in order to ameliorate the destabilization, and Cu the resulting change in culture.

$$P > S > \{ \ \} \, Co > Cu$$

We realize, of course, that real life is not as simple or as linear as this formula suggests, but we have found that this way of describing the development process resonates with the experience of many of those that we talk to and work with. The process of cultural change is also not a one-off, as implied by the notation, but evolves and unfolds over time. Often many sequences have to be gone through before a radically different culture emerges in a school.

Many heads and school leaders seem to adopt, albeit intuitively, a similar approach to the management of change. They seem to agree with Schein (1985, p. 2) that 'the only thing of real importance that leaders do is to create and manage culture'. They realize that the impact of successful change needs to be on the culture of the school, for it is culture that sustains innovation and conse-quently enhances the achievement of students. They therefore focus on culture first. It is almost as if they begin by asking 'What cultural changes are required?' and then, 'What priorities, strategies, and changes in conditions can bring this about?'. The link between setting priorities and the culture of the school is therefore of some importance. Sequencing priorities over time can help the successive shaping of school culture. In recognition of this, many school leaders 'think big, start small' in their planning for development. They also sequence priorities in such a way that they build on initial good practice and then on subsequent success. They manipulate strategy and conditions in order to affect culture, in the pursuit of enhancing the quality of educational outcomes and experience for all pupils. The process often unfolds as seen in the following sequence:

$$P1 > S1 > \{ \ \} \, Co1 > Cu1$$

$$P2 > S2 > \{ \ \} \, Co2 > Cu2$$

$$P3 > S3 > \{ \ \} \, Co3 > Cu3$$

When the process of cultural change is embarked on, it may be that Cu3 is the ultimate goal. To move there too quickly is impossible, so the various intermediate stages have to be traversed first. There are a number of interesting paradoxes here. Although real life is not as rational as this, we often need to have strategic maps in our minds as we embark on and sustain the journey of improvement. Also there is rarely any clarity about the nature of subsequent priorities or the cultural change they effect at the start of the journey. Priorities unfold almost organically as progress is made. This is not to say that everything is *ad hoc*. There is often a concomitant clarification of values within the school as the process unfolds that provides a framework for, and maintains the integrity and consistency of, the development work. In this sense the notion of vision, which is so popular nowadays, is more about the elaboration and articulation of a set of values that occurs throughout the development work than a concrete image given by the head at the outset. It also appears in our experience that the process unfolds unevenly. There are always highs and lows, peaks and troughs. Even in the most successful schools, development accelerates then levels off. When a new priority is set, energy flows once again. Sustaining momentum over time and appreciating the inevitability of such plateaux are consequently very important. This is especially the case because the process takes at least two years to work through, and consequently does not conform to neat planning cycles.

We have also found that something similar operates at the level of the teachers and the students. For the teachers, although the conditions may be eased and the internal turbulence reduced at the school level, the pressure of individual learning on their part often remains the same. The conditions in, and the culture of, the school are, however, increasingly supportive of their developmental efforts. As teachers experience a more supportive environment within the school, so they are more able to endure the threat of new learning. As they adapt the teaching and learning practices in their classrooms, they begin to see that the learning of their pupils is enhanced, and this evidence gives them confidence in the change and increases their commitment to the new approach.

Similarly, students will experience dissonance as a teacher provides different classroom experiences. As a result students too will have to make an adjustment to their conditions of learning before there is a pay-off in outcomes. This emphasizes the point we made earlier, that in order to reduce the internal turbulence for pupils they should become equal partners in development.

It is possible, at least theoretically, to see this process operating at the three levels of school, teacher and student, with each phase complementing and supporting the other. In the following sequences the priorities are consistent, although the strategies may well vary across the three levels. If the destabilization is to be coped with, then alterations to the conditions have to occur at the organizational, teaching and learning levels. Ideally, this will result in modifications to the culture of the school, the quality of the teaching process on the part of teachers, and the learning outcomes of students. It is in this way that the process of cultural change supports the learning of students.

School   P > S > { } Co > Culture
Organizational

Teacher P > S > { } Co > Teaching-learning
Teaching

Student P > S > { } Co > Outcomes
Learning

We hope that it is now clear that the main threat to successful cultural change through school improvement is the inevitable destabilization that the process brings with it. Some years ago Bruce Joyce remarked in a conversation with one of the authors that educational change is 'technically simple, but socially complex'. Although that statement has always had the ring of truth, it is only recently, as we have more thoroughly explored the process of cultural change, that we have experienced the full force of its profundity. We have always been alert to the social complexities involved in the school development process, but we now realize that it is inextricably connected to the internal turbulence so characteristic of successful school improvement.

This realization struck us most forcibly during a visit last year to one of 'our' secondary schools. The purpose of the visit was to discuss with the head and project coordinators the reasons for the success of the first year of the project. In this school the focus was the establishing of a new resource centre and the acquisition by the staff of a complementary range of teaching styles. In preparation for the meeting a member of the group had produced an elaborate time-line to inform the discussion. The discussion was, in retrospect, conducted at the level of strategy, with a liberal sprinkling of jargon or what we tend to call 'Cambridge-speak'. We drew the discussion to a close, congratulated each other on our success so far and made to leave.

As we were walking away from the head's room, the project coordinator asked, rhetorically, 'Do you want to know the real reason for the success of the project?' She told us that a section of the staff go down to the pub for lunch on Fridays. Among this group are a number of teachers who are significant 'opinion leaders'. Although these individuals were not all senior members of staff, the possibility of a policy proposal being accepted depended to a large degree on the reactions of this Friday pub group. Serendipitously a large number of the teachers involved in the resource-based learning initiative were also members of this group. Hence the 'success' of the project. If this fortunate coincidence had not taken place, then it is likely that the individuals in the pub group would have been highly resistant to the change.

This is a clear example of the role of informal groups. In the example, the norm of the informal group overlapped with the formal norm established by management. At a more general level and in our experience, formal groups initiate but informal groups tend to block or frustrate. A strategy for change, at least on the part of management, may mean deliberately destabilizing the informal group and in so doing limiting its ability to block. A more positive strategy would be deliberately to incorporate the informal group, or at least members of it, into the development team. This is what happened in this case, albeit by accident.

Another example of destabilization as a result of successful development work occurred in a large secondary school, where there was an expanded cadre group (see Chapter 12) whose task was to lead and support a particular curriculum development. The group consisted of three coordinators designated by the headteacher, and about twenty other teachers who volunteered to take part. It was fairly representative of the whole school, with members from all subject departments, including colleagues with a wide variety of status and experience. Over a twelve-month period the group proved to be very successful in pursuing its tasks and, in particular, in influencing thinking and practice throughout the school — so much so that the group came to be seen as the central mechanism for policy development. Turbulence gradually became apparent as certain staff, including members of the senior management team, perceived themselves as losing influence as a result of the system that had been created. Indeed, one of the deputy headteachers became aware that he was only hearing about key policy discussions days after they had occurred. Eventually tensions came to the surface at a meeting of the senior management team, where this deputy headteacher complained to his colleagues about how he felt that they as a group had been marginalized within the school.

When we first experienced this kind of destabilization our instincts were to want to help schools avoid these problems. Schools and teachers are very busy and actions that create negative efforts are inevitably unwelcome. We have come to the view, however, that often it is not a matter of avoiding the turbulence but rather of finding ways of coping with it.

We also began to realize how profoundly important the attitudes and behaviour of headteachers and other senior staff clearly are in creating conditions for supporting change. We can, of course, quote many examples of headteachers who seem to be successful in their own ways in carrying out this critical task. Regrettably we also observe examples of headteachers who seem to struggle in this area. We think, for example, of a primary school headteacher who seems so burdened with the day-to-day problems he perceives that he seems to reiterate continually to his staff why nothing can be achieved. His regular comments about limited resources, lack of time and, perhaps worst of all, the limitations of the pupils encourage an atmosphere of low expectations. Similarly the head of a secondary school who seems committed to giving staff space to influence policy development appears to his staff as being so indecisive that they feel uncertain about what is expected of them. This malaise seems to strike senior staff most of all — so much so that two of them were reported to have spent two weeks together typing the text for a school brochure into the word processor. By all accounts this was perceived by some staff as an avoidance strategy by colleagues who felt unsupported in taking a lead in more significant areas of school life. In these two schools little progress will be made, because the school leaders are themselves paralysed by the thought of change. In these cases the developmental initiatives barely reached the wall of destabilization.

These are a few examples of what happens in schools that are coming to terms with the complexity of social change. In many of 'our' most successful schools, however, there is a recognition that the cultural aspects of change are at least as important as the more technical emphasis on prioritization and strategic planning. It is through such an approach to school development, which recognizes the social and cultural complexity of change, that some schools are managing to achieve quality in times of change. Implicit in this discussion is a view that school improvement, if it is to be successful, needs to come from *within* the schools. The challenge, as we see in the following section, is to find ways of working that are consistent with that aspiration.

WHAT HAVE WE LEARNT ABOUT INTERVENTION, AND HOW CAN WE BUILD ON THIS?

So far we have summarized our current thinking with respect to the technical, cultural and social strategies that seem to be effective in supporting school improvement initiatives. We are now faced with the conundrum of how we can best support schools through this complex process. Part of the difficulty facing us in working in our chosen way is seen in Figure 14.1. Traditional inservice provision seems to concentrate in the main on knowledge. Inspectors, on the other hand, are usually interested only in classroom behaviour. We know from experience and research that attitudes are crucial if knowledge is to be put into practice. Our style of working cuts across all three. This is necessary if successful change is to result, but makes the nature of intervention extremely complex. We have already described in Chapter 7 the nature of our strategy of intervention, which is summarized below:

- the contract between the partners;
- the logic and journey of school improvement;
- the project manual:
  - staff development;
  - involvement:
  - inquiry and reflection;
  - leadership;
  - coordination;
  - collaborative planning;
- working across the levels:
  - cadre;
  - extended cadre;

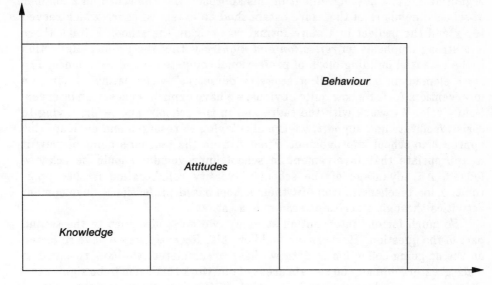

Figure 14.1 *How people change (Hersey and Blanchard, 1972; West and Ainscow, 1991).*

 — senior management;
 — leadership;
- reflection and inquiry;
- 'ourselves':
 — guardians of the contract;
 — providing and modelling staff development;
 — pressure and support;
 — visits;
 — consultancy and technical support;
- accreditation.

In simple terms our strategy, or the nature of our intervention, consists of seven elements. The first is the *contract* between the partners in the project — the school and its teachers, in some cases the LEA or sponsoring agency, and ourselves. This defines the parameters of the project and the obligations of those involved to each other. The second element is our knowledge of the change process, which we refer to as the *logic and journey of school improvement*. Our framework for school improvement maps the territory of our engagement with the schools. The third element is the *manual* that we have produced to support our staff development work with the schools. This contains our best shot at summarizing the conditions necessary for successful school improvement, as seen in Part 3 of this book. From the beginning of the project we were determined that we would attempt to affect all *levels* of the school, and this is the fourth element. One of the things that we had learned from the research and our previous work is that change will not be successful unless it impacts on and is owned at all levels of the organization. The key ingredient in this approach was the cadre; in a number of schools members of the cadre established an extended cadre which served to extend the project in a more formal way within the school. Fifthly, there is a strong emphasis on *reflection and inquiry* within the project. Reflection is the essential building block of professional competence and confidence. The sixth element in our overall strategy is '*ourselves*' — the nature of our own intervention. As is by now quite obvious, we have explicitly chosen an interventionist role. We work with the cadre and in the schools, and, while trying to assist, facilitate and support, we are also trying to research and evaluate this approach to school improvement. Finally, from the teacher's point of view it is appropriate that involvement in school improvement should be acknowledged. An advantage of the school-university collaboration is the opportunities for teachers to *accredit* their school-based professional development activities through a series of academic awards.

So much for our intervention strategy; we must now turn to the second part of the question, 'How can we build on this? Recently, as we have reflected on the on-going collection of data we have accumulated, we have resolved to place greater emphasis on certain areas of our work that seem to be significant. This is particularly the case in relation to the four types of school whose cultures we described in Chapter 6. For ease of exposition we have grouped our reflections under the main headings of the framework for school improvement: conditions, priorities, strategies and outcomes.

Conditions

A clear pattern that we have noted is that unless a school is prepared to make tangible changes in conditions in order to support staff in working towards the priorities, little progress can be anticipated. Unfortunately, some schools seem to find it almost impossible to make such changes. All sorts of explanations may be offered but at the heart of these there seems to be an unwillingness to take the risk of disrupting day-to-day practices. In such a school we feel that the only response we can offer is to press the point home: it is necessary to invest existing resources in order to achieve development. This applies particularly to what we have called *stuck* schools. Often these schools require sustained work on their conditions before they are ready to engage in development work.

Beyond this general point, we have found that a number of areas seem to be particularly significant. For example, organizational structures such as senior management teams and the use of school-wide task groups seem at times to have a dramatic impact on development activities. We also have a sufficient range of examples of the involvement (or lack of involvement) of the head-teacher in the project to encourage us to be far more explicit with individual heads as to what we anticipate of their involvement.

We are still understanding the implications of the nature of staff development when working in this way. Certainly, we need to be more explicit about training the cadre in staff development. In this regard we have found the distinction between workshop and workplace very helpful in sharpening our thinking about the location of our staff development efforts and the links to the conditions. The distinction between the two increasingly pervades our work. We also feel that there needs to be a better integration of cadre training and school-based work. Although we should spend some time doing whole-staff training in the schools, our priority should be to help cadre members sequence and use whole-staff training in their schools more effectively.

Priorities

On some occasions we have found it necessary to intervene more directly in order to assist with decision making about priorities. Some schools attempt too many priorities and, as a result, suffer from self-imposed overload. Others operate with a priority that is so general as to be meaningless. Certainly the title given to the priority in the school seems to be vital. What is needed is a form of words that has meaning and relevance to all staff, indicating that the project is going to make a useful contribution to their professional lives. This advice often applies to what we have described as *wandering* schools. They are often trying to do too much, with the consequence that they do little of it very well and there is not much classroom impact resulting from it. Our main task with these schools is to assist them in focusing down, to narrow the agenda to issues of real importance. This should then enable them to carry out these crucial developmental tasks as well as they can.

We have also come to recognize that achieving clarity among staff as to what a particular development priority means is often a complex and time-consuming process. Furthermore, this is probably inevitable if such a priority is to be adopted by those involved. Adoption means achieving a level of understanding among individuals, and this takes time. Priorities of the sort we have been working with in IQEA schools, such as differentiation, autonomous learning and resource-based learning, are not simple concepts. They require people to develop an understanding of what they mean and to explore the implications of them for practice. It is not simply about implementing differentiation, but about understanding, criticizing and adapting differentiation through engaging with it in classroom settings. Consequently, in the project schools we are encouraging coordinators to be sensitive to this process of adult learning and to invest energy and resources in creating conditions that will enable it to occur. We also insist that they address the relationship between the priority and student learning.

Strategies

The ideas presented in the earlier sections of this chapter provide us with a basis for intensifying our activities in helping schools to formulate powerful intervention strategies. This is certainly the case with *promenading* schools. They need help to correct the imbalance between maintenance and development, and to build on past achievements with more energy and an eye to the future. Clearly these strategies have to operate at a formal and an informal level, and must include responses to technical issues as well as the challenge of the social complexity of change. More specifically, our experience leads us to emphasize the following elements:

- *being reflective* — seeking to understand experience with a view to informing planning and action;

- *seeking greater clarity* — scrutinizing decisions in order to achieve better definitions of what is intended;

- *coping with destabilization* — providing forms of support that enable individuals to handle pressures experienced during change;

- *pressing for commitments* — ensuring that all those involved are responding in the ways that were agreed in the contract;

- *involving students* — overcoming barriers to change presented by students and, wherever possible, providing them with a positive role;

- *widening the involvement of the whole staff* — avoiding situations where groups of staff feel excluded from project activities;

- *using significant staff development events* — creating conditions that mean that these events can have a long-term impact;

- *using outside consultants* — clarifying expectations in order for these consultants to provide maximum support to staff;

- *intensive inquiry* — using in-depth inquiry procedures to inform policy decisions and implementation strategies.

In combination, these strategies can lead to the redesign of the workplace and, in so doing, provide strong support to individual members of staff as they seek to develop aspects of their practice. There also needs to be more time found for teachers to talk about and observe each other teaching. In this respect, we should also emphasize the need for more specific and more rigorous classroom observation, and the development of a common vocabulary which will enable all members of the school staff to discuss classroom events and experiences.

Outcomes

In the past, many school improvement projects have rightly been criticized for their lack of emphasis on student outcomes, however broadly defined. We need, therefore, to emphasize continually the importance of evaluating and monitoring all types of outcome and to integrate this information into the development process. This applies to all types of schools, including those that we have characterized as *moving*. Currently we are encouraging project schools to define their priorities in terms of success criteria; that is, to give operational definitions of what the priorities mean and how their achievement will be recognized. They need to be continually searching for clarity in their chosen priorities, and becoming more specific and aware of what they wish to achieve as teachers and for their students. This, in turn, leads us all to focus our evaluations on classroom processes and, of course, student learning.

In addition we have been encouraging task groups and working teams to be far more explicit about the intended outcomes of their work by gathering information related to priorities. All of this has implications for the content of cadre days and may also involve us in more classroom visits in order to collect evaluation data.

Outcomes, however, do not relate just to students. The project is also about supporting teacher learning and the strengthening of the school's organization. The process of setting success criteria should help everyone to be clearer about the knowledge, attitudes and skills that staff require to develop in order to achieve the priorities. We need also to gather information on conditions and strategies in order to monitor how well the school as a whole is building its capacity to manage change.

To assist in this process we find it useful to construct frameworks for discussion and planning. These offer outline maps for tracing the process of improvement and a common terminology that can be used to facilitate planning. This approach is perhaps similar to the one outlined by Donald Schon (1987, p. 4), when he suggests that through 'complementary acts of naming and framing, the practitioner selects things for attention and organises them, guided by an appreciation of the situation that gives it coherence and sets a direction for action'. What we are introducing into the schools are frames and names that are common across the project and, therefore, encourage collaboration. Obvious examples would be the conditions and our framework for school improvement.

Within the discussions that are fostered by these frames, our roles vary from time to time and from place to place. On some occasions this may involve us in questioning our school-based colleagues in order to encourage them to 'think aloud' about their work. Often they tell us that simply having an outsider who poses questions in a supportive way and then assists in setting deadlines is very helpful.

In addition, of course, we may contribute ideas and suggestions from our own experience and knowledge of the research literature. It is important to note, however, that we see such inputs as contributing further resources to the process of internal review and development. They are *not* intended to refocus decision making on us as external consultants.

A further significant role within discussions created by our various planning frames is that of 'critical friend'. Having established a long-term agreement to collaborate with colleagues in a school, and then invested time in creating a working relationship with those colleagues, it is appropriate that we should be prepared to offer a critique of their proposals and actions. In this way we are seeking to balance our support with a degree of pressure that is intended to push their thinking forward.

It is important to add at this stage that, despite what we have written earlier, we do at times elect to adopt more proactive roles in project schools. We do so in order to provide specific support to school coordinators at particular times. For example, we often contribute to school-based staff development programmes, working in partnership with school colleagues. Sometimes this involves us in team teaching in order to provide demonstrations, practice and feedback related to particular staff development techniques. We may also assist in the planning and processing of significant meetings. So, for example, one of us recently helped a headteacher and certain of his senior colleagues devise a plan for a key meeting of staff. This involved modelling how the meeting might be managed and then providing feedback as the headteacher and deputy head practised how they would carry out their tasks during the meeting.

The various frames used within the project fulfil a further function with respect to our research activities. In a sense they provide organizing mechanisms for the collection and analysis of data. In this way the data we collect are used to develop the frames further, thus providing us with insights as to how the process of development occurs within the schools, and an understanding of the impact of our own actions. In other words, we are using the data from schools to help refine our intervention.

These public exhortations to ourselves provide us with an immediate agenda for action. They also, we believe, go some way to demonstrate the research potential of working closely with particular schools as they struggle to bring about developments in policy and practice. It is this thought that we wish to return to in concluding this chapter and the book.

CODA: ON WORKING WITH, RATHER THAN ON

Our commitment to working with, rather than on, schools presents many difficulties and dilemmas. For example, it requires us to be juggling continually with the competing demands of giving support to innovation while, at the same time, making sense of the processes involved for research purposes. It also poses many questions about what our roles should be with respect to the process of change in each school.

In a more traditional project we might well have chosen to introduce the schools to an existing model of development based upon previous research activities. Then, having set the initiative going, our task would have been to stand back and record the process and outcomes of the intervention. In IQEA we have deliberately chosen to adopt a very different approach, based upon an alternative perspective as to how change can be facilitated. Rather than seeking to impose externally validated models of improvement, we are attempting to support schools in creating their own models. Our assumption is that such an approach, which builds upon the biographies and circumstances of particular organizations, is much more likely to bring about and help sustain significant improvements in the quality of schooling.

Early on in the IQEA project we experienced considerable stress as a result of our wish to adopt a flexible and responsive stance in our work with the schools involved. At times, for example, we felt under some pressure to become more directive and to offer more specific and tangible advice. It was as if colleagues in the schools wanted us to impose ready-made solutions to the problems they faced. In such a climate it is very tempting to respond in the desired way in order to ensure credibility; stating that we see our role as being to help schools formulate their own solutions seems a rather limp response. We have to say, however, that time has convinced us that in the longer run this is a much more powerful form of help.

So we see our intervention as being chiefly about helping colleagues in schools to become clearer about the issues they face as they seek to bring about improvements in their work. Specifically this means helping them to make sense of the knowledge and expertise that exist within their schools and to formulate strategies for making use of available resources. Consequently much of our work involves us in improvisation. While we may well formulate plans for helping particular schools beforehand, during our visits these plans often have to be adapted or even abandoned in order to take account of the circumstances we find. Essentially we have to operate within the agendas created within the school.

Finally, a comment on the metaphor of the journey that we have been using when talking about the progress of development over time. It is a helpful image, implying as it does a dynamic view of development and change. But, to be literal, where does it lead? One of the problems with previous approaches to school improvement is that they have taken a short-term view of change. In many cases this has meant focusing on the implementation of a single issue or a given curriculum development. We now live in a change-rich environment, where multiple policy initiatives and innovation overload can easily oppress schools. In order to cope with change of this magnitude and complexity, we need to adopt a long-term perspective. We need to focus on the *management of change in general*, on the creation of effective and flexible structures and on the empowering of individuals, rather than on the implementation of specific, but usually minor, changes. This is why we have chosen to journey with our schools rather than to search for quick-fix solutions. It is inevitable that this account of our travels with the moving school is reflective and interim, because there is no clearly defined beginning or end to our work together. Simply, we journey on.

Appendix

The Conditions Scale

This rating scale is concerned with the conditions that appear to be important for school improvement. We are interested in your opinion of how far these conditions apply to your own school. This information is confidential and your individual responses will not be divulged to any member of the school. The aggregate results will be used as a basis for development work in your school.

Attached is a series of twenty-four statements about the school. We would like to know how far you feel these statements match *your own* perception of the school. There are no right answers; simply indicate in each area the response which most closely matches your views.

Please indicate whether you consider your present post to be a:

senior management role ☐
middle management role ☐
other ☐

Responses:
1 = Strong disagreement (never the case).
2 = Disagreement (rarely the case).
3 = Agreement (sometimes the case).
4 = Strong agreement (always the case).

Please circle

1 There is an appropriate whole-school policy for staff development. 1 2 3 4

2 There are procedures for ensuring that the staff development policy responds to changes in staff needs. 1 2 3 4

3 I know whom to talk to about my staff development needs. 1 2 3 4

4 Staff support one another in development activities. 1 2 3 4

5 There is an agreed policy to involve pupils in decisions. 1 2 3 4

6 There are clear procedures for involving pupils in decision making. 1 2 3 4

7 Pupils know whom to approach if they wish to comment on school policies. 1 2 3 4

8 Pupils frequently comment to me about aspects of school life.   1   2   3   4

9 There is a policy of using staff experience to guide development decisions.   1   2   3   4

10 Information is collected systematically as part of the planning process.   1   2   3   4

11 All colleagues have a role in contributing to and interpreting information for planning purposes.   1   2   3   4

12 I feel able to express my views freely about school policies and practices.   1   2   3   4

13 Staff are frequently encouraged to take a lead in developments.   1   2   3   4

14 Staff undertaking leadership roles are given appropriate support.   1   2   3   4

15 I know whom to approach for advice/direction on different aspects of my work.   1   2   3   4

16 I find that the styles of leadership used are generally appropriate to the task in hand.   1   2   3   4

17 The school has a policy for keeping people informed about development priorities.   1   2   3   4

18 The links and overlaps between activities are well coordinated.   1   2   3   4

19 Staff are clear about their and other people's responsibilities.   1   2   3   4

20 Informal contacts with colleagues make a positive contribution to my work.   1   2   3   4

21 Plans reflect agreed priorities.   1   2   3   4

22 There are well-established procedures for planning.   1   2   3   4

23 I know how I can contribute to school planning processes.   1   2   3   4

24 Our planning processes encourage good working relationships.   1   2   3   4

DIAGNOSING THE CONDITIONS WITHIN YOUR OWN SCHOOL

In order to estimate your own school's 'conditions' add together the score on items 1-4 and enter on the 'staff development' dimension; items 5-8 on the 'involvement' dimension; items 9-12 on the 'inquiry and reflection' dimension; items 13-16 on the 'leadership' dimension; items 17-20 on the 'coordinators' dimensions; items 21-24 on the 'planning' dimension. 'Eyeballing' these scores gives an indication of your own school's conditions that can be used as a basis for discussion.

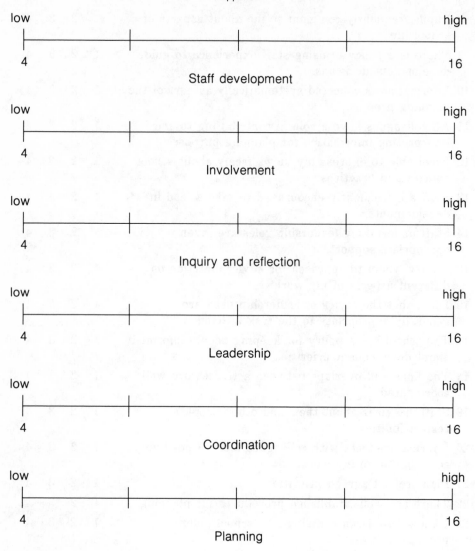

The scale also allows you to estimate some of the norms that characterize your school. Add together items 1, 5, 9, 13, 17, 21 and enter on the *objectives* dimension; add together items 2, 6, 10, 14, 18, 22 and enter on the *structures* dimension; add together items 3, 7, 11, 15, 19 and 23 and enter on the *roles* dimensions; and add together items 4, 8, 12, 16, 20 and 24 and enter on the *relationship* dimension. 'Eyeballing' these dimensions gives an indication of the norms that characterize the management of your school that can be used as a basis for discussion.

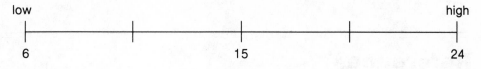

Objectives — norms relating to the purposes of the school, shared understanding of goals and priorities.

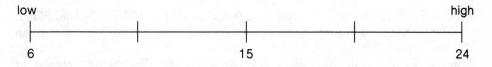

Structures — norms about the interrelationship between jobs, about responsibilities between jobs and obligations between job-holders.

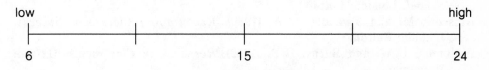

Roles — norms about how a person in a particular position should perform or how two persons should interact and behave.

low   high
├──────────────┼──────────────┼──────────────┤
6   15   24

Relationships — norms about the levels of informal support colleagues expect from and give to one another.

References

Abbott, R., Birchenough, M. and Steadman, S. (1988). *GRIDS School Hand-books*. (Second edition, primary and secondary versions). York: Longman for the SCDC.

Acheson, K. and Gall, M. (1980). *Techniques in the Clinical Supervision of Teachers*. New York: Longman.

Ainscow, M. and Hopkins, D. (1992). 'Aboard the moving school'. *Educational Leadership*, 50(3), 79-81.

Ainscow, M. and Muncey, J. (1989). *Meeting Individual Needs in the Primary School*. London: Fulton.

Ainscow, M. and Tweddle, D.A. (1988). *Encouraging Classroom Success*. London: Fulton.

Anderson, L.W. and Burns, R.B. (1989). *Research in Classrooms*. Oxford: Pergamon.

Angus, L. (1989). '"New" leadership and the possibility of educational reform'. In J. Smyth (ed.), *Critical Perspectives on Educational Leadership*. Lewes: Falmer Press.

Aoki, T. (1984). 'Towards a reconceptualisation of curriculum implementation'. In D. Hopkins and M. Wideen (eds), *Alternative Perspectives on School Improvement*. London: Falmer Press.

Armstrong, M. (1980). *Closely Observed Children*. London: Writers and Readers.

Asch, D. and Bowman, C. (1987). *Strategic Management*. London: Macmillan.

Ball, S.J. (1981). *Beachside Comprehensive*. Cambridge: Cambridge University Press.

Ball, S.J. (1987). *The Micro-politics of the School*. London: Methuen.

Barth, R. (1990). *Improving Schools from Within*. San Francisco: Jossey-Bass.

Beare, H., Caldwell, B.J. and Millikan, R.H. (1989). *Creating an Excellent School*. London: Routledge.

Becher, T., Eraut, M. and Knight, J. (1981). *Policies for Educational Account-ability*. London: Heinemann.

Bennett, N. (1991). 'The quality of classroom learning experiences for children with special educational needs.' In M. Ainscow (ed.), *Effective Schools for All*. London: Fulton.

Bennett, N., Desforges, C., Cockburn, A. and Wilkinson, B. (1984). *The Quality of Pupil Learning Experiences*. London: Erlbaum.

Bennis, W.E., Benne, K. and Chin, R. (1969). *The Planning of Change*. London: Holt, Rinehart & Winston.

Berman, P. and McLaughlin, M. (1978). 'Implementation of educational innovation'. *Educational Forum*, 40(3), 345-70.

Bernstein, B. (1970). 'Education cannot compensate for society'. *New Society*, 387, 344-7.

Bickel, E. and Bickel, D. D. (1986). 'Effective schools, classrooms and instruction: implications for special education'. *Exceptional Children*, 52(6), 489-500.

Binns, P. (1992). 'The theory of the learning organisation'. Mimeo, Ashridge Consulting Group.

Bolam, R. (1975). 'The management of educational change: towards a conceptual framework'. In A. Harris, M. Lawn and W. Prescott (eds), *Curriculum Innovation*. London: Croom Helm.

Bollen, R. and Hopkins, D. (1987). *School Based Review: Towards a Praxis*. Leuven, Belgium: ACCO.

Bollington, R. and Hopkins, D. (1989). 'School based review — as a strategy for the implementation of teacher appraisal and school improvement'. *Educational Change and Development*, 10, 8-17.

Bowles, S. and Gintis, H. (1976). *Schooling in Capitalist America*. New York: Basic Books.

Brophy, J. E. (1983). 'Classroom organisation and management'. *The Elementary School Journal*, 82, 266-85.

Brophy, J. and Good, T. (1986). 'Teacher behavior and student achievement'. In M. Wittrock (ed.), *Handbook of Research on Teaching* (3rd edition). New York: Macmillan.

Burns, T. and Stalker, G. M. (1961). *The Management of Innovation*. London: Tavistock.

Cabinet Office (1981). *Scrutiny of HM Inspectors of Schools in Scotland*. Edinburgh: Scottish Office.

Caldwell, B. J. and Spinks, J. M. (1988). *The Self-managing School*. Lewes: Falmer Press.

Caldwell, B. J. and Spinks, J. M. (1992). *Leading the Self-managing School*. Lewes: Falmer Press.

Charters, W. and Jones, J. (1973). 'On the risk of appraising non-events in program evaluation'. *Educational Leadership*, 2(11), 5-7.

Clift, P., Nuttall, D. and McCormick, R. (1987). *Studies in School Self-Evaluation*. Lewes: Falmer Press.

Coleman, J. (1966). *Equality of Educational Opportunity*. Washington, DC: USPO.

Comer, J. (1988). 'Educating poor minority children'. *Scientific American*, November, 42-8.

Corbett, H. D. and Rossman, G. (1989). 'Three paths to implementing change'. *Curriculum Inquiry*, 19(2), 163-90.

Crandall, D. et al. (1982). *People, Policies and Practice: Examining the Chain of School Improvement* (Vols 1-10). Andover, MA: The Network.

Crandall, D., Eiseman, J. and Louis, K. (1986). 'Strategic planning issues that bear on the success of school improvement efforts'. *Educational Administration Quarterly*, 22(2), 21-53.

Croll, P. (1986). *Systematic Classroom Observation*. Lewes: Falmer Press.

Cuban, L. (1983). 'Effective schools: a friendly but cautionary note'. *Phi Delta Kappan*, 64(10), 695-6.

Cuttance, P. (1992). 'Evaluating the effectiveness of schools'. In D. Reynolds and P. Cuttance (eds), *School Effectiveness*. London: Cassell.

Dalin, P., with Rolff, H.-G. and Kleekamp, B. (1993). *Changing the School Culture*. London: Cassell.

David, J. (1989). 'Synthesis of research on school based management'. *Educational Leadership*, 48(8), 45-53.

Deal, T. and Kennedy, A. (1983). 'Culture and school performance'. *Educational Leadership*, 40(5), 14-15.

Delamont, S. (1983). *Interaction in the Classroom*. London: Methuen.

DES (1977). *Ten Good Schools*. London: Department of Education and Science.

Dewey, J. (1929). *The Sources of a Science of Education*. New York: Liveright.

Doyle, W. (1987). 'Research on teaching effects as a resource for improving instruction'. In M. Wideen and I. Andrews (eds), *Staff Development for School Improvement*. Lewes: Falmer Press.

Drucker, P. (1985). *Innovation and Entrepeneurship*. New York: Harper & Row.

Duignan, P. and Macpherson, R. (1987). 'The Educative Leadership project'. *Educational Management and Administration*, 15, 49-62.

Edmonds, R. (1978). 'A discussion of the literature and issues related to effective schooling'. Paper prepared for the National Conference on Urban Education, Cemrel, St Louis.

Edmonds, R, (1979). 'Effective schools for the urban poor'. *Educational Leadership*, 39, 15-27.

Eisner, E. W. (1990). 'The meaning of alternative pradigms for practice'. In E. G. Guba (ed.), *The Paradigm Dialog*. London: Sage.

Elmore, R. (1990). *Restructuring Schools*. Oakland, CA: Jossey-Bass.

Evans, M. and Hopkins, D. (1988). 'School climate and the psychological state of the individual teacher as factors affecting the use of educational ideas following an in-service course'. *British Educational Research Journal*, 14(3), 211-30.

Flanders, N. (1970). *Analyzing Teaching Behavior*. Reading, MA: Addison-Wesley.

Fullan, M. (1985). 'Change processes and strategies at the local level'. *The Elementary School Journal*, 85(3), 391-421.

Fullan, M. (1991). *The New Meaning of Educational Change*. London: Cassell.

Fullan, M. (1992a). *What Is Worth Fighting For in Headship?* Buckingham: Open University Press.

Fullan, M. (1992b). 'We do not have the choice of avoiding change just because it is messy!'. *Times Educational Supplement*, 9 October.

Fullan, M. and Hargreaves, A. (1992). *What's Worth Fighting For in Your School?* Buckingham: Open University Press.

Fullan, M. and Miles, M. (1992). 'Getting reform right: what works and what doesn't'. *Phi Delta Kappan*, 73(10), 745-52.

Fullan, M. and Park, P. (1981). *Curriculum Implementation*. Toronto: Ontario Ministry of Education.

Fullan, M. and Pomfret, A. (1987). 'Research on curriculum and instruction implementation'. *Review of Educational Research*, 47(1), 335-97.

Fullan, M., Anderson, S. and Newton, E. (1986). *Support Systems for Implementing Curriculum in School Boards*. Toronto: Ontario Ministry of Education.

Fullan, M., Bennett, B. and Rolheiser-Bennett, C. (1990). 'Linking classroom and school improvement'. *Educational Leadership*, 47(8), 13-19.

Galton, M. (1978). *British Mirrors*. Leicester: University of Leicester School of Education.

Glickman, C. (1990). 'Pushing school reforms to a new edge: the seven ironies of school empowerment'. *Phi Delta Kappan*, 68-75.

Glickman, C. (1991). 'Pretending not to know what we know'. *Educational Leadership*, May, 4-10.

Good, T. L. and Brophy, J. E. (1987). *Looking in Classrooms*. New York: Harper & Row.

Gray, H. L. (1988). *Management Consultancy in Schools*. London: Cassell.

Gray, J. (1981). 'A competitive edge: examination results and the probable limits of secondary school effectiveness'. *Educational Review*, 33(1), 25-35.

Gray, J. (1990). 'The quality of schooling: frameworks for judgement'. *British Journal of Educational Studies*, 38, 203-23.

Gray, J., Jesson, D. and Sime, N. (1990). 'Estimating differences in the examination performances of secondary schools in six counties'. *Oxford Review of Education*, 16(2), 13-58.

Guba, E. and Clark, D. (1965). 'Examination of political change roles in education'. *Strategies for Educational Group Newsletter*, 2, October.

Guba, E. and Clark, D. (1975). 'The configurational perspective'. *Educational Researcher*, 4(4), 6-9.

Hall, G. and Hord, S. (1987). *Change in Schools*. New York: State University of New York Press.

Hall, G. and Loucks, S. (1977). 'A developmental model for determining whether the treatment is actually implemented'. *American Educational Research Journal*, 14, 236-70.

Hall, G. and Loucks, S. (1978). 'Teachers' concerns as a basis for facilitating and personalising staff development'. *Teachers College Record*, 80(1), 36-53.

Hall, V., Mackay, H. and Morgan, C. (1986). *Headteachers at Work*. Milton Keynes: Open University Press.

Handy, C. and Aitken, R. (1986). *Understanding Schools as Organisations*. Harmondsworth: Penguin.

Hargreaves, A. (n.d.). 'Restructuring restructuring: post modernity and the prospects for educational change' (mimeo).

Hargreaves, A. (1986). *Two Cultures of Schooling*. London: Falmer Press.

Hargreaves, A. (1991). 'Contrived collegiality: the micropolitics of teacher collaboration'. In J. Blase (ed.), *The Politics of Life in Schools*. Newbury Park, CA: Sage.

Hargreaves, A. (1992). 'Cultures of teaching: a focus for change'. In A. Hargreaves and M. Fullan (eds), *Understanding Teacher Development*. London: Cassell.

Hargreaves, A. (1993). 'Individualism and individuality: reinterpreting the teacher culture'. In J. Little and W. McLaughlin (eds), *Teachers' Work*. New York: Teachers College Press.

Hargreaves, D. H. (1967). *Social Relations in a Secondary School*. London: Routledge & Kegan Paul.

Hargreaves, D. H. (1982). *The Challenge for the Comprehensive School*. London: Routledge.

Hargreaves, D. H. (Chair) (1984). *Improving Secondary Schools*. London: ILEA.

Hargreaves, D. H. (1990). 'Accountability and school improvement in the work of LEA inspectorates: the rhetoric and beyond'. *Journal of Education Policy*, 5(3), 230-9.

Hargreaves, D. H. and Hopkins, D. (1991). *The Empowered School*. London: Cassell.

Hargreaves, D. H., Hopkins, D., Leask, M., Connolly, J. and Robinson, P. (1989). *Planning for School Development*. London: Department of Education and Science.

Harris, A., Lawn, M. and Prescott, W. (eds) (1975). *Curriculum Innovation*. London: Croom Helm.

Havelock, R. (1975). 'The utilisation of educational change and development'. In A. Harris, M. Lawn and W. Prescott (eds), *Curriculum Innovation*. London: Croom Helm.

Heckman, P. (1987). 'Understanding school culture'. In J. Goodlad (ed.), *The Ecology of School Renewal (the 86th NSSE Yearbook)*. Chicago: NSSE.

Hersey, P. and Blanchard, K. (1972). *Management of Organizational Behavior*. Englewood Cliffs, NJ: Prentice-Hall.

Hewton, E. (1988). *School Focused Staff Development: Guidelines for Staff Development*. Lewes: Falmer Press.

HMI (1988). *Secondary Schools: An Appraisal*. London: HMSO.

HMI/Scottish Education Department (1988a). *Effective Secondary Schools*. Edinburgh: HMSO.

HMI/Scottish Education Department (1988b). *Effective Primary Schools*. Edinburgh: HMSO.

Holt, J. (1964). *How Children Fail*. London: Penguin.

Hook, C. (1981). *Studying Classrooms*. Geelong, Vic.: Deakin University Press.

Hopkins, D. (1984). 'Change and the organisational character of teacher education'. *Studies in Higher Education*, 9(1), 37-45.

Hopkins, D. (1987a). *Knowledge Information Skills and the Curriculum*. London: British Library.

Hopkins, D. (1987b). *Improving the Quality of Schooling*. Lewes: Falmer Press.

Hopkins, D. (1990a). 'The International School Improvement Project (ISIP) and Effective Schooling: towards a synthesis'. *School Organization*, 10(2-3), 174-94.

Hopkins, D. (1990b). 'Integrating staff development and school improvement'. In B. Joyce (ed.), *Changing School Culture through Staff Development (1990 Year Book)*. Alexandria, VA: ASCD.

Hopkins, D. (1993). *A Teacher's Guide to Classroom Research* (2nd edition). Buckingham: Open University Press.

Hopkins, D. (1994). 'Process indicators for school improvement'. In A. Tuijman (ed.), *Educational Indicators*. Paris: OECD.

Hopkins, D. and Wideen, M. (eds) (1984). *Alternative Perspectives on School Improvement*. London: Falmer Press.

House, E. (1979). 'Technology and craft: a ten year perspective on innovation'. *Journal of Curriculum Studies*, 11(1), 1-15.

Hoyle, E. (1976). 'Strategies of Curriculum Change'. Unit 23 Open University Course: Curriculum Design and Development. Milton Keynes: Open University Press.

Hoyle, E. (1986). *The Politics of School Management*. London: Hodder & Stoughton.

Huberman, M. (1992). 'Critical introduction'. In M. Fullan, *Successful School Improvement*. Milton Keynes: Open University Press.

Huberman, M. and Miles, M. (1984). *Innovation Up Close*. New York: Plenum.

Hull, R. (1985). *The Language Gap*. London: Methuen.

ILEA (1990). *Differences in Examination Performance*. London: Research and Statistics (RS 1277/90).

Jensen, A. (1969). 'How much can we boost IQ and scholastic achievement?'. *Educational Review*, 34, 1-123.

Johnson, D. W., and Johnson, F. P. (1982). *Joining Together*. Englewood Cliffs, NJ: Prentice-Hall.

Johnson, D. W. and Johnson, R. T. (1989). *Leading the Cooperative School*. Edina: Interaction Book Company.

Johnson, D. W., Johnson, R. T. and Holubec, E. J. (1986). *Circles of Learning: Cooperation in the Classroom*. Edina: Interaction Book Company.

Jones, A. (1987). *Leadership for Tomorrow's Schools*. Oxford: Blackwell.

Joyce, B. (ed.) (1990). *Changing School Culture through Staff Development (1990 Year Book)*. Alexandria, VA: ASCD.

Joyce, B. (1991). 'The doors to school improvement'. *Educational Leadership*, 48(8), 59-62.

Joyce, B. (1992). 'Cooperative learning and staff development: teaching the method with the method'. *Cooperative Learning*, 12(2), 10-13.

Joyce, B. and Showers, B. (1980). 'Improving in-service training: the messages of research'. *Educational Leadership*, 37(5), 379-85.

Joyce, B. and Showers, B. (1984). 'Transfer of training: the contribution of coaching'. In D. Hopkins and M. Wideen (eds), *Alternative Perspectives on School Improvement*. Lewes: Falmer Press.

Joyce, B. and Showers, B. (1988). *Student Achievement through Staff Development*. New York: Longman.

Joyce, B. and Showers, B. (1991). *Information-Processing: Models of Teaching*. Aptos, CA: Booksend Laboratories.

Joyce, B., Hersh, R. and McKibbin, M. (1983). *The Structure of School Improvement*. New York: Longman.

Joyce, B., Showers, B. and Rolheiser-Bennett, C. (1987). 'Staff development and student learning: a synthesis of research on models of teaching'. *Educational Leadership*, 47(2), 11-23.

Joyce, B., Murphy, C., Showers, B. and Murphy, J. (1989). 'School renewal as cultural change'. *Educational Leadership*, 47(3), 11-23.

Joyce, B., Showers, B. and Weil, M. (1992). *Models of Teaching* (4th edn). Englewood Cliffs, NJ: Prentice-Hall.

Kanter, R. M. (1990). *When Giants Learn to Dance*. London: Routledge.

Keddie, N. (1971). 'Classroom knowledge'. In M. F. D. Young (ed.), *Knowledge and Control*. London: Collier Macmillan.

Kyriacou, C. (1986). *Effective Teaching in Schools*. Oxford: Blackwell.

Kyriacou, C. (1991). *Essential Teaching Skills*. Oxford: Blackwell.

Lawton, D. (1989). *Education Culture and the National Curriculum*. London: Hodder & Stoughton.

Levine, D. and Eubanks, D. (1989). 'Site based management: engine for reform or pipe dream?' (mimeo).

Levine, D. U. (1992). 'An interpretive review of US research and practice dealing with unusually effective schools'. In D. Reynolds and P. Cuttance (eds), *School Effectiveness*. London: Cassell.

Levine, D. U. and Lezotte, L. W. (1990). *Unusually Effective Schools: A Review and Analysis of Research and Practice*. Madison: National Center for Effective Schools Research.

Lippitt, R., Hooyman, G., Sashkin, M. and Kaplan, J. (1978). *Resource Book for Planned Change*. Ann Arbor: Human Resource Development Association.

Little, J. (1981). *The Power of Organizational Setting*. Washington, DC: National Institute of Education.

Little, J. (1990). 'The persistence of privacy: autonomy and initiative in teachers' professional relations'. *Teachers College Record*, 91(4), 509-35.

Loucks-Horsley, S. and Hergert, L. (1985). *An Action Guide to School Improvement*. Alexandria, VA: ASCD/The Network.

Louden, W. (1991). *Understanding Teaching*. London: Cassell; New York: Teachers College Press.

Louis, K. S. and Miles, M. B. (1990). *Improving the Urban High School: What Works and Why*. New York: Teachers College Press.

Macdonald, B. and Walker, R. (1976). *Changing the Curriculum*. London: Open Books.

McLaughlin, M. (1990). 'The Rand Change Agent Study revisited: macro perspectives, micro realities'. *Educational Researcher*, 19(9), 11-16.

Miles, M. (1981). 'Mapping the common properties of schools'. In R. Lehming and M. Kane (eds), *Improving Schools: Using What We Know*. Beverly Hills, CA: Sage.

Miles, M. (1983). 'Unravelling the mysteries of institutionalisation'. *Educational Leadership*, 41(3), 14-19.

Miles, M. (1986). 'Research findings on the stages of school improvement' (mimeo). Center for Policy Research, New York.

Miles, M. (1992). '40 years of change in schools: some personal reflections' (mimeo). Invited address to Division A (Administration), American Educational Research Association meeting, San Francisco, 23 April, Center for Policy Research, New York.

Miles, M., Ekholm, M. and Vandenberghe, R. (eds) (1987). *Lasting School Improvement: Exploring the Process of Institutionalization*. Leuven, Belgium: ACCO.

Millman, J. (ed.) (1981). *Handbook of Teacher Evaluation*. Beverly Hills, CA: Sage.

Mortimore, P. (1991). 'School effectiveness research: which way at the crossroads?'. *School Effectiveness and School Improvement*, 2(3), 213-29.

Mortimore, P., Sammons, P., Stoll, L., Lewis, D. and Ecob, R. (1988). *School Matters*. London: Open Books.

Murgatroyd, S. and Morgan, C. (1993). *Total Quality Management and the School*. Buckingham: Open University Press.

Murphy, J. (1991). *Restructuring Schools: Capturing and Assessing the Phenomena*. New York: Teachers College Press.

Murphy, J. (1992a). 'School effectiveness and school restructuring: contributions to educational improvement'. *School Effectiveness and School Improvement*, 3(2), 90-109.

Murphy, J. (1992b). 'Effective schools: legacy and future directions'. In D. Reynolds and P. Cuttance (eds), *School Effectiveness*. London: Cassell.

NCC (1990). *Curriculum Guidance: The Whole Curriculum*. London: NCC.

Nias, J. (1989). 'Refining the cultural perspective'. *Cambridge Journal of Education*, 19(2), 143-6.

Nias, J., Southworth, G. and Yeomans, R. (1989). *Staff Relationships in the Primary School*. London: Cassell.

Nuttall, D., Goldstein, H., Prosser, R. and Rashash, J. (1989). 'Differential school effectiveness'. *International Journal of Education Research*, 13(10), 769-76.

OECD (1989). *Decentralisation and School Improvement*. Paris: OECD/CERI.

OFSTED (1992). *The Handbook for the Inspection of Schools*. London: Department for Education.

Owens, R. G. (1987). *Organizational Behavior in Education* (3rd edition). Englewood Cliffs, NJ: Prentice-Hall.

Patterson, J., Purkey, S. and Parker, J. (1986). *Productive School Systems for a Non-rational World*. Alexandria, VA: ASCD.

Pearce, J. (1986). *Standards and the LEA*. Windsor: NFER-Nelson.

Persell, C. H. *et al.* (1982). 'Effective principals: what do we know from various educational literatures?' Paper prepared for the National Institute of Education.

Plant, R. (1987). *Managing Change and Making It Stick*. Aldershot: Gower.

Plowden Report (1967). *Children and Their Primary Schools*. London: HMSO.

Pollard, A. (1985). *The Social World of the Primary School*. London: Cassell.

Pollard, A. and Tann, S. (1987). *Reflective Teaching in the Primary School*. London: Cassell. (2nd edition 1993.)

Porter, A. C. and Brophy, J. E. (1988). 'Synthesis of research on good teaching: insights from the work of the Institute of Research on Teaching'. *Educational Leadership*, 48(8), 74-85.

Purkey, S. C. and Smith, M. S. (1983). 'Effective schools — a review'. *The Elementary School Journal*, 4, 427-52.

Purkey, S. C. and Smith, M. S. (1985). 'School reform: the district policy implications of the effective schools literature'. *The Elementary School Journal*, 85(3), 352-89.

Quinn, B. J. (1980). 'Strategies for change'. Reprinted in H. Mintzberg and B. J. Quinn (eds), *The Strategy Process*. Englewood Cliffs, NJ: Prentice-Hall.

Reynolds, D. (1985). *Studying School Effectiveness*. London: Falmer Press.

Reynolds, D. (1991). 'Changing ineffective schools'. In M. Ainscow (ed.), *Effective Schools for All*. London: Fulton.

Reynolds, D. (1992). 'School effectiveness and school improvement'. In D. Reynolds and P. Cuttance (eds), *School Effectiveness*. London: Cassell.

Reynolds, D. and Cuttance, P. (eds) (1992). *School Effectiveness*. London: Cassell.

Reynolds, D., Hopkins, D. and Stoll, L. (1993). 'Linking school effectiveness knowledge and school improvement practice: towards a synergy'. *School Effectiveness and School Improvement*, 4(1), 37-58.

Reynolds, D. and Sullivan, M. with Murgatroyd, S. (1987). *The Comprehensive Experiment*. London: Falmer Press.

Rosenholtz, S. (1985). 'Effective schools: interpreting the evidence'. *American Journal of Education*, 93, 352-88.

Rosenholtz, S. (1989). *Teachers' Workplace: The Social Organization of Schools*. New York: Longman.

Rosenshine, B. (1983). 'Teaching functions in instructional programs'. *The Elementary School Journal*, 83(4) 335-51.

Rowland, S. (1984). *The Enquiring Classroom*. London: Falmer Press.

Rubin, L. (1985). *Artistry and Teaching*. New York: Random House.

Rudduck, J. (1984). 'Introducing innovation to pupils'. In D. Hopkins and M. Wideen (eds), *Alternative Perspectives on School Improvement*. London: Falmer Press.

Rudduck, J. (1991). *Innovation and Change*. Milton Keynes: Open University Press.

Rutter, M., Maughan, B., Mortimore, P. and Ouston, J., with Smith, A. (1979). *Fifteen Thousand Hours*. London: Open Books.

Sarason, S. (1982). *The Culture of the School and the Problem of Change* (2nd edition). Boston: Allyn & Bacon.

Scheerens, J. (1992). *School Effectiveness*. London: Cassell.

Schein, E. (1985). *Organization Culture and Leadership: A Dynamic View*. San Francisco: Jossey-Bass.

Schmuck, R. A. and Runkel, P. J. (1985). *The Handbook of Organizational Development in Schools* (3rd edition). Palo Alto, CA: Mayfield.

Schon, D. A. (1983). *The Reflective Practitioner*. New York: Basic Books.

Schon, D. A. (1987). *Educating the Reflective Practitioner*. San Francisco: Jossey-Bass.

Sergiovanni, T. (1987). 'The theoretical basis for cultural leadership'. In L. T. Sheive and M. B. Schoenheit (eds), *1987 Yearbook of the Association for Supervision and Curriculum Development*. Alexandria, VA: ASCA.

Shulman, L. S. (1988). 'The dangers of dichotomous thinking in education'. In P. P. Grimmett and G. L. Erickson (eds), *Reflection in Teacher Education*. New York: Teachers College Press.

Sizer, T. (1989). 'Diverse practice, shared ideas. The essential school'. In H. Walberg and J. Lane (eds), *Organizing for Learning: Towards the Twenty First Century*. Reston, VA: NASSP.

Skilbeck, M. (1984). *School Based Curriculum Development*. London: Harper & Row.

Slavin, R. E. (1983). *Cooperative Learning*. London: Longman.

Slavin, R. (1989). 'PET and the pendulum: faddism in education and how to stop it'. *Phi Delta Kappan*, 752-8.

Smith, D. and Tomlinson, S. (1989). *The School Effect*. London: Policy Studies Institute.

Snyder, K. J. and Anderson, R. H. (1986). *Managing Productive Schools: Towards an Ecology*. Orlando, FL: Academic Press.

Stenhouse, L. (anonymously) (1970). *The Humanities Project: An Introduction*, London: Heinemann Educational Books.

Stenhouse, L. (1975). *An Introduction to Curriculum Research and Development*. London: Heinemann Educational Books.

Stenhouse, L. (1980). *Curriculum Research and Development in Action*. London: Heinemann Educational Books.

Stenhouse, L. (1983). *Authority, Education and Emancipation*. London: Heinemann Educational Books.

Stillman, A. and Grant, M. (1989). *The LEA Adviser — A Changing Role*. Windsor: NFER-Nelson.

Stoll, L. (1991). 'School effectiveness in action: supporting growth in schools and classrooms'. In M. Ainscow (ed.), *Effective Schools for All*. London: Fulton.

Stoll, L. and Fink, D. (1992). 'Effecting school change: the Halton approach'. *School Effectiveness and School Improvement*, 3(1), 19-41.

Stringfield, S. (1993). 'Lessons being learned from research on educational improvement programs in the United States'. (mimeo). Paper presented at Tamtec Conference, Oslo, Norway, January.

Stringfield, S. and Teddlie, C. (1988). 'A time to summarise: the Louisiana School Effectiveness Study'. *Educational Leadership*, 46(2), 43-9.

Stringfield, S. and Teddlie, C. (1991). 'Observers as predictors of schools' effectiveness status'. *The Elementary School Journal*, 91(4), 357-76.

Stringfield, S. *et al.* (1992). *Urban and Suburban/Rural Special Strategies for Educating Disadvantaged Children (First Year Report)*. Baltimore, MD: Johns Hopkins University.

van Velzen, W., Miles, M., Ekholm, M., Hameyer, U, and Robin, D. (1985). *Making School Improvement Work*. Leuven, Belgium: ACCO.

Walberg, H. (1990). 'Productive teaching and instruction: assessing the knowledge base'. *Phi Delta Kappan*, 71(6), 470-8.

Wang, M. C. (1991). 'Adaptive instruction: an alternative approach to providing for student diversity'. In M. Ainscow (ed.), *Effective Schools for All*. London: Fulton.

Weick, K. E. (1985). 'Sources of order in underorganized systems: themes in recent organizational theory'. In Y. S. Lincoln (ed.), *Organizational Theory and Inquiry*. Beverly Hills, CA: Sage.

West, M. and Ainscow, M. (1991). *Managing School Development: A Practical Guide*. London: Fulton.

Willis, P. (1977). *Learning to Labour*. London: Saxon House.

Willms, J. D. (1992). *Monitoring School Performance: A Guide for Educators*. Lewes: Falmer Press.

Wilson, B. L. and Corcoran, T. B. (1988). *Successful Secondary Schools*. Lewes: Falmer Press.

Winkley, D. (1985). *Diplomats and Detectives: LEA Advisers at Work*. London: Robert Royce.

Woods, P. (1979). *The Divided School*. London: Routledge & Kegan Paul.

Woods, P. (1980). *Pupil Strategies: Explorations in the Sociology of the School*. London: Croom Helm.

Woods, P. (1986). *Inside Schools*. London: Routledge & Kegan Paul.

Name Index

Subject Index